# Working-Class Literature(s)
## Historical and International Perspectives

*Edited by John Lennon & Magnus Nilsson*

**STOCKHOLM**
UNIVERSITY PRESS

Published by
Stockholm University Press
Stockholm University
SE-106 91 Stockholm, Sweden
www.stockholmuniversitypress.se

Supporting Agency (funding): The publication of this book has been made possible by a generous grant from The Crafoord Foundation

First published 2017
Cover Illustration: Photo by Max LaRochelle on Unsplash
Cover image copyright and license: https://unsplash.com/license
Cover designed by Karl Edqvist, SUP

Stockholm Studies in Culture and Aesthetics ISSN: 2002-3227

ISBN (Paperback): 978-91-7635-051-5
ISBN (PDF): 978-91-7635-048-5
ISBN (EPUB): 978-91-7635-049-2
ISBN (Mobi/Kindle): 978-91-7635-050-8

DOI: https://doi.org/10.16993/bam

Suggested citation:
John Lennon & Magnus Nilsson (eds.). 2017 *Working-Class Literature(s): Historical and International Perspectives*. Stockholm: Stockholm University Press. DOI: https://doi.org/10.16993/bam. License: CC-BY

# Stockholm Studies in Culture and Aesthetics

Stockholm Studies in Culture and Aesthetics (SiCA) (ISSN 2002-3227) is a peer-reviewed series of monographs and edited volumes published by Stockholm University Press. SiCA strives to provide a broad forum for research on culture and aesthetics, including the disciplines of Art History, Heritage Studies, Curating Art, History of Ideas, Literary Studies, Musicology, and Performance and Dance Studies.

In terms of subjects and methods, the orientation is wide: critical theory, cultural studies and historiography, modernism and modernity, materiality and mediality, performativity and visual culture, children's literature and children's theatre, queer and gender studies.

It is the ambition of SiCA to place equally high demands on the academic quality of the manuscripts it accepts as those applied by refereed international journals and academic publishers of a similar orientation. SiCA accepts manuscripts in English, Swedish, Danish, and Norwegian.

## Editorial Board

Kristina Fjelkestam, Professor of Gender Studies at the Department of Ethnology, History of Religions and Gender Studies at Stockholm University

Malin Hedlin Hayden, Professor of Art History at the Department of Culture and Aesthetics at Stockholm University

Christer Johansson (coordination and communication), PhD Literature, Research Officer at the Department of Culture and Aesthetics at Stockholm University

Jacob Lund, Associate Professor of Aesthetics and Culture at the School of Communication and Culture, Aarhus University

Catharina Nolin, Associate Professor of Art History at the Department of Culture and Aesthetics at Stockholm University

Ulf Olsson (chairperson), Professor of Literature at the Department of Culture and Aesthetics at Stockholm University

Meike Wagner, Professor of Theatre Studies at the Department of Culture and Aesthetics at Stockholm University

## Titles in the series

1. Rosenberg, T. 2016. *Don't Be Quiet, Start a Riot! Essays on Feminism and Performance.* Stockholm: Stockholm University Press. DOI: https://doi.org/10.16993/baf. License: CC-BY 4.0

2. Lennon, J. & Nilsson, M. (eds.) 2017. *Working-Class Literature(s): Historical and International Perspectives.* Stockholm: Stockholm University Press. DOI: https://doi.org/10.16993/bam. License: CC-BY 4.0

# Peer Review Policies

## Guidelines for peer review

Stockholm University Press ensures that all book publications are peer-reviewed in two stages. Each book proposal submitted to the Press will be sent to a dedicated Editorial Board of experts in the subject area as well as two independent experts. The full manuscript will be peer reviewed by chapter or as a whole by two independent experts.

A full description of Stockholm University Press' peer-review policies can be found on the website: http://www.stockholm universitypress.se/site/peer-review-policies/

## Recognition for reviewers

The Editorial Board of Stockholm Studies in Culture and Aesthetics applies single-blind review during proposal and manuscript assessment. We would like to thank all reviewers involved in this process.

Special thanks to the reviewers who have been doing the peer review of the manuscript of this book.

# Contents

Introduction   ix
*John Lennon & Magnus Nilsson*

Working-Class Literature and/or Proletarian Literature: Polemics of
the Russian and Soviet Literary Left   1
*Katerina Clark*

The Race of Class: The Role of Racial Identity Production in the Long
History of U.S. Working-Class Writing   31
*Benjamin Balthaser*

Writing of a Different Class? The First 120 years of Working-Class
Fiction in Finland   65
*Elsi Hyttinen & Kati Launis*

The Making of Swedish Working-Class Literature   95
*Magnus Nilsson*

Mexican Working-Class Literature, or The Work of Literature in
Mexico   128
*Eugenio Di Stefano*

British Working-Class Writing: Paradox and Tension as Genre
Motif   159
*Simon Lee*

Afterword   197
*John Lennon & Magnus Nilsson*

Contributors   207
Index   211

# Introduction

*John Lennon & Magnus Nilsson*

The idea for this collection was born out of a chance encounter over coffee in a U.S. Starbucks. Over a wide-ranging conversation, we discussed the state of working-class literature as a field, the decline of Marxism in academia, our favorite working-class authors, and the lack of good coffe shops on U.S. campuses. We both generally laid out the various trajectories of scholarly reception of working-class literature in our respective countries and realized that while there were similar trends, there were also stark differences. The conversation became a bug that, in the coming weeks, we could not squash: Why, for example, was working-class literature recognized as a central strand in national literature in Sweden while often discounted and marginalized in the U.S.? We each separately and ineffectively chased that bug to no avail. Over email conversations, we tried to find common ground between these two national understandings but even that was difficult because we weren't sure how the other defined fundamental terms. We contemplated how we define and categorize working-class literature and questioned whether a common definition could translate across the Atlantic Ocean? Researching comparative approaches on Swedish-U.S. working-class literature quickly showed a dearth of scholarship on this particular relationship but even more importantly, we found that that there was very little comparative research on working-class literature across national boundaries at all. We quickly decided to co-write an essay specifically on Swedish and U.S. working-class literatures as a way to jump start this discussion.

---

**How to cite this book chapter:**
Lennon, J. and Nilsson, M. 2017. Introduction. In: Lennon, J. and Nilsson, M. (eds.) *Working-Class Literature(s): Historical and International Perspectives.* Pp. ix–xviii. Stockholm: Stockholm University Press. DOI: https://doi.org/10.16993/bam.a. License: CC-BY

Working on this together allowed us to know more about each other's literary histories, as well as our own. There was value in our discussions, an opening dialogue that expanded definitions and raised larger questions about working-class literature from a global perspective. So why weren't more researchers doing this comparative work? This question was followed by the next logical one—why aren't we doing more? From that question emerged what would eventually become this edited collection. Our idea was to invite authors from a variety of nations who would write a compact history of the working-class literature of their country. If read as stand-alone chapters, each contribution gives an overview of the history and research of a particular nation's working-class literature. If read as an edited collection (which we hope you do), they contribute toward a more complex understanding of the global phenomenon of working-class literature(s).

At this particular historical moment—when the disparities between classes are growing, while conversations about class are becoming more marginalized (except for the plethora of opinion pieces assigning blame for Donald Trump's U.S. election or Great Britain's vote to leave the European Union on the rural lower classes)—a comparative analysis of working-class literature is needed. For decades, the conceptual triumvirate of *race, gender, and class* has set the agenda for much literary research. Triumvirates, however, are seldom egalitarian. Today, for example, two members of the famous second Roman triumvirate – Mark Anthony and Augustus Octavian – are much more well-known than its third member: Marcus Aemilius Lepidus. Class, it could be argued, is the Marcus Aemilius Lepidus of contemporary literary studies, as well as in academia in general. Viewed as being important, yes, but certainly, class does not garner the same attention as other phenomena. As Julian Markels (2003, p. 68) puts it in *The Marxian Imagination: Representing Class in Literature*, "class has become for so much recent scholarship the lip-service afterthought to gender and ethnicity." In recent years, increased attention given by scholars to phenomena such as sexuality, disability, and species has pushed class even further down on the agenda. In fact, scholars interested in class are often not even invited to the academic "diversity banquet" (Russo and Linkon, 2005, p. 13).

One indication of the relative neglect of class in contemporary academia is that, whereas scholarship on literatures connected to, for instance, race and gender – such as African-American literature, feminist literature, postcolonial literatures, écriture feminine, etc. – has multiplied, research on working-class literature has often stagnated or diminished. As an example, the most comprehensive works about German working-class literature – such as Gerald Stieg and Bernd Witte's, *Abriss einer Geschichte der deutschen Arbeiterliteratur* (1973), or Rüdiger Safranski's, *Studien zur Entwicklung der Arbeiterliteratur in der Bundesrepublik,* (1976) – were published more than 40 years ago.

Obviously, this neglect is a significant problem. Works published in the 1970s have long ago ceased to be comprehensive. This lack of contemporary research may also have contributed to the fact that working-class literature is often ghettoized and examined from a long-gone "glory-days" perspective. In a recent text about German working-class literature, Thomas Ernst (2011, p. 338) argues that in the 1960s, working-class authors deserved a place in German literary history, but that today, they do not.

The fact that much research on working-class literature is anchored in the past means that it is often steeped in outdated critical discourses. The theoretical foundation for Safranski's research on this literature, for example, is a version of Marxism-Leninism that was in vogue in radical academic circles in West-Germany in the 1970s, but which has long ago both been abandoned by Safranski and lost its attraction within literary studies. Much contemporary research on working-class literature also remains theoretically backward. Unlike the multivariate and evolving theoretical framings used when examining race and gender, there has not been a significant development of analytical tools to understand class from a literary perspective. Pointedly, in U.S. working-class studies – where much of the most interesting research on U.S. working-class literature is carried out – one finds a marked hostility toward (contemporary) literary theory (Nilsson & Lennon, 2016, p. 43).

Our argument—that there is a relative lack of research on working-class literature in contemporary academia and that much of the existing research is dated or theoretically backward—does not mean to suggest that contemporary and innovative scholarship on working-class literature does not exist. On the contrary, in recent years, a range of scholars has produced highly interesting works, which, for various reasons, have not received the attention they deserve. One interesting example of this is the publication of a great deal of innovative research on Japanese working-class literature by, among others, Samuel Perry (2014), Heather Bowen-Struyk (2011), and Mats Karlsson (2016). Another example is the plethora of working-class literature scholarship in the Nordic Countries that within the last couple of years has resulted in the publication of a series of edited collections of research (Jonsson et al., 2011; Jonsson et al. 2014; Agrell et al., 2016; Hamm et al., 2017).

However, like older research on working-class literature, much of this new research is characterized by a rather narrow national perspective. Although working-class literature is often internationally influenced due to factors such as translations of literature, migration, and the internationalist ideology of the labor movement, scholarship on this literature often only looks internally within national borders. In their essay about Finnish working-class literature in this volume, for example, Elsi Hyttinen and Kati Launis highlight that many of this literature's "transnational connections [...] remain underresearched." Similarly, in his article about Swedish working-class literature, Magnus Nilsson shows that its history has been written as a national narrative that obscures its international connections. This is true also for the research on other working-class literatures. Two good illustrations of this are Michelle Tokarczyk's (ed.) *Critical Approaches to American Working-Class Literature* (Routledge, 2011) and Niclas Coles and Janet Zandy's (eds.) *American Working-Class Literature* (Routledge, 2006), which, as the titles suggest, focus entirely on working-class literature in the U.S. While both works have many strong qualities, including an expansion of what can be considered "working-class literature," the lack of a global focus is a noted absence. Because of the unfortunate national compartmentalization of literary studies, there has been a general lack of comparative discussions among literary scholars examining different national working-class literatures. A further problem is that much of the scholarship on national working-class literatures – such as, working-class literatures from Germany and the Nordic countries – is seldom published in English. Thus, research about working-class literature is often fragmented according to language barriers or myopic views of nation states.

Nevertheless, some attempts have been made to dismantle this national perspective. One example is the recent publication of an issue of the English-language *Journal of Finnish Studies* (vol. 18, no. 2) about Finnish working-class literature. Another is the argument put forward by Sonali Perera in her monograph, *No Country: Working-Class Writing in the Age of Globalization* (2014), which asserts that national borders and literatures have become less relevant for the study of working-class literature. We are excited by Perera's non-Eurocentric view of working-class literature and applaud her international perspective, which bypasses arbitrary global North-South binaries. We feel, however, that nation-states have been and, to some extent, still are important localizing forces on literature. In other words, we contend that working-class literature(s) cannot be properly understood without national comparisons. In the second decade of the twenty-first century, national border walls (both physical and ideological) are becoming larger and more imposing. Book markets and fields of literary production etc. are still often anchored nationally, or in languages without global reach, despite increasing globalization. Thus, although we praise Perera's willingness to look outside of a specific national context, we feel that it is only a start. There needs to be more robust conversations connecting literatures and time-periods from a larger number of nations around the globe.

The essays collected in this volume – all of which are original contributions, written by prominent and emerging scholars who are experts in working-class literatures of particular nations – describe and analyze such literatures from Russia/The Soviet Union, The United States, Finland, Sweden, Mexico, and Great Britain. The aim of collecting them is to respond to the problems described above.

Unlike most of the existing research on working-class literature, these essays do not confine their arguments to narrow chronological periods or particular authors. Instead, they have a wide-angle

view that follows the historical and thematic threads of particular nations' working-class literary traditions. Together, they map
a substantial terrain: the history of working-class literature(s) in
different parts of the world. In effect, each essay gives a thor-
ough presentation of a particular nation's working-class literary
history, while together, they give a complex – albeit far from comprehensive – picture of working-class literature(s) from a global
perspective. Thus, this collection of essays highlights similarities
and differences between different working-class literatures and
brings to the fore how they are rooted both in international and
in national contexts. Through this perspective – which is elab-
orated further in the afterword – the collection challenges the
narrow national(istic) perspective characteristic of much research
on working-class literature, while still acknowledging national
specificities. In other words, the essays collected here present
working-class literature as parts of *working-class literature(s)* –
a totality made up of relatively autonomous but interrelated,
or even overdetermined, parts that simultaneously encompass a
global and a national phenomenon.

We feel it is important to mention that the contributing authors have not been asked to apply any given universal definition
of the phenomenon of working-class literature to their articles.
Instead, they have been encouraged to apply definitions that are
relevant within their respective national contexts and from their
respective theoretical perspectives. In this way, the essays do not
only map the histories of working-class literature(s), but also the
construction of them as such. The essays also focus on a wide
range of different aspects of these literatures, such as their relationships to other literary traditions, their contributions to the
construction of working-class subjectivities, their connections to
political struggles, etc. They are not toothless general histories;
each article engages with specific questions about their nation's
working-class literature.

Katrina Clark's essay examines Russian/Soviet proletarian literature from its birth towards the end of the nineteenth century until the collapse of the Soviet Union a hundred years later. Clark's
focus is primarily on the dialectic tension between two understandings of the concept of "proletarian" literature: as a literature

of or by workers, or as literature of or by the workers' political vanguard, i.e. the socialist intellectual, who may or may not be of working-class origin. On the one hand, self-educated workers' writing have been promoted as true proletarian authors whose work embody valuable experiences and ideals. However, on the other hand, proletarian literature, written by intellectual party members, has been promoted as a means for inculcating workers with political enlightenment. The outcome of this dialectic has been a highly heterogeneous literary history encompassing grand documentary projects supported by the communist party such as "The History of the Factories," as well as poetry written by self-educated workers and the socialist-realist production novel.

Benjamin Balthaser's essay on U.S. working-class literature places emphasis on the way that the production of class in this country has always been intertwined with racial looking, identification, and solidarity. Specifically, he explores the evolution of black nationalism, emphasizing how this political movement is also centrally concerned with class. Using Lukács' *History and Class Consciousness* (1923) and *The Autobiography of Malcolm X* (1965) as central texts, Balthaser reads widely across working-class literature in the U.S. to analyze how it produces working-class subjectivity that is centrally concerned with racial identity.

Elsi Hyttinen & Kati Launis's article on 120 years of working-class fiction in Finland mirrors many of the other literary histories presented in this volume, stressing that there is no accepted unifying definition of the term *working-class literature*. Emerging from the labor movement and labor press at the turn of the 20th century and transforming dramatically in the immediate years after the Civil War of 1918 (before being reevaluated yet again in the 1960s as the political environment in the country shifted), working-class literature in Finland has developed among the contested and fluid fault lines of class-awareness, political commitment, and aesthetic form. Chronologically mapping working-class literature onto Finish history, Hyttinen and Launis demonstrate how one significant historical moment—the Civil War—has powerful limiting effects on what is (and what is not) understood as *working-class literature*. Literary scholars, however, have reexamined accepted definitions of this term, thereby calling into question the term itself. As Finnish literature enters a new aesthetic period of experimentation and form in the 21$^{st}$ century, this lack of a set definition allows for a more robust debate on the framing of working-class literature.

Magnus Nilsson offers an overview of the history of Swedish working-class literature, focusing on how this literature has been conceptualized in different ways, at different times, and in different contexts, thereby challenging established understandings of it. Among other things, he demonstrates how connections to working-class literatures in other countries have been obscured. Nilsson argues that the conceptualization of working-class literature's relationship to national and bourgeois literature, as well as to the working class, has been debated for more than a century.

Eugenio Di Stefano's article looks at Mexican working-class literature over a hundred-year period, specifically exploring the 1920s-1930s, the 1960s-1980s, and the early 2000s. Comparing and contrasting different labor literatures with specific foci on proletarian and testimonio literatures, Di Stefano argues that each working-class literature subgenre relates to the various modernization projects throughout modern Mexican history. Moreover, reading the literature of the present day, he notes an aesthetic transition from proletarian and testimonio literatures. Di Stefano states that present day working-class literature argues less for some fictional 'authenticity' and instead insists on experimental aesthetic forms that create spaces to interrogate a political subjectivity. In a post-modern, neo-liberal world where everything is commodified, Di Stefano stresses a need for an aesthetic commitment to the forms of working-class literature that accentuate artistic invention rather than a fictional 'authentic' reproduction of working-class life.

Simon Lee's article on British working-class literature examines the genre's rich lineage, arguing that its primary focus is the tension between aesthetic and political objectives. Matching a substantial review of the scholarship of the genre with an examination of a range of literature from the Chartists to the Kitchen Sink authors, Lee contends that each period in British history continually reinvents what is "British working-class literature." Each era, therefore, infuses contemporary social concerns with adapted literary techniques that resist commodification and stagnation of the term, rendering the genre fluid and thus consistently politically- and aesthetically-engaged.

By capturing a wide range of definitions and literatures, this collection wants to give a broad and rich picture of the many-facetted phenomenon of working-class literature(s), disrupt narrow understandings of the concept and phenomenon, as well as identify and discuss some of the most important theoretical and historical questions brought to the fore by the study of this litera- ture. Thereby we want to make possible the forging of a more ro- bust, politically useful, and theoretically elaborate understanding of working-class literature(s).

## Acknowledgments

The authors would like to thank Jasmin Salih, Neal Fischer, and Heather Fox for their professionalism and wonderful help in copyediting and indexing this book. We are also grateful to our respective universities, The University of South Florida and Malmo University, who were helpful in facilitating us in meeting and working on this endeavor (a special thanks to Dr. Joe Moxely for the introduction). The making of the book was made possible by a generous grant from The Crafoord Foundation.

## References

Agrell, B. et. al., eds. (2016). *"Inte kan jag berätta allas historia?"*: *Föresällningar om nordisk arbetarlitteratur*. Göteborg: LIR.skrifter.

Bowen-Struyk, H. (2011). Streets of Promise, Streets of Sorrow: Bobayashi Takiji and the Proletarian Movement. *Japanese Studies*, 31 (3), pp. 305–318.

Coles, N. and Zandy, J. eds. (2006). *American Working-Class Literature*. London and New York: Routledge.

Ernst, T. (2011). Warum es keine Gruppe 2011 gibt: Die Literatur und die flexiblen und digitalen Arbeitswelten der Gegenwart. In: G. Cepl-Kaufmann and J. Grande eds., *Schreibwelten – erschriebene Welten*. Essen: Klartext, pp. 340–246.

Hamm, C. et. al., eds. (2017). *Hva er arbeiderlitteratur?: Begrepsbruk, kartlegging, forskningstradisjon*. Bergen: Alvheim og Eide.

Jonsson, B. et. al., eds. (2011). *Från Nexø till Alakoski: Aspekter på nordisk arbetarlitteratur*. Lund: Absalon.

Jonsson, B. et. al., eds. (2014). *Från Bruket till Yarden: Nordiska perspektiv på arbetarlitteratur*. Lund: Absalon.

Karlsson, M. (2016). The Proletarian Literature Movement: Experiment and Experience. In: R. Hutchinson and L. Morton, eds., *Routledge Handbook of Modern Japanese Literature*. Abingdon and New York: Routledge, pp. 111–124.

Markels, J. (2003). *The Marxian Imagination: Representing Class in Literature*. New York: Montly Review Press.

Nilsson, M. and Lennon, J. (2016). Defining Working-Class Literature(s): A Comparative Approach Between U.S. Working-Class Studies and Swedish Literary History. *New Proposals*, 8 (2), pp 39–61.

Perera, S. (2014). *No Country: Working-Class Writing in the Age of Globalization*. New York: Columbia University Press.

Perry, S. (2014). *Recasting Red Culture in Proletarian Japan: Childhood, Korea and the Historical Avant-Garde*. Honolulu: University of Hawai'i Press.

Russo, J. and Linkon, S. L. (2005). *New Working-Class Studies*. Oxford: IRL Press.

Safranski, R. (1976). *Studien zur Entwicklung der Arbeiterliteratur in der Bundesrepublik*. Berlin: Freie Universität.

Stieg, G. and Witte, B. (1973). *Abriss einer Geschichte der deutschen Arbeiterliteratur*. Stuttgart: Ernst Klett.

Tokarczyk, M. ed. (2011). *Critical Approaches to American Working-Class Literature*. New York and London: Routledge.

# Working-Class Literature and/or Proletarian Literature: Polemics of the Russian and Soviet Literary Left

*Katerina Clark*

What did working-class literature mean in the Russian, and espe-cially the Soviet, context? Actually, in the pre-revolutionary years when working-class literature first began to be published on any scale, but most particularly during the Soviet period, literature produced by, or about, the working classes was standardly re-ferred to not as "working class" but rather as "proletarian liter-ature" [*proletarskaia literature*]. This is an important distinction because in Bolshevik parlance the term "proletarian" had two main meanings: either of or by the working classes, or of or by the vanguard of the proletariat, i.e. of the Russian-cum-Soviet Communist Party. The latter definition dominated throughout the Soviet period, although in the first decades there was a significant lobby of writers who were fierce proponents of a "working-class literature" in the sense of a literature of and about the working classes—and so not necessarily by or about members of the Party.

In Marxist-Leninist writings any "proletarian" was ideally, or at least in his or her sympathies, not only a Party member but also working class. Hence, as if to smooth over the disparity between "proletarian" (as of the Party) and "proletarian" (as of the work-ers), most of the heroes of the classic novels of Soviet literature were workers (or poor peasants) or at least of working class or-igins. Their roles as workers and as Party members intertwined, although greater stress was laid on their roles in the Party than as workers. In the pre-revolutionary period, however, proletarian literature tended to be a literature about the working classes *tout*

How to cite this book chapter:
Clark, K. 2017. Working-Class Literature and/or Proletarian Literature: Polemics of the Russian and Soviet Literary Left. In: Lennon, J. and Nilsson, M. (eds.) *Working-Class Literature(s): Historical and International Perspectives.* Pp. 1–30. Stockholm: Stockholm University Press. DOI: https://doi.org/ 10.16993/bam.b. License: CC-BY

*court.* Much of it was written by actual workers about their lives and there was a common belief that it should be independently generated from within their ranks. During the Soviet years, there was a further complication—the interpretation of who could be included under the rubric "proletarian" shifted over time. At times, in addition to Party members and factory workers, those of poor peasant origin or agricultural laborers were viewed as "proletarians." At other times, one had to be a factory or construction worker to qualify.

This article focuses on industrial workers rather than agricultural laborers and follows "proletarian literature" from its beginnings in the 1890s through the demise of the Soviet Union a century later. Given the complexity of the topic, I have divided the text into several sub-sections, each of which discusses a particular phase or aspect of the interpretation and practice of "proletarian literature" in relation to its treatment of workers.

The article reviews successive trends in the representation of proletarians and proletarian writers as they are related to representations of intellectuals. The tension between the educated intellectual and the proletarian (whether a worker or a Party member) was already an important issue in the pre-revolutionary period but became an obsession of Soviet literature. Many questions associated with the issue were debated, directly or indirectly, in the literature and criticism of these years. The questions included: Should proletarians learn from the better educated professional intellectuals or were they too tainted by their bourgeois class identities? Could intellectuals, indeed, ever be integrated into, or play a positive role in, proletarian culture? Or rather, should the proletariat generate its own intelligentsia from within—as Gramsci in his *Prison Notebooks* advocated for with the development of an "organic intelligentsia" which might assume hegemony—and a penetration throughout society of their own system of values and beliefs that would counteract bourgeois intellectual hegemony? Did all men have the capacity to function as intellectuals and writers, and how could workers, especially the predominantly illiterate or semi-literate workers of imperial Russia, be enabled to create their own literature, to express themselves? In the Soviet period especially, the ultimate question was *What was, or should be, the relationship to each other of workers, intellectuals and the Party?*

## Working-Class Literature of the Pre-Revolutionary Years

In the late decades of tsarism – from approximately the 1890s until the Revolution in 1917 – there emerged a working-class literature in the sense of a literature by workers and about their lives. Even though the Russian working classes were heavily illiterate, many workers, often self-taught, produced poems, fiction and other works during these years, some of which were published in trade union, Bolshevik or specialized papers and journals (Volkov, 1951). Between 1905 and 1913 almost every issue of a trade union or socialist party newspaper included at least a couple of poems by self-identified workers. There were also several publishing ventures that targeted the poorly educated, such as *Gazeta-kopeika* [the penny newspaper]. Additionally, concerned or idealistic Bolsheviks and leftists of assorted stripes acted as patrons to the worker writers and collectors of their literary efforts (Steinberg, 2002).

In the early twentieth century, the leading player and patron of this movement for a literature of the masses was Maxim Gorky, himself of lower-class background and self-educated but by then a famous writer. Gorky played an influential role in fostering a literature of the "self-taught writers," partly though his association with the publishing venture Znanie. Znanie operated from 1898 to 1913 and Gorky joined its editorial board in 1900, becoming its leader in 1902. Under Gorky's leadership Znanie began, in addition to publishing established authors who were disaffected by tsarism, to provide an outlet for a rising generation of young lower class authors. But even after he severed his ties with the publishing house in 1912, he continued to act as a broker for lower class writers. However, post-1912, he increasingly differentiated between different categories of lower class writer, singling out proletarian writers in particular, and shepherding into print, for example, a series of anthologies of writings by "proletarian writers": *Nashi pesni* (1913), *Pervyi proletarskii sbornik* (1914) and *Proletarskii sbornik* (1917). Gorky also wrote (while residing temporarily in the U.S. in 1906) *The Mother* (Mat'), a novel about factory workers who become revolutionaries. The novel is loosely based on actual incidents in Sormovo in 1902. Its two main characters are a mother and her son, both impoverished factory workers. The son seems set on a life of dissolution and drunkenness, until he comes into contact with revolutionaries. And, since the text is by Gorky who would soon start the Capri school, the son starts reading the books they give him. His illiterate mother is, in turn, attracted to the revolutionary cause, though less by reading than by a profound love for her son. At the end of the novel, she dies a martyr's death: She picks up the party banner from a fallen comrade during a demonstration and is mowed down. This novel was to become a model for socialist realism (see below), where the political education and development of the "positive hero" provided a given novel's overarching plot structure.

Gorky was not only a firm believer in educating workers. He also contended that the uneducated workers should be encouraged to speak for themselves and acted as a patron for the self-taught, neophyte writers. In his article "On Self-Educated Writers" [*O pisateliakh-samouchkakh*] (1911), he reports between 1906 and 1910 that he received over 400 manuscripts from what he called "writers from the masses." In these relatively early years "proletarian literature" was virtually not yet a separate category and less than half of the manuscripts were from industrial workers. Given these writers' low level of education, most of their products were relatively primitive, abounding in grammatical errors and with little sense of how to construct a literary work. But to Gorky, this was not the point. "Please remember," he enjoined the readers of the article, "that I am talking not of talented people, not of art, but of the truth, about life, and above all about those who are capable of action, upbeat and can love what is eternally alive and all that is growing and noble – human" (Gor'kii, 1911). The workers were for their part passionate about the need to express themselves. As one worker from a train depot Gorky cites in the article puts it: "I would like to learn a little more (*pod"uchit'sia*), so that what has stored up in my soul could flow out freely in words, and these words of mine and thoughts and feelings would be read by those around me....," while another writer, a metal worker who was self-educated, reported that "some unknown force is making me turn to writing."

Gorky's work in helping the downtrodden and marginal find their "voice" may have been in part influenced by, or was at least

parallel to, a comparable movement in the United States for having workers (and other marginalized figures) write the stories of
their lives, or at least relate them to ghost writers. By giving the
downtrodden a "voice," it was felt, they might acquire full status
in society. In America, this movement was centered around the
journal *The Independent*, which, between 1902 and 1906, published some 75 autobiographies of workers, immigrants, blacks,
and native Americans. The journal's idealist editor, Hamilton
Holt, setting great store by the enterprise, was moved to declare
that "the history of the world is essentially the history of the coming into their own of the common people" (Holt, 1906; as cited in
Stein and Taft, 1971). In keeping with the consequent need to ensure that the stories were authentic, each of them was, whenever
possible, written by its narrator or, in the case of those unable or
too impatient to write, set down from interviews and then read
and approved by the person telling his or her life story. In 1906,
the year Gorky visited America, Holt published *The Life Stories
of Americans as Told by Themselves,* which selected sixteen "life-
lets" from those that appeared in *The Independent* and, it is speculated, further reinforced Gorky's conviction that the underclass
must be helped to write their own story.

"The coming into their own of the common people" was a cause
Gorky was fervently committed to. While in exile on Capri he
and other Party leaders, such as Alexander Bogdanov and Anatoly
Lunacharsky, established a school for workers at his house that
was set up to educate future leaders of the revolutionary movement, in order to make it possible for workers to play greater roles
in the leadership of the Party (it ran from 1909-1910); Gorky lec-
tured there on Russian literature. The Capri teachers lamented the
absence of "conscious leaders" among the workers in the Party
and claimed this was because the Bolsheviks had not adequately
addressed their intellectual development. Lenin was opposed to
the school because he saw it as too independent of Party leadership, and indeed while there, Gorky and his associates developed
a new concept for communists, *Godbuilding* [*bogostroitel'stvo*],
which sought to recapture the power of myth for the revolution
and to create a religious atheism that would elicit all the passion
and sense of wonderment of religion but replace religion's god

figure with man (collective humanity). Godbuilding was ridiculed by Lenin, who was also not an advocate of workerist literature. Rather, he insisted that Bolshevik intellectuals should inculcate political enlightenment in the proletarians and contended that a cogent revolutionary program could never emerge from a narrow worker milieu where their mental world was limited to everyday experiences.

Gorky, however, retained a faith in the capacities of the lower classes – especially workers (he was somewhat dismissive of peasants). He even asserted, in concluding his article on self-taught writers, that "precisely today, after [the revolution of] 1905, the intellectual should look to the growth of new ideas, new forces among the masses." To him the most significant finding in the writings of the uneducated masses he received was a marked "negative attitude towards the intelligentsia" and "skepticism and mistrust" among the lower classes, regardless of their political orientation. Often, he reported, this attitude takes the form of rabid hostility and anger. In general, writers from the masses depict the intellectual as "a sort of gentleman who is used to giving orders" and lashing out violently at the downtrodden, while also being "weak-willed and always ill-acquainted with reality and a coward in moments of danger." These reported attitudes largely coincide with Gorky's own. He himself shared some of their prejudices against elite intellectuals, though he tended to articulate them in terms of movements in the literary world. Particular bêtes noirs for him were modernist and decadent writers (even Dostoevsky fell into this category for him). In this article, he remarks that "If one were to contrast their [lower class] hard lives and their cheerful voices with the hysterical, capricious maneuvers of established literati … one would understand the hostile attitude of the masses to the intellectuals."

After the failure of the 1905 revolution in Russia, many advocated promoting a literature of the workers specifically, rather than of the broader category of the masses or the downtrodden. "Proletarian literature" became their banner term. Worker suspicion of educated elites became more pronounced and many writers wanted to throw off any tutelage from them (sometimes including from the Capri school). They expressed skepticism that intellectuals could ever fully express a truly working class point of view, commonly alleging that intellectuals could write about workers but could never really feel as workers do. The caricatured image of the "bourgeois" intellectual lingered throughout the Soviet period and reappeared in several examples of Soviet literature, as we shall see. But, in the meantime, many working-class writers advocated forming a fully independent literary movement, to be headed by truly proletarian intellectuals. The opposition to "bourgeois" intellectuals came not only because of their condescending, paternalistic attitudes, but also because supporters of a genuinely working-class literature had begun to aspire for it to be more than a niche literature. They often sought its hegemony as "proletarian literature."

## The Early Soviet years

The polemics surrounding the issue of what was "proletarian literature," who could be considered a proletarian writer, and the jostling for dominance among contending claimants to the title "leader of proletarian literature" continued well after the Revolution of 1917 and the institution of Soviet power. In the "workers state," however, the stakes had become higher and debates on the meaning of proletarian literature only intensified. During the 1920s the different positions in the arguments were espoused by different Party leaders and also by different and new, self-styled "proletarian" literary associations. The polemics continued for the entire decade until they were more or less ended by the formation of the Writers Union in 1932.

The first major Soviet organization for "proletarian literature" was the Proletcult (Proletarian Culture or *Proletarskaia kul'tura*), founded on 16 October 1917, one week before the Bolsheviks took power – an indication in itself of the way 1917 was no absolute dividing line in the story of Soviet proletarian literature. It was founded when nearly 200 representatives of workers' cultural-enlightenment societies, including the Capri veterans, trade union and factory committees, and members of assorted parties of the left attended the meeting in Petrograd, which aimed to establish a new cultural organization for workers. With support of the

Bolsheviks, the Proletcult developed into a national organization, though it was extremely variegated in its membership and their aesthetic orientations and so never really comprised a coherent movement (Malley, 1990). In the post-revolutionary years, the Proletcult was the only major cultural organization prepared to assert that literature should be working class without necessarily being Party-minded (Brodskii et al., 1929).

In this early phase of Soviet proletarian literature, most of the texts published as "proletarian" were poetry, as was also true of the pre-revolutionary movement. Of the 429 texts that the "self-taught" writers sent to Gorky between 1906 and 1910, only 67 were stories or plays, the rest were poems (Gorky, 1911). Many of the poems of the early post-revolutionary period were marked by a utopian universalism (sometimes called "Cosmism"). In this era of revolutionary fervor the hyperbolic and ecstatic were in vogue, but also a key theme was identifying the worker with the machines and metals he worked with. As Vladimir Kirillov wrote in 1918, "We have grown close to metal and fused our souls with machines." In a much-anthologized poem, "We grow out of iron" ["*My rastem iz zheleza*"], another prominent proletarian writer, Alexei Gastev, wrote of the revolutionary poet as developing into a mythic giant, reaching the height of smokestacks, as iron blood flows into his veins—in effect challenging the effete bourgeois poet who did not have such privileged access to metals or machines. The worker poets were self-declaredly trading the effete eloquence of the educated bourgeois for directness, virility, power and the toughness of metals. As one literary critic described it in the Petrograd Proletcult journal *Griadushchee* [*The Future*], in contemporary Russian literature two class perspectives were in conflict: the antiquated bourgeois "poetry of gold and ornament" and the new proletarian "poetry of iron" (Bogdat'eva, 1918, as cited in Steinberg, 2002).

Despite such bombastic rhetoric in its poetry, many leaders of Proletcult, such as Bogdanov, came from elite educated backgrounds, which partly contributed to the movement eventually losing favor. By 1920, it was no longer a major presence in Soviet Russia. By then, new proletarian literary organizations, which favored prose rather than poetry, were emerging. Initially, the most important of them was Smithy [*Kuznitsa*], which was formed from a group of writers that broke away from Proletcult on February 1 of that year on the grounds that it was too dominated by non-proletarians and hampering the development of a proletarian literature. That May, the group began a journal, *Smithy*, after which the breakaway group then came to be known. In October of the same year, the First Congress of Proletarian Writers was held in Moscow and established a new body that was to assume great importance in the literary history of the 1920s: the All-Russian Union of Proletarian Writers (VSPP), later renamed the Association (VAPP).

Among groups advocating a proletarian literature, the great division between those who believed it should be by or of the working classes and those who believed it should be by or of the Party was becoming exacerbated. In 1922, a new proletarian writers' organization, *October* [*Oktiabr'*] was formed of militant Party members, both the first and the main such body to agitate for Party commitment as the first principle of Soviet literature (Oktiabr', 1922). Shortly thereafter, *October* gained control of a new literary polemical journal *On Guard* [*Na postu*] (1923-25), which became conspicuous for its attacks on rivals—a category which included not only so-called fellow travelers [*poputchiki*] but also writers of *Smithy* who were branded unproletarian for their failure to insist on a Party orientation in literature. The group lacked strong support from Soviet officialdom, however, and had trouble getting funding for the journal which was closed in 1925. Nonetheless, it was restarted as *On Literary Guard* [*Na literaturnom postu*] in 1927, by which time the group had become the most powerful and most feared in Soviet literature. They had assumed the leadership of first MAPP (the Moscow branch of VAPP) and enjoyed such an overwhelming control of RAPP (the Russian sector of it) that they came to be known as RAPP.

Though the two groups (Smithy and RAPP) were the chief, rival claimants to the title "proletarian literature," almost none of the leaders of either organization were, in fact, of a working-class background. Most of the prominent writers in *Smithy* were of peasant or petty bourgeois origins (as was also true of most Proletcult writers), while the main writers in RAPP were characteristically from the provinces and of petty bourgeois origins.

In both cases, the writers tended to have a background in Soviet journalism before becoming writers, though many of the writers in *Smithy* had also contributed to pre-revolutionary proletarian literature (Clark, 2000). Thus, their claim to represent proletarians was somewhat tenuous, though less problematical for the RAPPists, since they identified "proletarian" with "the vanguard of the proletariat," i.e. the Party. *Smithy* urged proletarian writers to become Party-minded, but this was not considered a sine qua non, as it was on the RAPP platform, nor was it as prominent in the Smithy platform as the demand that all Soviet literature be *of the working classes*. Many members of Smithy were not in the Party though its most famous writer, Fedor Gladkov, joined the Party in 1920.

Both groups were, in their writings of the 1920s, obsessed with the question of what were the respective roles of intellectuals, Party officials, and workers in the new Soviet society. Their positions largely echo those of pre-revolutionary debates on proletarian literature, except that now, of course, the Party had to be a factor in any formulation. Smithy members largely insisted on an authentically working-class hero, while RAPP writers appropriated that topos for Party members; in their fiction no intellectual could feel at home in the Party.

The contrast between the Smithy and RAPP conceptions of the role of the proletarian can be seen in a comparison of two works: *A Week* (Nedelia, 1922) by Iurii Libedinskii who was to function in the second half of the 1920s as the leading theoretician of RAPP, and *Cement* (Tsement, 1925) by Fedor Gladkov, a leader of Smithy. Many of the differences between Libedinskii's and Gladkov's fiction that are relevant here can be attributed to the two writers' different orientations within proletarian literature. Libedinskii's first story, "A Week," was hailed repeatedly (at the time) as the first "successful" or "realistic" work of proletarian literature (Gorbachev, 1928). Set in the Party administration of a Siberian town during the Civil War, it shows an obsessive preoccupation with the question of how (or whether) a person of education or intellectual interests could (or should) be incorporated into the Party, or into the institutions of Bolshevik society. As the story progresses, it soon becomes clear that the author is judging his characters according to whether they are capable of spontaneous and, therefore, reliable attachment to the Party. The Party is described as a "family" whose members have a sense of belonging to one another (Libekinskii, 1922). This bond is the "proletarian point of view" and their commitment to its purposes. The proletarian Bolsheviks report that their espousal of this point of view comes from *feeling* rather than from *reason*, that it is natural to them (Ibid.). By contrast, those Bolsheviks who have an intellectual mindset appear as wanting, through rational conviction, to join the family, but destined to remain outsiders in it. The Party ethos and gut sense of belonging simply do not come naturally to them, and they are torn by inner conflicts. In a critical moment during a counterrevolutionary raid, the main example of the intellectual, Martynov, hesitates before pulling the trigger. In other words, he is depicted as "weak-willed and a coward in the face of danger," in the same way that Gorky reported of the way bourgeois intellectuals were often represented in the pre-revolutionary writings of the masses.

Gladkov's *Cement* is one of the two main and most popular exemplars of socialist realism, the other being Nikolai Ostrovsky's *How the Steel Was Tempered* (Not coincidentally, Ostrovsky's novel is also about the Civil War. However, unlike Gladkov's novel, the protagonist primarily identifies himself as a Civil War hero and not with his working-class origins). *Cement*'s plot concerns the restoration of a pre-revolutionary factory in a provincial town as the Civil War is winding down, amidst trying conditions of food and fuel shortages, periodic raids by White Guards, and general chaos. In other words, the situation is comparable to that of *A Week*, except that, appropriately enough, the center of action is the factory itself, not the Party headquarters. Furthermore, the main protagonist (and hero), Gleb Chumalov, is portrayed as being a worker above all. Although it is also true that Gleb is a Party member, and, indeed, is made head of the factory's Party committee shortly after the action of the novel commences, the essential image of him projected in the novel is of a young worker. Moreover, the restoration of the factory to efficient production came about not by the dutiful execution of Party directives but rather as Gleb stood up to his superiors. The mandate for this disregard for authority comes from Gleb being identified not only as a worker but also as a returning hero from the Civil War. The sorts of qualities which ensured his success in war now define his actions at the factory.

Gleb represents a new and dynamic kind of hero. He—as became true of most heroes from 1930's fiction—is all "struggle," "vigilance," heroic achievement, energy, and another cluster of qualities similar to the "true grit" of the American frontier: "stick-ability" [vyderzhka], "hard as flint" [kremen'], and "will" [volia]. The worker, then, was now a man of action, virile like the man of iron from early post-revolutionary poetry and like the workers of that poetry presented in hyperbolic terms. And yet, Gleb was identified less with the machine than with the bogatyr', the mythical knight of the Russian folk tradition now grafted onto a narrative of production. Ostensibly, Cement is a novel about postwar reconstruction and has as its subjects problems of supply, administration, labor relations, technology and guerilla insurgency on the part of counterrevolutionaries. Gleb charges over the novel's world with the greatest of ease, taking on all manner of fierce, unremitting obstacles, each one of which he manages to overcome with amazing dispatch. One admiring onlooker remarks as he watches Gleb set every corner of the economy in motion with his incredible energy: "Dammit, Chumalov old man! Harness yourself to the factory instead of the dynamos, and you'll be able to make it work all by yourself" (Gladkov, 1925, 53).

Despite this apparent privileging of the new man over technology, Cement contains a scene of what could be called 'the industrial sublime,' as Gleb visits his factory's gleaming machine. As in countless other Soviet – and especially Stalinist texts—the hero is overwhelmed when he comes across the colossus of a new construction site or, as here, part of a factory (the machine room, a veritable proletarian cathedral). The novel also draws on common tropes for representing the intellectual (in contrast to the worker) that were common in pre-revolutionary working-class literature. The main example of the intellectual in this text is Sergei, the dedicated Party member from the educated bourgeoisie. His father inhabits a clichéd musty world of books and is cut off from the real world, while Sergei, in a virtual illustration of a point made by Gramsci, displays great eloquence when addressing the workers. The workers, however, soon lose interest in his speech while Gleb, though poor in words, speaks with passion and rouses them for the cause. Similarly, when, in the novel's final scene at the celebration of the factory's reopening, Gleb, is called upon to speak, he feels that words are inadequate to express the moment. And yet, when he does address the gathered crowd, his words are met by a thunder of applause. Ultimately, Sergei, for all his devotion to the Party and self-sacrifice, has to recognize that he is alien in the Party and accept being purged from it, despite his devastation.

However, in the works of these years, the militantly "proletarian" stance of both Smithy and RAPP writers was effectively mitigated by the Leninist doctrine of the "*spets*" (i.e. the specialist or in other words the professionally educated expert). Lenin directed that, though such figures were from the bourgeoisie, their expertise was essential at a time when the country was seeking to establish itself. He decided that they should not be persecuted, but rather encouraged to accept Soviet power and work for it. Consequently, though Libedinskii in his articles insisted that only someone with the "proletarian point of view" should be able to take part in the creation of Soviet literature, he allowed that those who did not have it could acquire it in the process of class struggle (Libedinskii, 1924). In "A Week" specifically and in proletarian literature of this period generally, the fact that a given protagonist possessed a bourgeois education is represented as a reason for caution, but not for outright rejection. For instance, in *Cement,* the issue of the *spec* is largely tackled through another character, the engineer Kleist, who (like Sergei) is from the bourgeois intelligentsia. The story of Kleist provides a version of the narrative of the *spets*. Initially, Kleist is a far more sinister figure than Sergei; far from being a Party member, he had been a counterrevolutionary and, like Sergei's father, shuts himself away in an isolated world. But Kleist (in effect obeying the doctrine of the spec) has to learn to rein in his class hatred and work with the engineer. Ultimately, Kleist is moved to dedicate himself to the cause of reconstruction and Soviet power.

By no means were all of the Party leadership in favor of a proletarian literature. Lenin, especially in his 1905 essay "Party

Organization and Party Literature," insisted that there could be no independent literature and that all writers should essentially subordinate themselves to the policies and needs of the party so that literature would become "a cog or a screw" in the great Party effort. And Trotsky, especially in a series of essays he published in *Pravda* during the early 1920s and later put together as *Literature and Revolution* [*Literatura i revoliutsiia*] (1925), argued that the workers were as yet not sufficiently educated to generate a quality literature of their own and that consequently (during the interim while they gained more education and culture) so-called fellow-travelers should be the mainstay of Soviet literature. In effect, the Soviet Union would bypass proletarian literature and aim to develop a single "socialist" literature and culture.

But then Lenin died in 1924 and Trotsky lost out in the struggle for leadership. In October 1927, he was expelled from the Central Committee and in November from the Party. His supporters were expelled that December, and he was exiled in 1929. The demise of Trotsky meant the closing down or shake-up of the leading publishing houses and journals where he had acted as patron and which promoted fellow-traveler writers. In consequence, the stakes of RAPP, hitherto the chief opponent of fellow-traveler literature, rose. By 1928, it was fairly apparent that the Party favored the institution of a proletarian literature in the Soviet Union and that it had in mind primarily Party-oriented literature.[1] RAPP became extremely powerful and was well positioned to lead a proposed cultural revolution.

## Literature of the First Five-Year Plan

In 1928, the First Five Year Plan was launched, which constituted an ambitious program for large-scale industrialization and collectivization to be accompanied by a cultural revolution. The leadership aimed not only to modernize but also to eliminate the tensions between the workers and the bourgeoisie by privileging workers. "Proletarianization" became a centerpiece of the Party platform. Bourgeois professionals were replaced by proletarians (whether working class or from the Party) on a huge scale. In literature, the professional writer was denigrated and expected to compensate for having the wrong class identity by subordinating him or herself to the economic cause and its main actors: the worker masses. In a reversal of status within culture, workers were to become writers, and writers were to attempt to merge with the working classes. In ways similar to what Walter Benjamin has outlined in "The Author as Producer" (itself heavily influenced by the cultural ethos of the Soviet First Five-Year Plan), the image of the writer as a genius-creator was debunked, and the producer was to be the author for the new age. A great deal of effort in the literary world was put into having workers write about their own work place experiences. As for professional Soviet writers, they were to be auxiliaries to this cause and so were organized in "brigades" and sent to the main construction and production sites to enjoy such service roles as tutoring the workers in writing, and organizing the enterprise's wall newspaper or its library.

RAPP played the leading role in organizing the worker literary effort in the plan years. It encouraged workers, particularly record setting workers [*udarniki*], to write about their achievements at work for the benefit of others.[2] The resulting literature, largely comprising "sketches" [*ocherki*], tended to be highly journalistic and to provide a wealth of detail about technical aspects of a production process and how the worker-author's workplace was organized. In other words, this literature, though more literally working class, was somewhat pedestrian by comparison with the fiction of Gladkov, which was so much more colorful, action-packed and hyperbolic in style. Several writers sought to atone for their sin of not being purely working class and spent extended time on the new construction sites and giant factories. Some major novels were generated from their experiences, such as Gladkov's *Energy*, also known as *Power* [*Energiia*] (1932-38), based on his time in the gigantic construction project, Dneprostroi, in southeast Ukraine; Marietta Shaginian's *HydroCentral* [*Gidrotsentral*] (1929), set in the Dzorages' hydroelectric dam in her native Armenia; and Valentin Kataev's *Time, Forward!* [*Vremia, Vpered!*] (1933), set in Magnitostroi a new industrial complex being built just beyond the Urals.

Kataev's fast-paced and suspenseful *Time, Forward!* is the most successful and most readable of all the plan-years' fiction.

It concerns a team of concrete workers at Magnitostroi who are trying to break the national record for how much concrete was poured in one shift. The emphasis, then, is on pace. The ever quickening pace of the concrete workers is matched by the ever quickening pace with which the very landscape around them is transformed. The hero finds that the terrain changes so radically every day that he keeps having to rechart his route to work (Kataev, 1932).

## "The History of the Factories" as a Factory of History

Gorky returned to the Soviet Union permanently in 1930 and continued—now on an enhanced scale—his pre-revolutionary work helping the untutored masses become competent writers. To this end he founded the journal *Literary Study* [*Literaturnaia ucheba*] in 1930 to give advice to beginner writers; many of those associated with the journal subsequently became important names in Soviet literature (Dobrenko, 1997).

Gorky also devoted a lot of attention to having workers write about their own experiences in the workplace. The masses were to be allegedly transformed by writing their own lives. In the first half of the 1930s, this attempt at "writing Soviet man" was focused on two series of monographs, both founded in 1931 on order of the Central Committee of the Party but also primarily on Gorky's initiative. The first of these was "The History of the Civil War," founded on July 30. The second, one of Gorky's pet ventures and our main concern here, was "The History of the Factories" [*Istoriia fabrik i zavodov*, or *Istoriia zavodov*] established by decree of October 1931.

In the American 1930s, especially under the New Deal, the government sponsored the writing of life stories by workers and other ordinary Americans (Denning, 1996).[3] However ,"The History of the Factories" was a more ambitious undertaking. The idea was to have each major factory write its own history. These histories were to be collectively written but largely comprised of individual autobiographical accounts by workers of their time at the given factory or construction site. All the members of a given factory were to be potentially involved in writing them. In so doing, they were to draw on the memoirs of old workers from the factory, especially of Old Bolsheviks, on archival material, and on approved, Marxist accounts of history, as well. In the first instance, 102 of the country's largest enterprises were involved (primarily in the Russian Republic and Ukraine). Later, 200 more were added, but it was an aim to have a department for "The History of the Factories" in *every* major factory. In the heyday of this scheme between 1932 and 1935, as many as 88 journalists and writers worked full-time on it, in addition to others co-opted on a part-time basis. The yield in actual books was not so high. By the Second World War, over twenty books had been published in the series, and factories that did not manage a book generally produced more modest publications of some sort (Bachilo, 1959).

These histories were not only to be about factories, literally, but also about railways, the metro, canals and other such construction projects. The "factory" was to be the site of radical transformation. At the center of all these histories—whether of new factories and construction sites or those of prerevolutionary Russia—had to be the absolute contrast between the BC of prerevolutionary Russia and the AD of the enterprise under the Bolsheviks, typically described as going from an era of "rapacious barbarism," in which "everywhere one found backwardness and ignorance… the unenlightened poor and the downtrodden," to a situation where it could be said of the workers that, whatever their position in the factory, labor had become for them "creative, rich in meaning, and joyous" (Gorky and Mirskii, 1935). In other words, the temporal dimension, which was not very marked in the largely presentist accounts of workers' lives written during the years of the First Five-Year Plan, was central.

The project's main purpose was to reinforce or even create a particular consciousness, both in those who wrote and in their readers. It was not so much a working-class consciousness but rather a Bolshevik one. Gorky, in a much-quoted remark, called the project "a special kind of communist university [*Komvuz*]" offering a "process of Leninist study" ("Uskorit'", 1932). The factory, then, was no longer just the site for the production of material goods. Its primary function was as a site for the production of subjects. In this aspect the factory was not self-sufficient, as it might have seemed to be in the immediately preceding, proletarian phase of Soviet culture during the First Five-Year Plan. Production of material goods, such as pouring concrete in Valentin Kataev's *Time, Forward!* was no longer an end in itself.

Gorky in his comments on the project always insisted that the worker must "speak for himself" as a necessary condition in "the working class's striving for self-consciousness" (1931). But in reality that was far from the case. The many accounts of the organization of the project, especially in its own organ—the journal *Istoriia zavodov*—give the distinct impression that it was largely directed by the Party, on the one hand, and by professional writers who were assigned to particular enterprises, on the other.[4] Additionally, in an effort to ensure that the workers' recollections fit the desired narrative, not only were they assigned specific texts to read but also a number of state and Party bodies that dealt with ideology were sent to help the factories and their workers with the histories: Party organizations, the Komsomol, Istpart (a body that oversaw the history of the Party), the Trade Unions, the Communist Academy, the Academy of Sciences, and the management and Party heads of individual factories and construction projects ("Sozdadim", 1933). Also, questionnaires were distributed to the workers in advance, as a way of generating brief, standardized outlines of individual workers' careers. Those responsible for collecting oral narratives were advised that they should in no way record them directly (Nishchinskii, 1933; Rabinovich, 1933). Moreover, once the ostensibly "own stories" of workers were collected, they were subjected to a "working over" by professional writers, sometimes to repeated workings over.

In "The History of the Factories," then, the workers' autobiographies were presented as the spontaneous outpourings of poorly educated individuals. The distinction between third-person and first-person narration (never an absolute one) was particularly blurred, as was the line between self-expression and boiler-plate narrative. One egregious example occurred when a small team of professional writers were charged with putting together the final version of *The White-Sea Baltic Canal* [*Belomorsko-Baltiiskii kanal imeni Stalina*]. Set in an infamous forced-labor camp, these writers began interpolating "bits" of one individual worker's narrative into another's to streamline the book. Hence, many of the (auto)biographies presented in the book were actually composites of different narratives. In seeking to make the shifts from a "bit" of one worker's biography to a "bit" of another's the formalist, Victor Shklovsky, a member of the team, came up with a system of three varieties of "montage" to be used (Gauzner, 1934).

"The History of the Factories" was that privileged department of each factory, which was designated to manufacture texts rather than goods, a higher-order process. But even as the texts would be perfected in the constant "working over," so too would be the worker author-readers, so that, in this process, they too would approach becoming perfect texts. They could become higher-order selves once they had inscribed themselves/been inscribed into the (auto)biographical narratives. Thus, the question has to be asked: "Who writes whom?" Are the workers merely written, or do they discover the capacity to write and, through writing, inscribe themselves into the national narrative with a reinforced working-class identity?

## Socialist Realism

A year after "The History of the Factories" project was launched Soviet literature underwent a profound change. By Central Committee decree of 23 April 1932, all independent writers' organizations were abolished and all Soviet writers were to join a single body: the Union of Soviet Writers. Gorky was made its titular head. The list of organizations to be eliminated surprisingly included the proletarian organization, RAPP, which had as recently as 1931 seemed to enjoy so much favor with the Party that there was a distinct danger all literary organizations would be subsumed under it. A month later, in May 1932, a new term, *socialist realism*, was coined as *the* "method," or theory for a mandated unified approach to the writing of literature. The term *proletarian* had been largely replaced in Bolshevik rhetoric by "socialist." In other words, there is a real question as to whether socialist realist literature, even if by workers or about workers, could be considered "working class."

As I have argued in *The Soviet Novel: History as Ritual*, what the new term came to mean in practice was that literature and in particular the novel, or principal genre of socialist realism, was organized by a de facto masterplot that charted the "positive" hero's progress to a high level of political consciousness. The novel was then ritualized, as were in effect most of the "autobiographies" in "The History of the Factories" series, although the standard outline of a worker's life in works from that series – from ignorance and exploitation in the pre-revolutionary factory to education, greater consciousness and a superior workplace in the Soviet period – was a little different from the standard trajectory of the Soviet novel. The principal difference derived from the fact that in the standard socialist realist novel the Party and the Party hierarchy played a dominant role; a given novel's "positive hero" occupied a clear position on this hierarchy and moved up it in tandem with his political development. "Proletarian" now meant that any worker-hero was most likely a Party member and his development over the course of the novel generally led to his promotion within the Party or local administration. Commonly, at the end of a novel, he assumed leadership in the microcosm of the Soviet society in which the novel was set in a factory, suburb, collective farm or region. This outcome generally coincides with the successful completion of a task in the economic sphere (over-fulfilling the plan, building a dam, etc.), and very likely with a resolution in the hero's private life as well (boy gets girl). In the course of his progression in political consciousness and self-mastery (to greater discipline), the positive hero is guided by someone superior in the Party hierarchy and, in *The Soviet Novel,* I have analyzed the process as a version of an initiation ritual with the older Party official as a mentor figure. In other words, while the worker in "The History of the Factories" revealed in his autobiographical account how he had achieved a *greater* degree of consciousness, the socialist realist positive hero achieved (allegorically) complete consciousness. Moreover, a mentor figure from the Party hierarchy is not a factor in these worker autobiographies and the "author" is rarely a Party member, so that they represent mutations of the pre-revolutionary workerist literature that likewise had Gorky as its patron. I might add that, although *Cement* is considered an all-time classic of socialist realism, it was really only embryonically so: Gleb's superiors in the Party, far from fulfilling the mentor

function, have strong negative traits and are even his antago-
nists whom he must defy in order to have the factory restored.
Furthermore, at the end of the novel, he is not promoted, and they
remain in their positions.[5]

The masterplot is not my subject here, however, but rather the
proletarian hero in a socialist realist novel. Several generalizations
can be made. First, although a Party-guided political and behav-
ioral progression provided the central arc of a standard socialist
realist plot, a proletarian identity for the hero, or at least a poor
peasant identity, was essential. Equally essential was some past of
military engagement as revolutionary struggle. In the inter-war
years, most literary heroes had fought for the Reds in the Soviet
Civil War of 1918-21. After the Second World War, this criterion became less viable and a heroic record in the Second World
War became *de rigueur*; ideally the hero would have fought from
Stalingrad to Berlin' as virtual stations of the cross of Soviet my-
thology. The two – proletarian identity and military heroism –
were essentially twin criteria for positive hero status. For example, in Nikolai Ostrovsky's novel *How the Steel Was Tempered*
[Kak zakalialas's stal'] (1932-34), a candidate for the status
of *the* socialist realist novel, the hero Pavel Korchagin, was an
indefatigable fighter in the Civil War whose grave injury and life-
threatening illness did not deter him for most of the novel. He was
of working-class origins and had been a worker in a train depot
before joining the Red Army.

An important distinction from the fiction of the First Five-Year
Plan, however, was that in fully-fledged socialist realism, some
proletarian status, such as working in a factory, was no longer
enough for a socialist realist hero. Stalin had reversed the Five-
Year-Plan tide of militant "proletarianization" with, inter alia, the
slogan derived from his speech to the graduates from the Red
Army Academies of 4 May 1935 "Cadres Decide Everything"
[kadry reshaiut vse], i.e. qualified persons in command positions
have priority. The positive heroes of the 1930s fiction (and to a
lesser extent of the 1940s) follow the trajectory of the nation as a
whole to greater education and even higher education. Most strik-
ingly, many worker-heroes aspire to become engineers. They thirst
for an education that ensures social mobility and essentially cross

class lines, leaving their working-class lives behind as they become engineers and managers or showing greater reverence for
intellectual activity than their 1920s predecessors. In *How the
Steel Was Tempered*, for example, Pavel Korchagin, far from feeling alienated from "the musty world of books," is shown as being
drawn to books at a very early age. The humble worker borrows
them from a bourgeois friend and, though he must eventually
recognize that she is his class enemy in later years, he is guided by
Party people in more directed reading and devours books in a fre-
netic attempt to educate himself. Throughout his military career,
Pavel is inspired by Ethel Voynich's *The Gadfly* (1897), a novel
about an Italian revolutionary from an upper-class background
that was written by a similarly upper-class Englishwoman who
was married to a Polish revolutionary. On the eve of a major
battle, Pavel reads the book to a rapt audience of soldiers as an
inspirational text.

We will recall here the slogan used at the First Writers Congress
of 1934: "Engineers of Human Souls." As a *Literary Gazette*
[*Literaturnaia gazeta*] editorial published on the opening day of
the Congress makes particularly clear (citing words attributed
to Stalin), the model for the writer is now tied to the model for
the engineer ("Segodnia", 1934). Writers were no longer to overcome their tainted, bourgeois pasts and aspire to a working-class
mentality, as during the First Five-Year Plan but were rather to
lead and mold – construct – workers and peasants. This reval-
orization of the educated and professionally trained sometimes
even led to someone of that category assuming a mentor role for
the young worker rather than a senior member of the local Party
hierarchy. One example of this would be Vasilii Grossman's novel
*Stepan Kol'chugin* (1938). Set in a Donbass mining town, the novel
chronicles the progress of its eponymous hero, somewhat along
the lines of Gorky's socialist realist paradigm *The Mother*, from
callow and oppressed working class lad to a conscious Bolshevik
revolutionary. A major distinction, however, would be that, while
the son, Pavel, in *Mother* is propelled onto his path to consciousness through contact with revolutionaries among his fellow workers, for Stepan, a major step forward on that path occurs when he
is taken under the wing of a chemist who works at his factory's

laboratory and instructs him, not in ideology, but in the natural sciences. Moreover, Stepan conceives the progress to communism in terms of building a city that is new, rationally organized, and monumentally proportioned (Grossman, 1938). This shift from an emphasis on production of material goods to building a model city could be related to the great Stalinist project of the 1930s. The project reconstructs Moscow as the nation's capital and emblem, but is also symptomatic of the way the emphasis on sheer output of material goods had characterized fiction of the plan years, or what Kataev was often attacked for as fetishization of production in a "concrete hysteria."[6] This emphasis was now often subordinated in literary texts to the output of a human product, as in "The History of the Factory" series. The reconstruction of Moscow was a project of great symbolic resonance and connected with the centralization of the country in a hierarchy of power, so that the shift of emphasis from the production of material goods to the creation of a new city also stood for fealty not to a proletarian identity so much as to the political status quo.

It should not be assumed that the shift to a mentor for the working-class hero from among specialist intellectuals was general in the literature of the 1930s. More often, the mentor figure was the proletarian Bolshevik leader with or without professional training. But the Party organizer, among the various characters in a given work, most frequently functions as the "engineer" as the one most directly responsible for producing *both* the industrial complex or its material output and its new man. This is particularly the case in what is probably the most prominent socialist realist production novel of the 1930s: Aleksandr Malyshkin's *People of the Backwoods* [*Liudi iz zakholust'ia*] (1938). At the core of *People from the Backwoods* is material Malyshkin gathered during trips he made to Magnitostroi in 1931 and 1932, together with Valentin Kataev. Inasmuch as the material Kataev gathered there formed the basis for *Time, Forward!*, a comparison of the two novels helps highlight how the values of the early 1930s contrast with those of the plan years. *People from the Backwoods*, having taken so long to write, straddles the plan years and the 1930s. Consequently, it became a First-Five-Year Plan novel that has been largely influenced with the values of the

Stalinist 1930s. So while Kataev's novel is completely concerned with the protagonists on a particular construction site trying to break the national record for pouring concrete in one shift, Malyshkin's downplays the production aspect of Magnitostroi and shifts the focus of the action from the production site – the *stroi* – to the town—Magnitogorsk—which houses the workers. Moreover, Kataev attempts to provide a comprehensive account of the great changes taking place in 'the thirties,' his original title for the novel. Hence, he relates events in Magnitogorsk, not just to their local significance but to the situation of the country in agriculture, industry, politics, and intellectual life, no less.

The plot of *People from the Backwoods* is played out as a Manichaean drama wherein protagonists oscillate between identifying with the "backwoods" (chaos, ignorance, primitivism, a mercantilist mentality, and an interest in luxury and comfort – not to mention perfume, the foxtrot and the tango) and identifying with "Moscow" (Malyshkin, 1956). Magnitogorsk itself represents an intermediate point in a tri-partite hierarchy of place. When a wavering soul is won for the light, however, it is not because he is captivated by the poetry of collective labor or because he gets a thrill as the first tractor comes of the assembly line, as tended to be the case in fiction of the First Five-Year Plan. In fiction of this period, such thrills are definitely downgraded inasmuch as they are now relegated to the province of women (such as, in *People from the Backwoods*, the erstwhile gadfly, whose principal identity is as an errant wife; mended her ways after an encounter with the almighty tractor). Instead, male heroes are now overwhelmed by gigantic construction projects and, above all, by the new socialist town. The most crucial conversion in Malyshkin's novel – that of the youngest protagonist, a former farm laborer – occurs when the Party organizer paints for him an enticing picture of the path he could take in life, culminating in his becoming an engineer. We sense, however, that the lad (Petr) is more likely destined to become a political leader than a designer of factories or machinery. (This development would have taken place in Part II which, due to Malyshkin's early death in 1938, was never completed.) Another factory worker (Pashka), dreams of enrolling in a literary school, though he ultimately opts to join a new construction project (ibid.).

The teleological structure of 1930s socialist realist novels, then, charts not only political Bildung for workers and their personal maturation but also their social mobility. Though their young heroes do not want to stay in the working classes, they reject the educated intellectuals of the old dispensation who, as Malyshkin puts it, are "puffed up with their learning" and highly eloquent but live in the "half light," of a "spiritual backwoods" [*dukhovnoe zakholust'e*] cut off from the contemporary milieu. They read books by Nietzsche, Bergson and such émigré philosophers as Semyon Frank, Nikolai Berdiaev and Nikolai Lossky (ibid.). So while the young proletarian heroes aspire to an education, it is essentially to make them part of a new working-class intelligentsia, in order to supplant the rotten old one. Many of the attitudes expressed by the narrator and by "positive" protagonists are reminiscent of those to be found in Gladkov's *Cement*. For example, the great sacrifices made in the Civil War should serve as a model for workers in the present-day (ibid.). But a crucial difference between the representations of the workers in the two novels is found in the trajectory of social mobility through advanced education, which was outside the mental universe of Gleb in *Cement*.

In the post-war, late Stalin years, literature about industrial production or construction dispensed almost completely with worker-heroes and largely concerned clashes within the elite: state management, Party officialdom and engineers. Many of the central tropes of Gladkov's *Cement* were used (not entirely surprising given that between 1945 and 1948 he headed the Literary Institute that trained writers). In particular, the representation of the positive hero as a dynamo, or a ball of energy who pulls off the impossible in the workplace against the advice of professional engineers and diehard bureaucrats, reoccurs. And yet, there is an important distinction here, to be seen, for example, in Vasilii Azhaev's Stalin-prize winning *Far from Moscow* (Daleko ot Moskvy, 1948): the "impossible" feat pulled off in the workplace is no longer due to the initiative of a dedicated worker. Rather, it constitutes the main hero's insistence on placing him (or her) self within the political hierarchy, in which this feat *must* be pulled off, no matter the odds because that is what "Moscow" has ordered (and, of course, it is) (Azhaev, 1948).

In the literature of the "thaws" that came under Khrushchev after Stalin died in 1953, pushing the pace of production is debunked as Stalinist excess. The conventional opposition—between the conscientious Party member of working-class origins and the engineer who effectively impedes the pace of progress with his timidity and rejects the worker's bold plan on the grounds that it is not feasible scientifically—was now inverted. Most of the main works that engage industrial themes feature scientists who have invented superior machines or theories, but are thwarted in getting them adopted by corrupt or "careerist" bureaucrats blocking their approval. This is the detriment of the common good. However, the inventor figures in this literature are no genial workers. On the contrary, in the most famous and incendiary of these texts, V. Dudintsev's *Not by Bread Alone* [*Ne khlebom edinym*] (1956), the corrupt factory manager (nemesis of the hero-inventor) is a Party member of proletarian origins, while the inventor has a university degree. The only prominent author to champion the workers in these years, Vsevolod Kochetov, produced two major novels about dynasties of workers: *The Zhurbins* (*Zhurbiny*, 1952) about shipbuilders and *The Ershov Brothers* [*Brat'ia Ershovy*] (1958) about metalworkers, written in response to Dudintsev's novel. Kochetov, though fiercely devoted to Party, proletariat (though not himself of worker origins), and somewhat xenophobic, was swimming against what was generally seen as a liberalizing tide. By the 1980s Era of Perestroika, Dudintsev was publishing *White Garments*, or *Raiments* [*Belye odezhdy*] (1987), an exposé of the infamous agrobiologist, Trofim Lysenko, who challenged conventional wisdom in genetics with his claims that one could cultivate plants in such a way that they could thrive despite environmental factors like climate. In *White Garments* scientists from working class backgrounds are represented as usurpers, a complete reversal of the common Stalinist image of the worker, as somehow endowed with an intuitive mastery of science and engineering. Yet, in a sign of the times, Dudintsev received a Lenin prize for the novel the following year.

These two moments bookend what has been called the period of "stagnation" under Leonid Brezhnev, a time of reaction against modernism and of nostalgia for an idealized "village" of pre-industrial Russia. The stock positive literary character tended to be a peasant and the author foregrounded how peasants tended their own land and traditional wooden cottages, rather than how they served as workers (agricultural laborers) in some state or collective farm. Had "proletarian literature" outlived its time even before the use-by date of Soviet power? Had the overdone cult of the "proletarian," so identified with Soviet rhetoric, effectively spelled the demise of proletarian literature? Or, was this but a local instance of a more universal trend?

## Notes

1. This can be seen, for instance, in the fact that it sent three very highly-placed officials to attend the All-Union Conference of Proletarian Writers in April 1928. Cf. A. Lunacharskii (1928) "S"ezd VAPPa," *Na literaturnom postu* (3), pp. 2–3.

2. See Katerina Clark, "Little Heroes and Big Deeds: Literature Responds to the First Five-Year Plan," in Sheila Fitzpatrick, ed. (1978) *Cultural Revolution in Russia, 1928–1931*. Bloomington, Indiana University Press.

3. See especially Chapter Five, "The Literary Class War: Rethinking Proletarian Literature."

4. E.g. "Partorganizatsiia v bor'be za bol'shevistskuiu istoriiu zavodov," *Istoriia zavodov* (1933) sbornik 4 (5), pp. 75–79; cf. Iu. Zygostei (1934) "Byli gory vysokoi." *Istoriia zavodov*, 3 (4), pp.120–127.

5. I have in mind here, in particular, the ambiguous superior the figure of Badin, the strong Party leader who is also a rapist and enemy of Gleb. In the novel there is a potential mentor figure for Gleb in the local head of the secret police, Chibis, but that relationship is not developed.

6. E.g. Iv. Anisimov (5 Feb. 1933) "Kniga o pafose novogo stroitel'st-va. 'Vremia, vpered.'" *Literaturnaia gazeta 6*.

## References

Anisimov, Iv. (1933). Kniga o pafose novogo stroitel'stva. 'Vremia, vpered'. *Literaturnaia gazeta*, no. 6 (February 5).

Azhaev, V. (1948). Daleko ot Moskvy. *Novyi mir*, (7), pp. 12–3, 20; (10), p. 138.

Bachilo, I. (1959). Predislovie. In: *A.M. Gor'kiĭ i sozdanie istorii fabrik i zavodov; Sbornik dokumentov i materialov v pomoshch' rabotaiūshchim nad istorieĭ fabrik i zavodov*. [Sostaviteli: L. M. Zak, S. S. Zimina]. Moscow: Izdatel'stvo sotsial'no ekonomicheskoi literatury, pp. 11.

Bogdat'eva, E. (1918). "Poeziia zolota i poeziia zheleza," *Griadushchee*, 3 (June). In: M. D. Steinberg, ed., *Proletarian Imagination: Self, Modernity, and the Sacred in Russia, 1910–1925*. Ithaca and London: Cornell University Press, pp. 193.

Brodskii et al., ed. (1929). Literaturnye *manifesty (ot simvolizma k oktiabriu). Sbornik materialov*. Moscow: Federatsiia, pp. 131.

Denning, M. (1996). *The Cultural Front: The Laboring of American Culture in the Twentieth Century*. London, New York: Verso.

Dobrenko, E. (1997). *The Making of the State Writer: Social and Aesthetic Origins of Soviet Literary Culture*. Stanford: Stanford University Press.

Gauzner, G. (1934). Kollektivnaia rabota pisatelei 'Belomorstroi'. *Istoriia zavodov*, sbornik 3–4, pp. 111–113.

Gladkov, F. (1925). *Tsement, Krasnaia nov'*, (3), p. 53; English version *Cement*, tr. A. S. Arthur and C. Ashleigh. New York: Frederick Ungar, pp. 113.

Gorbachev, G. (1928). *Sovremennaia russkaia literatura*. Leningrad: Priboi, pp. 142.

Gor'kii, M. (1911). O pisateliakh-samouchkakh. *Sovremennyi mir*, 2 (February).

Gor'kii, A. M. (1931). Za rabotu!. *Pravda*, 28 November.

Gor'kii, A. M. (1932). "Uskorit' sozdanie 'Istorii zavodov.' Pis'mo A. M. Gor'kogo k 26 zavodov i fabrik," *Pravda* 1932 (145) (May 27).

Gor'kii, A. M. and Averbakh, L. (1935). O knige. In: M. Gor'kii and D. Mirskii, eds., *Byli gory vysokoi. Rasskazy rabochikh Vysokogorskogo zhelznogo rudnika o staroi i novoi zhizni*. Moscow: Gosudarstvennoe izdatel'stvo "Istorii fabrik i zavodov."

Grossman, V. (1938). *Stepan Kol'chugin* Part II, *God XXII, almanakh chetyrnadtsatyi*. Moscow: GIKhL, pp. 97.

Kataev, V. (1932). *Vremia, vpered!*, Krasnaia nov', (1), p. 16.

Klark, K. (2000). RAPP i institutsializatsiia sovetskogo kul'turnogo polia v 1920-kh – nachale 1930-kh godov. In: Kh. Giunter and E. Dobrenko, eds., *Sotsrealisticheskii kanon*. Moscow: Akademicheskii proekt, pp. 209–224.

Libedinskii, I. U. (1922). *Nedelia* in *Nashi dni* 2, p. 75.

Libedinskii, I. U. (1924). Temy, kotorye zhdut svoikh avtorov. *Na ((omit literaturnom)) postu*, (2–3), pp. 118.

Malley, L. (1990). *Culture of the Future: The Proletkult Movement in Revolutionary Russia*. Berkeley/Los Angeles/Oxford: University of California Press.

Malyshkin, A. (1956). Liudi iz zakholut'ia. In: *Sobranie sochinenii v dvukh tomakh, vol. II*. Moscow: GIKhL, pp. 125, 126, 134, 139, 154, 234, 263, 272, 363, 317.

Mirskii, D. (1935). O rudnike. In: M. Gor'kii and D. Mirskii, eds., *Byli gory vysokoi. Rasskazy rabochikh Vysokogorskogo zhelznogo rudnika o staroi i novoi zhizni*. Moscow: Gosudarstvennoe izdatel'stvo "Istoriia fabrik i zavodov."

Nishchinskii. (1933). Kak my organizovali rabotu po istorii zavodov. Iz opyta redkollegii izd-va imeni K. Marksa v Leningrade. *Iztoriia zavodov*, sbornik 4–5, pp. 215–220

Oktiabr' (1922). "Pis'mo v redaktsiiu". *Pravda*, 12 December 1922, pp. 5.

Proletariat i iskusstvo. (1929). Rezoliutsiia predlozhennaia A. Bogdanovym na Pervoi vserossiiskoi konferentsii proletarskikh kul'turno-prosvetitel'nykh organizatsii. In: N. L.

Rabinovich, I. (1933). O zapisi vospominanii. *Istoriia zavodov*, sbornik 4–5, pp. 206–208.

Segodnia otkryvaetsia Vsesoiuznyi s"ezd pisateli. (1934). *Literaturnaia gazeta*. (104) (August 17), pp. 1.

Sozdadim istoriiu 'Krasnogo Manchestera'. Rezoliutsiia Biuro Ivanovskogo gorkoma VKP(b). (1933). *Istoriia zavodov*, sbornik 4–5, p. 81.

Stein, L. and Taft, P. (1971). Introduction. *Workers Speak. Self Portraits*. New York: Arno and the New York Times, pp. vii.

Steinberg, M. D. (2002). *Proletarian Imagination: Self, Modernity, and the Sacred in Russia, 1910–1925*. Ithaca and London: Cornell University Press, pp. 23.

Volkov, A. (1951). M. *Gor'kii i literaturnoe dvizhenie kontsa XIX i nachala XX veka*. Moscow: Sovetskii pisatel', pp. 340.

# The Race of Class: The Role of Racial Identity Production in the Long History of U.S. Working-Class Writing

*Benjamin Balthaser*

This essay would like to pose what may be a provocative question: What if we considered *The Autobiography of Malcolm X* (1965) as one of the most important U.S. working-class novels of the twentieth century? How might centering Malcolm X's text as part of the working-class literary canon challenge ideas of both working-class literary tradition as well as the political meaning of its genealogy? Critic Michelle Tokarczyk suggests in her recent edited volume *Critical Approaches to Working-Class Literature* that "working class literature is far broader than the literature produced by politically minded whites" during the "Red Decade" of the 1930s (2011). Certainly, work by critics, such as Alan Wald, Bill V. Mullen, Barbara Foley and many others, have broadened our conception of the racial coordinates of mid-century radical working-class writing, noting not only the contributions of writers of color but the importance of anti-racism to the literary left since the late 1920s (Wald, 2014; Foley, 1993; Mullen, 1999). And yet, I might take us a step further and suggest that U.S. working class literature has always been about the production of a class identity through modes of racial looking, identification, and solidarity. As Stuart Hall famously wrote, "race...is the modality through which class is 'lived,' the medium through which class relations are experienced," in literature as much as in the practices of daily life (1996). But before I step into an argument about how the boundary-crossing memoir may re-center our idea of a U.S. working class literary tradition, let us consider for a moment how

How to cite this book chapter:
Balthaser, B. 2017. The Race of Class: The Role of Racial Identity Production in the Long History of U.S. Working-Class Writing. In: Lennon, J. and Nilsson, M. (eds.) *Working-Class Literature(s): Historical and International Perspectives*. Pp. 31–64. Stockholm: Stockholm University Press. DOI: https://doi.org/10.16993/bam.c. License: CC-BY

the story of the political evolution of black nationalism is also the story of class in America.

*The Autobiography* is often remembered as one of the ur-texts of the black liberation movement, read alongside Eldridge Cleaver's *Soul on Ice* (1968) and Amiri Baraka's *Dutchman* (1964). Many of the scenes stand out as part of the text's collective memory, including a high school English teacher's advice to a precocious young Malcolm to become a carpenter, his legendary conk and his decision to let his hair grow "natural," his conversion to Islam in prison, and his trip to Africa speak to text's primacy of race as determining not only personal, but national and international politics. Yet, I would argue, the pivotal moment in the text occurs not when the young Malcolm converts to Islam, but rather when he rejects his sister Ella's middle-class "Hill" neighborhood for the working class "ghetto" of Roxbury. Up to this point, the young Malcolm has largely been passive, following the counsel of his elders and submitting, reluctantly, to the world as it presented itself to him. Walking literally and figuratively down the Hill and into "That world of grocery stores, walk-up flats, cheap restaurants, pool-rooms, bars, storefront churches, and pawnshops" marks the first intentional, and I would suggest, overtly political act of the text (Haley and X, 2015).

It is often assumed that the politics of black nationalism obscure or deflect economic differences within the black community (Naison, 1983).[1] Yet embedded in Malcolm X's "descent" from the middle class Hill into the world of pool halls, musicians, and small time thieves, was the beginning of a novel of distinct class resistance. What attracted the young Malcolm to the life of hipster and hustler had little to do with the politics of assimilation—it was as much a resistance to wage labor, authority, and the carceral state expressed through a racial politics. As he says of his hustling days, "only three things in the world scared me: jail, a job, and the army," or rather, the markers of ruling class power over working class life (ibid.). Shorty's slang for a job, "a slave," ties the hipster's critique of white supremacy to the world of waged work.

This is not to say hustlers and hipsters didn't work. Young Malcolm's first job as a boot-black was valuable not as source of money, but for the connections it provided so he could sell "reefer" and engage in other illegal small deals. And most importantly for Malcolm, it allowed him to enter the world of musicians and dance-hall life. Labor was not a value in and of itself, but rather a means to achieve a life of leisure. Wrapped up in this identification is an attack on the work-ethic itself. Malcolm's donning of the zoot suit, as scholars such as Robin D.G. Kelley, Kathy Peiss, and Eduardo Pagan suggest, contained many layers of cultural and representational politics, not the least of which is a rejection of work: rather than emphasize the masculinity of the wearer through broad shoulders and uniformity of style, the suit feminized the wearer through its curves and suggested idiosyncratic excess over discipline and uniformity.[2] It is a parody of the capitalist uniform.

Indeed, Malcolm X's opposition to the small black bourgeoisie seems less embedded in the cultural affect of assimilation – he continues his life as a hustler long after he abandons the zoot for conservative blue and black suits, noting "a banker might have worn my shoes" (Haley and X, 2015). Rather, Malcolm X objects to the black middle-class views of capitalism and militarism, expecting to rise just far enough to earn their own share of it. It would be easy to suggest that Malcolm criticizes the black middle class as "trying to imitate white people," and he often lampoons their pretensions to a middle class status that they cannot themselves achieve - janitors at banks describing themselves as "in banking," maids boasting of the distinguished families for which they work. Yet Malcolm also acknowledges that many of the African-Americans on the Hill did own their own houses, have professions, and are "strivers and scramblers," succeeding on their own terms (ibid.). His distaste for the "Hill clowns" cannot only be reduced to a simple delusion that they may achieve whiteness, but rather an entire set of attitudes around class, labor, sexuality, and the state. It's important to note that many of Malcolm X's most militant detractors - from the military nurse who rolls his eyes at him to the black professor he cuts down with "n-word" – are members of the black middle class who he opposes on political, rather than cultural grounds. They can hardly be described as people who have achieved nothing in terms of class status or upward mobility. Even Malcolm X's liaison with a married white woman, Sofia, is registered as an act of theft, rather than a form of integration or assimilation: "white women...were regarded as stolen property, booty seized in the ultimate hustle," as Robin Kelley observes (1994). In other words, it is not association with white people, per se, that the young hustler objected to, but the relationship of whiteness to class and power.

What obscures the *Autobiography's* class politics is often the retrospective voice of the narrator, one who emphasizes Malcolm X's rupture with his criminal past as a way to stress the text's narrative of uplift and redemption (Marable, 2011). Yet as Kelley points out, Malcolm X's later politics as a black nationalist are frequently indistinguishable from his earlier postures as a young hustler, especially as he "lampooned the black bourgeoisie before black working-class audiences" (1994). Malcolm X's most famous (or infamous) critique of the 1963 "March on Washington" is largely expressed through class terms. When X describes the original idea of the march, it's a portrait of working class and poor radical self-activity, "overalled rural Negroes, small town Negroes, Northern ghetto Negroes...getting to Washington anyway they could – in rickety old cars, on buses, hitchhiking" (Haley and X, 2015). And yet, when civil rights leaders took control of the march, this "black powder keg" that planned to "shut down Washington" was transformed not only into a choreographed spectacle, but the class nature of the march changed as well:"It was as if an electrical current shot through the ranks of bourgeois Negroes...any rickety carloads of angry, dusty, sweating small-town Negroes would have gotten lost among the chartered jet planes, railroad cars, and air-conditioned buses" (ibid.).

Integration for Malcolm X is not about a relationship between white people and black people, but rather the control of one class of already integrated African-Americans over their segregated lessors. Indeed, Malcolm X's claim to leadership lay in his specific ability to communicate and understand the needs of working-class African Americans in contrast to the middle-class black leaders. Approached by a young hustler on the street, the black "'downtown' leader was standing...looking as if he'd just heard Sanskrit" (ibid.). For all of Malcolm X's apparent dismissal of his life as a hustler, he comments after the exchange, "the most dangerous black man in America was the hustler,"or someone for whom the class power of the black elite holds no sway (ibid.). What emerges from the *Autobiography* is a subjective class-consciousness articulated through the expression of race. As Eresto Laclau and Chantal Mouffe argue, social antagonisms of class are not static or sociological categories - they are lived, subjective, and political.[3]

What then, to make of *Autobiography* as a working class text? Typically, discussions of working class U.S. literature run within two parallel trajectories. The first is to assume that by "working-class" we mean the trajectory of literature that begins with the Russian Revolution in 1917 and responds to the call for a global "proletarian literature," or "proletcult" (see Katerina Clark's essay in this volume). While the formal period of Soviet-sponsored "proletcult" was relatively brief and ended by the late 1920s, as Michael Denning notes, the call was answered and by the 1930s "a group of landmark proletarian novels emerged," including authors, such as John Dos Passos and Agnes Smedley in the U.S. but also Haiti's Jacques Roumain, Japan's Tokunago Sunao, Peru's Cesar Vallejo, Germany's Willi Bredel, and countless others (2004). Neither a movement in a sociological sense - as many of the authors were not themselves working class - nor reducible to the Party apparatus, one could think of the global proletarian novel as both a political and aesthetic project. In the U.S., the arc of proletarian literature is marked by touchstone essays, such as Mike Gold's "Toward Proletarian Art" (1921), Kenneth Burke's address to the 1935 Writers Congress, "Toward a Revolutionary Symbolism," Meridel Le Sueur's "Fetish of Being Outside," (1935), and Richard Wright's "Blueprint for Negro Writing" (1937). These widely divergent essays on proletarian writing in the 1920s and 1930s have less in common in terms of aesthetic proscriptions (as much as they all differ widely as writers) as they do with an idea that proletarian writing is a kind of working class avant-garde. Denning refers to this movement as the "third wave of modernism," the re-alignment of the global avant-garde with a working-class politics (ibid.; Denning, 1998). By this standard, proletarian literature is measured by the articulation of a specific proletarian point of view, the production of a new subjectivity. The task, as Le Sueur

argues in her manifesto on working class literature, is to "create...
the nucleus of a new condition" (1990). It is, as Marshall Berman
suggests about all modernist writing, positioned toward the perception of a new, industrialized reality (1982).

The second trajectory locates U.S. working-class literature
within a far longer history. David Roediger's *The Wages of
Whiteness* and Eric Shocket's *Vanishing Moments: Class and
American Literature* point to a genealogy of working-class literature that developed over the course of the nineteenth century,
in a dialectical engagement with the twin capitalist enterprises of
industrial production and plantation slavery. Reading Rebecca
Harding Davis' "Life in the Iron Mills" (1861), Shocket notes the
way in which literary responses to the emergence of an industrial proletariat relied on the racialized imagery of slavery (2000).
Davis' text serves to "jar readers with the misapprehension" that
the mill workers are "black" with soot, and Schoket argues that
Davis understands exploitation by industrial capital as through
the language of racialized bondage and chattel slavery (ibid.). For
Davis, the site of the wage laborer is not the emergence of a new
class so much as the extension of bondage to white men. While this
might have served to draw powerful links between white workers
and black slaves, such rhetoric more frequently worked to natu-
ralize slavery as a function of racial difference: it is the blackening
of white men, and not the condition of exploitation, that becomes
the text's locus of dread. Shocket also draws on the extensive an-
tebellum pro-slavery literature critical of wage labor, including
George Fitzhugh and Williame Gilmore Simms, who argue that
industrial labor degrades the worker and produces an "inferior
race of men" (ibid.). As David Roediger points out, languages of
race and class emerge at the same time and are co-constitutive
(1996). Race became the language through which forms of labor
exploitation came to be witnessed, exposed, and understood.

This emergence of class through the articulatory process of
race has another more interesting implication: We might begin to
think of slave narratives as the first working-class fiction in the
U.S. As C.L.R. James and W.E.B. Du Bois have argued, one cannot appreciate the importance of slavery to the global economy,
or the role of black resistance to slavery, without understanding

that black slaves were the mid-Atlantic's first proletariat (James, 1989; Du Bois, 1998). Uprooted from their origins, clan, and previous caste, slavery threw millions of people into a proto-industrial economy that mobilized advanced forms of credit, technics of labor discipline, and the new mobility of shipping to create an army of bonded labor.[4] Du Bois's description of the first "general strike" in the history of the U.S. to describe slaves walking off their plantations to Union Army lines emphasizes not only the agency of black labor but their understanding of themselves as a class. If seen this way, we can begin to think of slave narratives as a kind of working-class literature. Frederick Douglass's 1845 memoir *The Narrative of the Life of Frederick Douglass, an American Slave* details not only his efforts to free himself from bondage but to gain control over his body and thus his labor. His struggle— first over Covey and then to retain wages earned as a caulker— are inseparable from his plans to escape North. While Douglass' description of Boston Harbor at dawn can be read as utopian fiction—industrious shipyards, bustling masons and clerks, coppery light and clean salty air—it is nonetheless a tribute to the dignity of labor. Harriet Jacob's *Incidents in the Life of a Slave Girl* (1861) is equally a narrative about control over the narrator's labor, or in this particular case, her reproductive labor. Douglass retains mastery over his own body, while Jacobs retains control over her children – a radical act of self-possession, especially as establishing conventional gender roles for former slaves would be understood as an act of proving one's humanity.

It must be noted however, that most if not nearly all working-class literature from the 19th century was literature *about* working class people, seldom by them and even more rarely, from their perspective. Davis' *Life in the Iron Mills* is instructive here: The narrator is an omniscient middle class observer who leads the reader from a well- established home and into the lives of mill workers. In this sense, the novella is as much about the workers as it is about middle-class apprehensions about workers - their morality, their liminal racial status, and above all, their real and symbolic proximity to the narrator's home. Like Jacob Riis's 'Lantern Shows' of the urban working classes, 19th century literature about class was often an attempt to provide a kind of surveillance over the poor.

Benevolent at times, and reactionary at others, its function was to act as a layer of mediation between the poor and the ruling elite. This form of mediation is, in many ways, also the logic of the slave narrative. While Douglass's first-person memoir powerfully constructs his own self-possession, it is also a mediated text, verified by well-known white abolitionists who must testify to Douglass's character, especially his honesty, industry, and his "meekness." This seems a surprising claim for a man who wins his freedom, at least in part, by physically defeating a stronger and older, white overseer (Garrison, 1995). As Amy Kaplan articulates in *The Social Construction of American Realism*, the realist novel is constructed as a kind of literary Central Park, a well-mannered site at which all classes can converge and, it is hoped, form a lawful democratic polity (Kaplan, 1988). William Dean Howells novel, *A Hazard of New Fortunes* (1890), constructs this vision as a dinner party, at which an upper-middle class writer hosts a dinner for the owner of his magazine, as well as the working-class immigrant translator. One gets the sense that for Howells, had the dinner been successful, democracy might have been achieved.

The twin trajectories of working class literature – as an avant-garde movement of politically working-class writers and as a literature marked by racial modes of seeing and identification – came together in the 1930s, as an increasingly influential Communist Party and other left organizations placed race/ism at the center of anti-capitalist strategy and analysis. In the words of Hakim Adi, the Communist Party became the "era's sole international white-led movement ... formally dedicated to a revolutionary transformation of the global political *and* racial order" (2009). In the U.S., anti-racist Communist Party-USA (CPUSA) activity included expelling "white chauvinist" members after public trial, integrating labor unions and Party social events, recruiting African-American members, and most famously, defending the Scottsboro Boys from the death penalty (Naison, 1990). As scholars, such as Robin Kelley, Barbara Foley, James Smethurst, Alan Wald, and Bill Mullen noted, the Communist Party also became a major site for African-American cultural production.[5] While few African-American writers publically announced their membership as did Richard Wright and later W.E.B. Du Bois, nearly all

African-American writers in the 1930s were either members of the party or at least "fellow travelers," including Claude McKay, William Attaway, Frank Marshall Davis, Lorraine Hansberry, Audre Lorde, Ralph Ellison, Chester Himes, Sterling Brown, Langston Hughes, Paul Robeson, Countee Cullen, Alain Locke, Ossie Davis, Dorothy West, Robert Hayden, and many others (Wald, 2000).[6] The cultural impact of both Communist Party policy as well as the sheer number of African American intellectuals attracted to the Party at this time had a profound impact on U.S. political and literary culture, wedding anti-racism and the African-American freedom struggles to the left in ways that are still actively felt.

This is not to suggest the Communist Party invented the U.S. obsession with ways in which class and race are co-constituted; rather, one could say, it turned the abject fear of "racialized" waged-workers into a point of solidarity and revolutionary potential. As I will discuss below, recognizing or identifying one's racialized status as a worker or with other workers became a marker of political awareness. As Michael Denning reframes Stuart Halls's famous phrase, "ethnicity and race had become the modality through which working class peoples experienced their lives and mapped their communities" (1998). Clearly, *The Autobiography of Malcolm X* fits neatly within the trajectory of 19th century working class literature. The text pays tribute to Douglass's *Narrative*, from its opening with an act of racist violence, to the natal alienation he faces with the loss of his parents, from the struggle for self-possession and uplift through a growing political awakening, to the quest for literacy. And one could also say it is a text that ironically signifies on Douglass's *Narrative*, opening where Douglass closes – in the North. No longer a producer's republic of small craftsmen in Douglass's vision of Boston Harbor, the North is produced through racial and economic division, a division enforced in equal parts through deception and violence. *The Autobiography* returns back to the 19th century, when class was understood as a category produced in relation to a racialized institution of slavery. And yet one can also think of the *Autobiography* as an extended meditation on the class lines within the African American community, and how a politics of black liberation must recognize class as having its own discursive and material logic. Indeed, after his hajj to Mecca, Malcolm X articulates what racial theorists Michael Omi and Howard Winant would call a Gramscian theory of race: Whiteness is not a blood quantum or phenotype, but rather as Malcolm X says, "attitudes and actions toward the black man." In other words, it is a political project, one with a distinct class character (Haley and X, 2015). Rather than think of Malcolm X's politics of black nationalism as a rupture with the earlier 20th century proletarian movement, I would argue it is a fulfillment of it.

## Proletarian Literature: The Epistemology of the Working Class

Neither Malcolm X nor the much more conservative Alex Haley identified themselves with the proletarian literary movement in the U.S.; nonetheless, *The Autobiography* bears as much in common with theoretical aims of proletcult as it does with the long history of writing on class and race. *The Autobiography* is more than just a political tract - it powerfully argues for the *subjectivity* of working-class African Americans. The problem with integration for Malcolm X is as much a question of racial purity as it is the middle-class nature of integrationist organizations; the working-class hustler is under no such illusion. And yet, working-class literature is thought to be less a concern of working-class subjectivity and an inheritor of the particular class struggles of a given nation, but as a formal question of realism. Often when discussing the theoretical origins of proletarian literature, the genre of "social realism" is forwarded as a short-hand for the entire movement. Georg Lukacs' *The Historical Novel* (1937), with its examples rooted in nineteenth century authors and its call for a dialectic between surface transparency and social complexity, is understood to have articulated the intellectual framework of the genre. Yet as James Murphy states, even at the moment of proletcult's articulation during the Bolshevik Revolution, such a point of view was only one among many (1991). What is clear from his accounts of Party intellectual debates, proletcult was to give voice to worker-writers and display class struggle - yet questions of genre and style were left relatively open. As Michael Denning argues in *The Cultural Front* (1999), the proletarian literary movement should be considered an experimental avant-garde, stylistically innovative and self-reflexive (1998).[7] Indeed, I would suggest what unites post-Revolutionary working class literature is not a style but rather a particular epistemology toward the meaning of class.

It is not the Soviet literary critic of Lukacs' *Historical Novel*, but rather the 1920s avant-garde theoretician of Lukacs' *History and Class Consciousness* that should be seen as the intellectual framework for self-consciously working-class literature in the 20th century. As Frederic Jameson writes, Lukacs' *History and Class Consciousness* (1923) forcefully argues that the working class is defined by more than just a political project, rather the text is a "prophetic invocation of a radically different class logic— the praxis as well as the new epistemological capacities of the industrial working class" (2009). For Lukacs, the working class is confronted by twin crises: both its exploitation by another class, but also its reification, or the abstraction of both its life and its labor from a totality of being and into a thing—a commodity. The irony for Lukacs is that the very status of "worker" is a negative category, as it implies both the fragmentation and compulsion of their labor and self. The task of a proletarian political movement is to be aware of one's objectification within the processes of production and consumption. Indeed, for the bourgeoisie, their life and interests are identical with their objective position with the capitalist mode of production. For the working class, they must develop a point of view that is not only objective, but subjective as well. Quoting Hegel, Lukacs articulates such working-class subjectivity as the moment in which a class becomes "*conscious of its own essence*" and that it "possesses its absolute truth only in this recognition and not immediately in its *existence*" (1972). In other words, the consciousness of the proletariat exists not only in an accurate, factual representation of its own condition, but in a collective awareness of a future in which its labor and life are free from contradiction. Putting it more simply, Lukacs states that the only way to "break through this barrier" of reification "is to overcome it inwardly *from the very start* and develop its own point of view" (ibid.).

It would be incorrect to conflate realism with proletarian literature by this definition. Realism, to use William Dean Howells' formulation, desired to depict the "phrase and carriage of everyday life," an accurate depiction of reality based on the empirical facts of human observation. Harding Davis' *Life in the Iron Mills*, as with Howells' *Hazard of New Fortunes*, relies on an often 'neutral' observer, recording the world around them and offering mediation between the opposing class forces. For Lukacs, this kind of realism recalls the "static" world of bourgeois history, in which the "untranslated immediacy of facts" conceals not only the ongoing transformation of the "objective forms of life" through class struggle, but the reification of reality: the commodification of social relations appears as normal or naturalized (ibid.). Furthermore, for Lukacs, this form of narrative representation is the hallmark of bourgeois art, even when deployed for radical ends. Referring to such realism as "reflection theory," such art freezes reified social relations into place (ibid.). "Reality is by no means identical with empirical existence," Lukacs argues, suggesting that reality is a "complex of processes" that are always in motion, a "process of Becoming" (ibid.). Thus, the working class is both subject and object, or what Lukacs refers to as the "subject-object of history"— both captured within reified social relations, but also due to its particular standpoint, capable of overcoming and transforming its reified reality through a revolutionary movement.

One could say that for Lukacs, proletarian art is in tension with the reality it seeks to document—at once in need of exposing the class relations of production, while also critically undermining the very reality that produces such relations. It is a dialectical vision of art and reality, produced by the processes it seeks to undo. Frederic Jameson refers to Lukacs' theory of subjectivity as a prefiguration of "standpoint theory," which poses that one's reality is produced through membership in a particular social group (2009). And yet, unlike standpoint theory, identity for Lukacs is materially constructed, but never fixed. It is produced in a constant process of ongoing class relations and social forces. One can think of a standpoint emerging on a social terrain constantly in motion - materially fixed in one sense, but uneven, in process, and fluid in another. Often one can perceive this tension revealed in proletarian novels by their uneasy relationship with their own temporal range – contra the bourgeois novel, the span of one person's life. In Myra Pages's *The Gathering Storm* (1934), the novel refuses to concede the defeated textile strike as a finality and, rather, looks to a mobile and dynamic image of a storm on the horizon, yet to be realized. Likewise, the final pages of Mike Gold's *Jews without Money* (1930) points to a revolutionary future that will redeem the suffering of a "lonely, suicidal boy" (Gold, 2009). One can think of the temporal tensions between Malcolm X's hustler past and revolutionary present as caught between objects and subjects of history.

## Blueprint for (Working-Class) Negro Writing: A Question of Perspective

One essay, in particular, brings together the two tendencies of proletarian literature in the twentieth century - both the intersecting legacy of race and class in radical writing, as well as the dialectical tension of the "subject-object" of history. Richard Wright's essay, "Blueprint for Negro Writing" (1937), is a call for African-American writers to directly address the needs and concerns of working-class African Americans, while also bringing to bear a social analysis that ties together daily struggle with the workings of global capitalism. Wright signifies on W.E.B. Du Bois's formulation that the "talented tenth" of educated African-American men should be the political and moral leadership of the African-American community, pointing out that the African-American working classes are politically far ahead of the educated African-American intelligentsia:

> Lacking the handicaps of false ambition and property, [working-class African Americans] have access to a wide social vision and a deep social consciousness. They display a greater freedom and initiative in pushing their claims upon civilization than even the petty bourgeoisie. Their organizations show greater strength, adaptability, and efficiency than any other group in society. (Wright, 2007)

Like Lukacs' own theory of working class agency, the African-American working classes are materially positioned to resist identification with the ruling class; indeed, they are positioned to resist reification. Much like Malcolm X's critique of the black middle class, Wright condemns literary production of the "rising Negro bourgeoisie" as "decorous," couched in "servility" and emblematic of an entire class—"bloodless, petulant, mannered, and neurotic" (ibid.). He suggests that black middle-class writers are alienated even from their own works, that "at best, Negro writing has been external to the lives of educated Negroes themselves." Like Malcolm X's critique of the "Hill clowns," they are performing the alienation of a reified, capitalist society to which they wish to belong.

And yet, Wright believes there is a necessary role for literary production. Much like Lukacs' observation that to perceive one's "objective" status within a mode of production is necessary but not sufficient to produce a revolutionary consciousness, Wright also argues that working-class African-American "folklore" – blues songs, oral tradition, jazz – articulates "the collective sense of the Negroes' life in America" and marks the "vital beginnings of that recognition of value in life as it is lived." Yet Wright also acknowledges that African-American folklore by itself is not sufficient to lead a transformation of African-American political culture. He describes it as "nationalist" in orientation, and perhaps more than anything else, it lacks a global analysis of how the black liberation struggle fits within capitalism and colonialism. The nationalism of African-American folklore needs to be learned, respected, and understood; yet it is the role of the educated (or in Wright's case, self-educated) writer to re-construct a systemic analysis - what Lukacs would call "the social totality." This "aspiration to totality," which marks un-reified class consciousness for Lukacs, is a global understanding, to demonstrate how immediate events are complex, interconnected, and part of a larger system logic (Lukacs, 1972).

Wright refers as "a question of perspective" this understanding he feels is the special task of the African-American writer. I believe this is what Lukacs would refer to as "subjectivity." The relationship between the writer for Wright and revolutionary consciousness mirror one another. For Wright, it is the writer who must demonstrate the most advanced consciousness of the working class:

It means that Negro writers must learn to view the life of a Negro living in New York's Harlem or Chicago's South Side with the consciousness that one sixth of the earth's surface belongs to the working class. It means that Negro writers must create in their readers' minds a relationship between a Negro woman hoeing cotton in the South and the men who loll in swivel chairs in Wall Street and take the fruits of her toil. (Wright, 2007)

Meridel Le Sueur articulates a similar principle in her 1935 essay, "The Fetish of Being Outside," contending that it is the writer's "peculiar and prophetic function to stand for a belief in something that scarcely exists...the nucleus of a new condition and relationship to the individual and society" (1990). For Le Sueur (as for Lukacs), the role of the writer is both objective and subjective. Lukacs's tension between the documentary and revolutionary character of class consciousness is to be resolved by the revolutionary writer. She acknowledges that the "dark, chaotic, and passionate world of the proletariat" is not necessarily revolutionary, and yet articulates the role of "belief" as the writers' function to not just document but to also articulate an unreified social existence that does not yet exist. Yet for Wright, Le Sueur's metaphor of the "dark...passionate" world of the proletariat has very literal connotations: the black writer for Wright not only represents the working class, but the global non-white world.

## The Race of Class: The Proletarian Novel as Ethnic Bildungsroman

It would be impossible to talk about the development of working-class writing in the United States without a discussion of Mike Gold and his autobiographical novel, *Jews without Money*. Often taken to be the ur-proletarian novel of "Red Decade" of the 1930s, it was seen then and in retrospect as "a road marker to guide the proletarian literature that followed" (Rabinowitz, 1991). In part, this owed to Gold's already outsized role as editor of *The Liberator* and then *The New Masses*, both avant-garde intellectual publications of the CPUSA. As editor, Gold wrote columns and manifestos calling for and defining what proletarian literature in the U.S. should be. Much like Richard Wright and Meridel Le

Sueur's literary manifesto written over a decade later, Gold placed the subjectivity of the working-class writers at the center of his 1921 "Toward Proletarian Art." Writing that proletarian literature needs to be drawn "from the depths upward," Gold describes "Art" as the "tenement pouring out its soul through us" (1972). As a construction, the writer becomes a conduit not only for their personal experience but also for the entire social structure of capitalist inequity. Indeed, the writer's subjectivity is identical with his/her own positionality within a capitalist framework. The image of the depths moving toward the surface also calls to mind a deep materialism, in which the writer's psychological "depths" merge with the "base" of the literary superstructure. Much like the working-class literature of the proletarian movement that Lukacs theorized, Gold's essay calls for an objective-subjectivity.

Yet for the ur-text of proletarian literature, Gold's novel raises important questions about what the term means. Even though Gold calls his 1921 manifesto a work of literature about the "strike, boycott, mass-meeting, imprisonment, sacrifice, agitation, martyrdom, organization," *Jews without Money* is nearly free of any mention of revolutionary organizing until the final two-page invocation. As Michael Denning writes in *The Cultural Front*, the novel is a "ghetto pastoral," and the impact the novel had on American literature is less its call for revolution, but rather its placement of the urban, ethnic, immigrant landscape at the heart of the working-class imaginary. Often far too much attention is paid to the novel's call for revolution in its final pages. The content (what Denning refers to as its "form") is the "tenement pastoral," a genre "that Gold helped invent" and which went on to "became one of the central forms of proletarian fiction" (Denning, 1998). In other words, while Gold himself may refer to the Bolshevik revolution as his inspiration and Walt Whitman as his national icon, to locate the primal scene of proletarian literature in an immigrant ghetto is less a break with the past as a fulfillment of its contradictory impulses. It should thus come as little surprise that Gold's novel created such a sensation in revolutionary literary circles: It provided a model not so much for revolutionary agitprop, as it did to combine the call for proletarian writing with the racial matrix of class in the U.S. Furthermore, the book not only located race, language, national status, and ethnicity at the heart of the experience of class, but it also provided a ground for the narrator to locate his own racial and classed identity within a racially bound urban center.

As a novel about revolution, *Jews without Money* is fairly straightforward: Its young narrator observes through the multiple failures and defeats of his parents and comrades that there is no way out of his poverty but through collective, revolutionary action. And indeed, the novel is often derided as a "conversion" narrative, perhaps one of the easiest and least interesting modes by which a proletarian writer may overcome the Lukacian tension between proletarian literature's objective and subjective character. Yet as a novel about race, *Jews without Money* is profoundly complex in its treatment of the Jewish inhabitants of the New York City East Side ghetto. They are at once distinct as Jews, as immigrants and non-citizens, as non-whites, and equally as importantly, as non-blacks for whom full citizenship may at some future time hold promise. Indeed, the Soviet cultural formula, "national in form, proletarian in content," may refer not only to the novel's status as ethnic literature, but rather that the U.S. is a place in which class gets made through race. Thus, the decision the narrator has to make, in one sense, is what race he may decide himself to be. It is not a new question within Jewish literature - as Abraham Cahan's hapless narrator in *Yekl* (1896) abandons his dark, Orthodox "squaw" of a wife for the translucently white, secular Mamie, or more (in)famously, Jackie Rabinowitz becomes "Jack Robin" just long enough to leave the ghetto for uptown blackface performance in the 1927 film *The Jazz Singer*.

It should also be noted that the politics of immigration took a dramatic turn to the right during the years of Gold's radicalization in the 1920s. Responding in part to the rise of the 20th century Ku Klux Klan, the 1924 passage of the Johnson-Reed act enacted "national origin" quotas that were intended to reduce immigration from Southern and Eastern Europe to almost zero. The rise of the anti-immigrant and anti-Catholic/anti-Jewish Klan hardened racial lines in the 1920s, shifting national discourse from "melting pot" assimilation to an ideology of biological racial difference and often equating African-Americans and Southern/Eastern Europeans as not only culturally inferior (and in need of "Americanization"), but genetically inferior (Daniels, 1998). Jews, in particular, were singled out as "abnormally twisted" and "unassimilable," linking them phenotypically with African Americans and Asians (ibid.; Jacobson, 1999). The 1924 Act also divided the globe into East and West, marking all of Asia as one single racial category, while differentiating European immigrants by geographical proximity to Asia and Africa (Ngai, 2004). Gold's novel responds to the new racial matrix of non-Western European immigration by substituting a teleology of assimilation for a teleology of revolution. And yet Gold's teleology of revolution – based on Jewish-black identification – does not rely on a universal, unmarked subject. Rather, it is through Gold's identification with a racial marked Jewishness that he comes to his political awakening.

*Jews without Money* is the first prominent Jewish novel published in the U.S. to not only resist assimilation entirely, but to also embrace Jews' liminal racial status as a positive *class* marker of resistance. As William Maxwell points out, Gold came to the "conclusion that it was self-destructive for Jews to adopt the course of other European immigrant groups and inch toward the status of full-fledged white Americans by learning to loathe blackness" (1996). Maxwell continues by arguing the black haired, swarthy, broad-nosed, impoverished Jewish adolescent – described as a "gypsy" and nicknamed "Nigger" by the community – transgresses the boundaries of race at a moment in which racial difference was assumed to be biologically rooted (ibid.). In an historical moment in which racial categories were understood to be "self-evident" and "immutable," "Nigger" both undermines racial binaries but also locates race as a political relationship to power. In other words, it identifies with African Americans at a moment in which Jews were internally and externally pressured to assimilate.

"Nigger" was far from an outcast for Gold. Indeed, Mikey, the narrator, regarded him as one of the heroes of the text. "He was ready to die for justice," Mikey says of his adolescent friend after he resists a police officer's order to disperse from an illegal dice game. Mikey notes that the cops routinely harassed the children in the neighborhood, stealing money, sports gear, and violently treating the kids like "criminals" (Gold, 2009). Expected to forfeit the pennies to the cop after fleeing, "Nigger" leads the cop on a foot chase, finally leaping between buildings to avoid being caught. Continuing the criminalization of ghetto youth, Gold refers to the school as a "jail" and proudly boasts that "Nigger" hit a teacher "on the nose" after the teacher called Mikey a "little Kike" (ibid.). "Nigger" defied the racist and anti-Semitic authority against which Mikey and his friends fought, both on the street against rival Irish and Italian "Christian" gangs, as well as the official authority of the state manifested in the school system and the police.

While Baruch Goldfarb, a wealthy Jew, is described as a "Zionist leader," it is "Nigger" and the novel's other racially liminal gangster, "Louis One-Eye," who form "the valiant armies…in defense of the Jews" of Mikey's dreams (ibid.). It is "Nigger" who not only defends the young Mikey from his anti-Semitic teacher but also leads the gang against the other ethnic gangs of Irish and Italian youth in the Lower East Side. Equally, Louis One-Eye, while a predatory gangster and one of the villains of the book for entrapping Mikey's aunt into prostitution, defended the Jewish community against a mob of anti-Semitic Italian youths who assaulted elderly Jewish men (ibid). It should be noted that One-Eye (like "Nigger") received his education about the American state through the prison system, where One-Eye both lost his eye to police torture and also earned his reputation for fierceness.

Curiously, Mikey refers to "Nigger" as both someone who "scalped Indians" and "shot the most buffalo among the tenements," while also describing him (and the gang of which Gold was a part) as Indians, with "Nigger," the "chieftain of our brave savage tribe" (ibid.). As Richard Slotkin notes, the terrain around metaphors of the West underwent a profound shift in the 1930s, with the Western entering into a period of eclipse in the early 1930s, as urban crime dramas and gangster films portrayed a gritty world of poverty, criminality and desperation (Slotkin, 1998). As the city became a site of both crisis and political conflict in the deepening Depression, the ethnic gangster became a kind of "urban savage," tamed by the lawman of the city instead of the Indian-fighter of the frontier. Signifying on this trope, Gold both articulates "Nigger" as simultaneously the Indian-fighter *and* the "Indian" at the same

time, with Gold's gang figuring as both his "braves" and his dep-
uties. Gold never resolves this contradiction in the novel, even as
fantasies of both the Western, as well as "the charge up San Juan
Hill" by Teddy Roosevelt, figure frequently in the text as marks of
the narrator's "Americanized" imaginary. Rather than suggest their
lack of resolution poses a problem, I would say these seemingly
opposed and even contradictory images - in which Gold's gang is
both "Indian" and "Indian-fighter" - speak to the contradictory racial logic of the text. Mikey acknowledges not only his character's
whiteness in relation to African Americans in the text - especially
as his mother befriends black workers in the kitchen in which she
works - but also the liminal and othered racial status of the Jew.
Rather than see race as a fixed category, Gold mobilizes it as one of
political and class solidarity. "Nigger" is not "black" because of his
dark skin. Rather, his "blackness" emerges from his oppositional
stance and his defense of what Gold refers to as the "the Jewish
race". As perhaps the greatest irony for the "chieftain of a savage
tribe," "Nigger's" father hangs a poster of the Roosevelt's charge
up San Juan Hill in his living room, even as it is the very army ex-
terminating "the savage" abroad in U.S. colonial wars Gold spent
years opposing (Gold, 2009).

It should also be noted that such liminal racial identifications
are not in effect with members of the Jewish elite. Zechariah
Cohen, Mikey's father's boss, wants Mikey's father to buy real
estate in what were then Brooklyn suburbs. Cohen's wife, "glit-
tered like an ice-cream parlor" with her bleached hair and talked
only of how much money she can spend, the rich foods she eats,
and her expensive taste in clothing (ibid.). The suburb itself, for
"refined Jewish businessmen," is a site of emptiness and isolation, where "paved streets ran in rows between empty fields" and
in a "muddy pool where ducks paddled...a sign read 'Build Your
House in God's Country'" (ibid.). Gold represents the suburbs
through the figure of Mrs. Cohen, as a space of whiteness and
consumerism. They represent a rise in class status and a removal
from possible racial associations with non-whites. To represent
the suburbs as a site of emptiness and isolation suggests that
whiteness and economic success – "my fine expensive furniture,
my hand painted oil-paintings, my up-to-date water closet" – is

literally and figuratively a dead end, a site of empty houses and desolate lots (ibid.).

While the Jewish messiah who Mikey waits for is secularized into a call for "workers' Revolution" in the final page of the novel, what is clear in the text is that Mikey's path lay not with the frontier figures of his imagination nor the white suburbs of his father's dreams. Instead, Mikey joins "Nigger's crowd," which leads him, just a paragraph later, to wander into the fateful aura of the East Side soap-box oratory introducing him to his new life purpose (ibid.). While "Nigger" himself is not a revolutionary, the novel's arc only makes sense as a series of identifications in which the narrator learns less about his politics than about his identity. In other words, Mikey's politics are his identity. As a narrative, *Jews without Money* seems to have no plot. It is a series of anecdotes about Mikey's childhood on the Lower East Side. Yet, as a fictional narrative, the novel's tension lay in the narrator's decision to join with the "dark proletarian instinct" of his mother, rather than the dreams of whiteness imagined by his father (ibid.). The "darkness" of his proletarian instinct seems to have a distinct racial cast, as the phrase perhaps unwittingly suggests. If the tension in proletarian identity for Lukacs lay in the contradiction between the lived reified present and the social totality, the tension in *Jews without Money* is not resolved by the call to revolution. It is resolved through the narrator's decision to align himself *racially* with members of his own class, rather than abandon them for a dream of success or a flight of middle-class fancy.

Given the seminal nature of *Jews without Money* in defining U.S. working-class literature after the 1930s, it is interesting to note the direction that proletarian literature did *not* take in the decades following. At near the same time of *Jews without Money's* publication, a slew of novels exploded into the American literary scene, fictionalizing the Gastonia, North Carolina textile strike. These included novels by well-known writers and journalists, such as Sherwood Anderson's *Beyond Desire* (1932) and Mary Heaton Vorse's *Strike!* (1930), as well as intellectuals closer to the Communist Party orbit, such Grace Lumpkin's *To Make my Bread* (1932), Fielding Burke's *Call Home the Heart* (1932) and Myra Page's *Gathering Storm* (1932). Despite their coverage of political events and their far more open and direct treatment of collective labor organizing, the novels quickly faded from view (Denning, 1996). They received ample press attention, as did the strike they recorded. Two novels, *To Make my Bread* and *Gathering Storm*, even received prior publication in the Soviet Union and official state backing (Foley, 1993). Yet, as Denning notes, the authors were all "outsiders" and largely journalists, equated more with topical writing than with the proletarian tradition (Denning, 1996). That is to say, they lacked the quality of subjectivity and the production of identity that novels such as Gold's made central to their narrative arc.

These set-piece proletarian novels ended up as more of a footnote to literary history, rather than the beginning of a new literary movement – much as the actual Loray Mill strike at Gastonia failed to ignite a new interracial workers' movement, despite the heroism of the strikers and organizers. Many of the touchstone working class texts of the 1930s and 1940s, including James Farrell's *The Studs Lonigan Trilogy* (1935), Clifford Odets' *Awake and Sing* (1935), Philip Roth's *Call it Sleep* (1934), Nelsen Algren's *Never Come Morning* (1942), Chester Himes' *If He Hollers* (1945), Ann Petry's *The Street* (1946), Richard Wright's *Native Son* (1940), and Carlos Bulosan's *America is in the Heart* (1943), are more an exploration of the ethnic and/or racial self through the classed structure of power than they are truly novels of organized, working-class revolt. In this sense, Pietro Di Donato's 1939 *Christ in Concrete* is instructive. The novel opens with Geremio, a master brick layer in charge of his Italian-American crew, labeled as "wops" and "Dagos," justifying both the foreman and the building contractor to ignore the very safety violations that condemn Geremio to his "crucifixion" as the building collapses upon him (di Donato, 1993). A "wop," to the building contractor, is the status of a non-person, or a body to which full consideration need to be give, either during life, or after death. Geremio's wife learns this when she attempts to collect his death benefit – a benefit not awarded to non-citizens. Geremio refers to himself and friends as "Christians," denoting both their inherent value and equality before God, but also his submission to his foreman, or what the novel refers to as "Job." Both his dehumanization and submission before work are redeemed when his son, Paul, refuses both the cross and submission to his boss, telling his mother that he demands "justice" (ibid.). Yet what characterizes the novel is not so much the schema of the son's awakening, as the strange and often stilted language of the omniscient narrator, who details Italian-American life in an English that feels almost as though it is a translation. This strangeness, or duality within the language of the novel, is as much the "content" as Paul's final act of rebellion. They are inseparable from one another. Paul's first act of aggressive speech is also rendered against this mother's Italian-inflected phrasing, suggesting that their conflict is as much a question of identity as it is one of politics – or that the two are one and the same.

I would go so far as to suggest that, at least, part of the effective power of John Steinbeck's *Grapes of Wrath* (1939) - by far the most popular working class novel of the 20th century - lay precisely in the racialization of Tom Joad's body from white, protestant male to "Okie," signifying through the perception of difference the Joad's loss of class and racial status. The Joads understand themselves at the outset of the novel as not just farmers but as members of a pure racial stock. As Roxanne Dunbar-Ortiz points out, Steinbeck, as a result of his own racist views, got the racial self-image of the "Okie" migrants right: Many of the Okies were descendants of the original Scotch-Irish settlers and viewed themselves as Jacksonian Democrats, defenders of racially-defined, white, egalitarian virtue (2002). Their awareness of their new racial status is revealed slowly throughout the novel, charting Tom Joad's own subjective transformation from criminal to revolutionary. Bathing naked in a river, the Joads hear the word for the first time, spoken by another migrant who is returning back to Oklahoma from California. Asking what "Okie" means, the other bather replies, "Okie....means you're a dirty son-of-a-bitch. Okie means you're scum" (Steinbeck, 2006). The invocation of "dirt" and "scum" – particularly as the Joads are in the process of bathing – suggests a coloration of their bodies, a metaphoric darkening. Already poor, the Joads not only lose their land and must sell their labor to survive, but their bodies become targets of both the state as well as exploitation by large growers. The Joads become proletarianized in the novel, or another way to say it, they experience class through a process of racialization, of othering through a signification on the body. The tension of the novel is precisely between the objective nature of the Joad's class status and the subjective experience of losing their previous status as white people.

Up to this point, I've primary deployed examples of 1930s working class literature as written by white and/or white-ethnic authors. This has been deliberate, as I've hope to demonstrate how race and identity became the primary trope through which class identification was expressed, even for writers not typically thought of as "race writers." Of course, however, much this was true for white/ethnic writers, African-, Native, Asian- American and Latino/a writers of this period developed a complex and subjective vocabulary around racial identity similar to, but far more nuanced, than the white-ethnic writers I've mentioned thus far. Many of the seminal novels by writers of the color in the 1930s open with or feature a moment of racial dis-identification, in which the narrator's/character's own subjective sense of themselves is confronted by an understanding of the way they are interpellated within a system of racial dominance. One can think of Richard Wright's *Native Son*, in which Bigger expresses his understanding of race as both material and subjective: the plane he is not allowed to fly and his anxiety located at the center of his body. Or Ann Petry's Lutie Johnson of *The Street,* who reflects on her own domesticity while seeing an advertisement for a kitchen owned by white people. Or Carlos Bulosan's *America is in the Heart* that opens with the alienation of Allos watching what appears to be a stranger, but later revealed as his own brother, returning from the war he fought for the U.S. colonial power in Europe.

What connects these moments in the text is a Lukacian concept of subjectivity, one of that is both material and identitarian at the same time. Perhaps the most far-reaching and complex articulation of a subjective and objective view of racial history is Wright's *12 Million Black Voices* (1941), the second-person, non-fiction photo-essay, in which Wright narrates the Great Migration from the rural South to the urban core of Chicago. Wright uses the Great Migration as a means to explore his own sense of African-American subjectivity, in which he locates the double-consciousness

of African Americans as a consequence of living both within a feudal and modern capitalist economy at the same time.

> Standing now at the apex of the twentieth century, we look back
> over the road we have traveling and compare it with the road over
> which the white folk have traveled, and we see that three hundred
> years in the history of our lives are equivalent to two thousand
> years in the history of the lives of whites! .... Hurled from our
> native African homes into the very center of the most complex
> and highly industrialized civilization the world has ever known,
> we stand with a consciousness and memory such as few people
> possess. (Wright, 1941)

Taking a page from section 8 of Marx's *Capital*, Wright addresses
the unique context of the African American entrance into capitalist modernity. At once part of the primitive accumulation
of capital and at the center of the capitalist metropole, African
Americans are situated as no other group in the United States.
They exist at both the most brutal, underdeveloped and the most
advanced sections of capitalism simultaneously. For Wright, this
not only gives a material shape to African-American thought, he
offers this historical simultaneity as the particular subjective insight African Americans have into the West.

## Class in an Age of Fragmentation: Wither the Present?

Returning to *The Autobiography of Malcolm X*, I hope it should be
clear at this point how it is not a rupture so much as a fulfillment
of twentieth century traditions of self-conscious working-class writing. The development of both the racial and class consciousness and
identity of the narrator, its insistence on a unique and subjective expression of a racialized class politics, and the generic form of the bildungsroman all mark it within the tradition laid out by Mike Gold,
Richard Wright, Carlos Bulosan, Pietro Di Donato, James Farrell,
Ann Petry, and countless others. It should also come as no surprise
that Malcolm X himself developed theories of anti-capitalist and
socialist politics after his break with the Nation of Islam. Malcolm X
regularly spoke at labor union rallies and shared the stage with revolutionary socialists in the last year of his life. As George Breitman

points out, Malcolm X became increasingly critical not only of capitalism, but of theories and actions around racial liberation that did
not also address class exploitation as well (Breitman, 1970). And I
would suggest reading *The Autobiography* as not so much a change
of direction for Malcolm X than a further articulation of the politics
he already expressed throughout his life. The stylistic contours of his
autobiography position Malcolm X within the longer trajectory of
both working-class politics as well as working-class literary production. Similarly, in the revolutionary upsurge of the 1960s and early
1970s, we can think of Ernesto Galarza's 1971 *Barrio Boy*, and John
Rechy's 1963 *City of Night* as part of the same literary inheritance.

In terms of contemporary working-class literature, it seems little
surprise that Latino/a writers most self-consciously adhere to the
tradition laid out by an earlier generation of proletarian artists. In
one sense, working-class literature has often been the literature of
immigrants. As Mike Gold writes, America's wealth is the product
of "the tragedy of millions of immigrants," as migrants both then
and now often form a super-exploited class of workers (2009).[8]
And as Michael Denning points out, much of the revolutionary
culture of the 1930s was the product of the children of immigrants
(1998). I would also argue that immigration itself is a process of
racialization through class. As Mae Ngai and Lisa Lowe note, the
racial status of migrant workers is managed and reinforced by
their place on a labor hierarchy in the U.S. (Ngai, 2004; Lowe,
1996). But more than sociology, many migrants themselves hail
from countries in which the Left, and its traditions of working
class representation, are still part of public and popular discourse.
Processes of suburbanization, whiteness, and the unhealed scars of
the Cold War's multiple red scares have erased much of the memory of working-class literary production in the U.S. For complex
historical reasons, Latin America and the Caribbean, still maintain both the language and politics of working-class movements in
ways that are seldom evidenced in the United States among previous generations of migrants (Bacon, 2004).[9] The simple fact that
May 1st—a forgotten holiday for most Americans—was chosen as
the day for Migrant Rights marches across the country suggests a
great deal about how the memory of class and race speak to each
other in Latin American communities.

While poets such as Gary Soto, Martín Espada, Juan Felipe Herrera, Diana García, and playwright Luis Valdez carry on the working-class tradition of early proletarian writers, I would like to conclude with a reading of Helena Viramontes' 1995 novel, *Under the Feet of Jesus*. As one of the more comprehensive contemporary narrative explorations of the subjective consciousness of workers through the lens of citizenship and race, *Under the Feet of Jesus* also considers the ways in which the "objective" conditions of labor have changed and that these changes produce with them new forms of working class consciousness. The novel tells the story of the young teenager, Estrella, and her family of migrant farm-workers in the central valleys of California. Like many of the proletarian novels, it's what Barbara Foley refers to as a "radical bildungsroman." Estrella gains not only in maturity and insight throughout the text, but political awareness (1993).[10] Much of the early sections of the novel are dedicated to moments in which Estrella perceives her own identity in relationship to the class structure of the fields and towns through which she travels. In the first scene of Estrella working in the fields, we find her musing on the Sunmaid Raisins icon, a white woman in a red bonnet who "did not know" how hot, dirty, and dangerous the work is and whose bonnet would offer no protection in the harsh San Joaquin Valley sun (Viramontes, 1996). Likewise, Estrella's first lover, the college-bound Alejo who has fallen ill from pesticide poisoning, asks her if she intends to waste her life picking in the fields. Estrella's response, much like her reflection on the Sunmaid Raisin icon, asserts the value of her own labor in the face of classed assumptions of its value." What's wrong with picking peaches," she asks, a question that betrays a limited horizon of possibility but also the dignity of her work (ibid.).

Yet, unlike the revolutionary promise of Mike Gold's *Jews without Money* and Pietro di Donato's *Christ in Concrete*, the novel ends on an ambivalent note, with Estrella climbing to the top of a barn for a transcendent moment, gazing into stars that are her namesake. Ironically, however, it is the same barn that Perfecto will use the proceeds from demolishing to abandon her and her family. Indeed, the novel both asserts Estrella's dignity, value, and powerful subjective voice, while, far more often, trading in both surreal, disorienting imagery, liminal spaces, and ambiguous identities.

Perfecto, her mother's lover and a kind of step-father, lives in a "travesty of laws," neither documented nor married to Petra, Estrella's mother (ibid.). Estrella, herself, is neither a teenager - as she works full time and takes care of her ailing boyfriend - nor an adult. And the family is one of differing biological backgrounds, which encompass legal, national, and cultural relationships to both Mexico and the United States. Indeed, it is a novel of borders between citizen and non-citizen, family and non-family, childhood and adulthood—borders that are often obscure and uncertain from both a legal and subjective point of view.

Estrella's identity, often rooted in both her class and ethnic identity, also seems frequently on the verge splintering entirely. Coming across a baseball game after working in the fields, she is blinded by the lights and thinks for a moment that they were "the border patrol...and she tried to remember which side she was on" (ibid.). The baseball game further dissolves into "phantoms" as she wonders "where was home": the bat becomes a "blunt instrument against the skull"; the ball becomes a "peach" that one must run after in order to have money to eat. Estrella, who is a citizen, experiences her national identity as a moment not only of alienation, but of personal fragmentation - a game that is "America's national pastime" transforms into a border—on which side she stands, she doesn't know. The novel's title, *Under the Feet of Jesus*, refers to the papers that Estrella would need to show if she was ever stopped by *La Migra*, despite her birthright citizenship. While the novel certainly argues for Estrella's value and the dignity of her labor, her own sense of self is torn by her uneven relationship to family, age, and national status.

In a single dialectical image, she imagines herself both as drowning in the La Brea tar-pits she learns about from Alejo, and yet uses the image of tar to insist that it is the clinic at which she attempts to get Alejo treatment that owes her family. "Oil is made from our bones," Estrella thinks before she forcibly takes her family's last ten dollars back from a frightened nurse. She argues that the world literally runs on her labor like a car runs on gasoline, bringing her image of her own death into one of empowerment. Yet as the money is used to pay for the gas that will take Alejo to the hospital and away from her forever, it is an image that again returns back to a sense of ambiguity. If we return for a moment to Lukacs' subject-object of history, the idea of a unitary working class, or even a global working-class politics, may be as necessary as ever; but in the 1990s when *Under the Feet of Jesus* appears, this solidarity seems absent. There is a brief moment when United Farm Worker activists show up in the field, pass Estrella a leaflet, and then fade back into the heat and dust of the field. Estrella's identity is fragmented much as the working-class movement is fragmented - riven by tightened borders, by the smashing of unions, by the collapse of international socialist and anti-colonial projects. *Under the Feet of Jesus* encodes this loss within Estrella's fragmented consciousness. It is not a novel of despair so much as defeat. Estrella does not lack class consciousness so much as that consciousness is personal, private, and able to be expressed only in individual acts of resistance. The "revolutionary subject" of *History and Class Consciousness* is perhaps latent, but as the "subject of history," it lacks a teleology of the future that can resolve its contradiction.

As Sonali Perera and Michelle Tokarczyk suggest in recent scholarly works on working- class literature, many of the ideas around working-class literature have changed as ideas and formations of class have changed in the last few decades, due to globalization as well as post-Cold War revisions of twentieth century working-class movements (Perera, 2014; Tokarczyk, 2011). As the class conscious nature of the Movement for Black Lives policy platform recently reinforced with its call for union rights, free education, and free health care, race and class in this country are profoundly intertwined and will likely continue to be. As such, the inheritance of both the ethnic proletarian tradition, as well as the longer tradition of writing about class and race in fiction, will undoubtedly continue. Whether they will be novels of white backlash, such as Philip Meyers's *American Rust* (2011)—in which the enemies of the unemployed working class hero are sexually deviant, and racially-mixed homeless men—or they will be attempts to playfully reengage with the meaning of working-class oral traditions, such as Colson Whitehead's *John Henry Days* (2001) may be a function of future working class formations. Whether we can think of *The Autobiography of Malcolm X* as the high point of working class literature that is now receding, or a mid-point in a much longer wave, has yet to be seen. The "laboring of American culture" in Michael Denning's phrase may be moving in many contradictory ways, but social movements suggest that a literature of class will continue to be needed. Already, new magazines such as *Jacobin*, *Redwedge*, and *N+1* have foregrounded the class struggle and its connection to issues of race in new ways, similar to the Occupy movement and Black Lives Matter. Equally, as the globalized world dislocates an increasing number of migrants, these migrants bring with them organizing histories and political backgrounds that continue to produce new subjectivities and new life into working-class struggle. Hopefully, we can trust that novelists will emerge, who not only want to chronicle it but who lived it themselves.

## Notes

1. Naison describes the frequent tensions between Garveyite nationalists and the Communist Party over ideological questions such as black capitalism, the CP's attacks on black landlords, and of course, the centrality of race or class as a prime analytic.

2. For further treatment of the zoot suit and the rebel subcultures that surrounded it, see Robin D.G. Kelley (1994) "The Riddle of the Zoot: Malcolm Little and Black Cultural Politics During World War II." *Race Rebels: Culture, Politics, and the Black Working Class.* New York, The Free Press; Eduardo Pagán (2003) *Murder at the Sleepy Lagoon: Zoot Suits, Race, and Riot in Wartime L.A.* Chapel Hill, University of North Carolina Press; Kathy Peiss (2014) Zoot Suit: The Enigmatic Career of an Extreme Style. Philadelphia, University of Pennsylvania Press.

3. C.L.R. James famously refers to the black slaves of San Domingue as the world's "first proletariat" in the epilogue to his masterwork, *The Black Jacobins*, p. 392. For a more contemporary account of the origins of U.S. capitalism and finance through the institution of slavery, see Edward Baptiste (2014) *The Half that has Never Been Told: Slavery and the Making of American Capitalism.* New York, Basic Books.

4. See footnote 2; also see James Smethurst *The New Red Negro: The Literary Left and American Poetry, 1930–1946.* Oxford, Oxford University Press, 1999 and Robin D.G. Kelley, *Race Rebels: Culture,*

*Politics and the Black Working Class. New York: Simon and Schuster, 1996*, and *Hammer and Hoe: Alabma Communists: During the Great Depression.Chapel Hill, UNC Press, 1990.*

5. The full list of African American CPUSA members and "fellow travelers" that Wald lists in the review are here as follows: "Richard Wright...Margaret Walker, Lance Jeffers, Claude McKay, John Oliver Killens, Julian Mayfield, Alice Childress, Shirley Graham, Lloyd Brown, John Henrik Clarke, William Attaway, Frank Marshall Davis, Lorraine Hansberry, Douglas Turner Ward, Audre Lorde, W.E.B. Du Bois, and Harold Cruse were among those organizationally affiliated in individualized ways. A list of other African-American cultural workers who were, to varying degrees and at different points, fellow travelers, would probably include Ralph Ellison, Chester Himes, Sterling Brown, Langston Hughes, Paul Robeson, Theodore Ward, Countee Cullen, James Baldwin (as a teenager), Richard Durham, Alain Locke, Willard Motley, Rosa Guy, Sarah Wright, Jessie Fausett, Owen Dodson, Ossie Davis, Dorothy West, Marion Minus, Robert Hayden, Waring Cuney, and Lonne Elder III."

6. Denning, as do Foley and Wald, make very clear that despite the Soviet Union's formal call for socialist realism, few writers on the left followed the Party line with anything that could be described as orthodoxy or blind loyalty. The Cold War myth of the 1930s "writer in uniform" has, I hope, been firmly laid to rest.

7. Gold, *Jews without Money*, p. 41.

8. David Bacon makes the point that many Mexican and other Latin American immigrants bring with them the history of labor and social struggle that may help to re-energize the U.S. labor movement.

9. Barbara Foley coined the phrase "radical bildungsroman" to describe a key genre of 1930s proletarian literature.

# References

Adi, H. (2009). The Negro Question: The Communist International and Black Liberation in the Interwar Years. In: M. West, W. Martin, and F. Wilkins, eds., *From Toussaint to Tupac: The Black International since the Age of Revolution*. Chapel Hill, University of North Carolina Press, p. 155.

Bacon, D. (2004). *The Children of NAFTA: Labor Wars on the U.S./ Mexico Border*. Berkeley, University of California Press.

Berman, M. (1982). *All That is Solid Melts Into Air: The Experience of Modernity*. New York, Penguin Books.

Breitman, G. (1970). *The Last Year of Malcolm X: The Evolution of a Revolutionary*. New York, Pathfinder Press.

Daniels, R. (1998). *Not Like Us: Immigrants and Minorities in America: 1890–1924*. Chicago, Ivan R. Dee Publishers.

Denning, M. (1998). *The Cultural Front: The Laboring of American Culture*. New York, Verso.

Denning, M. (2004). *Culture in the Age of Three Worlds*. London, Verso.

di Donato, P. (1993). *Christ in* Concrete. New York, Signet Classic.

Du Bois, W. E. B. (1998). *Black Reconstruction in America: 1860–1880*. New York, The Free Press.

Dunbar-Ortiz, R. (2002). One or Two Things I Know About Us: Rethinking the Image and Role of the 'Okies'. *Monthly Review*, 54 (3) (July-August). Available at: http://monthlyreview. org/2002/07/01/one-or-two-things-i-know-about-us/ [Accessed 30 Aug 2016]

Foley, B. (1993). *Radical Representations: Politics and Form in U.S. Proletarian Fiction 1929–1941*. Durham, Duke University Press.

Garrison, W. L. (2009). Preface. In: *Narrative of the Life of Frederick Douglass*. New York, Dover Publications, pp. 87–101.

Gold, M. (1972). *Mike Gold: A Literary Anthology*, Michael Folsom, ed., New York, International Publishers.

Gold, M. (2009). *Jews without Money*. Philadelphia, Public Affairs.

Haley, A. and Malcolm X. (2015). *The Autobiography of Malcolm X as Told to Alex Haley*. New York, Ballantine Books.

Hall, S. (1996). Race, Articulation, and Societies Structured in Dominance. In: H. A. Baker, Jr., M. Diawara and R. Lindborg, eds., *Black British Cultural Studies Reader*. Chicago, University of Chicago Press, pp. 16–61.

Jacobson, M. F. (1999). *Whiteness of a Different Color: European Immigrants and the Alchemy of Race.* Cambridge, Harvard University Press.

James, C. L. R. (1998). *The Black Jacobins: Toussaint L'Ouverture and the San Domingo Revolution.* New York, Vintage.

Jameson, F. (2009). *Valences of the Dialectic.* London, Verso.

Kaplan, A. (1988). *The Social Construction of American Realism.* Chicago, University of Chicago Press.

Kelley, R. (1990). *Hammer and Hoe.* Durham, Duke University Press.

Kelley, R. (1994). *Race Rebels: Culture, Politics, and the Black Working Class.* New York, Free Press.

Le Sueur, M. (1990). The Fetish of Being Outside. In: *Harvest Song.* Albuquerque, West End Press.

Lowe, L. (1996). *Immigrant Acts: On Asian American Cultural Politics.* Chapel Hill, Duke University Press.

Lukács, G. (1972). *History and Class Consciousness: Studies in Marxist Dialects,* trans. Rodney Livingston. Boston, MIT Press.

Marable, M. (2011). *Malcolm X: A Life of Reinvention.* New York, Viking.

Maxwell, W. (1996). The Proletarian as New Negro: Mike Gold's Harlem Renaissance. In: B. Mullen and S. Linkon, eds., *Radical Revisions: Rereading 1930s Culture.* Urbana-Champaign, University of Illinois Press, 91–120.

Mullen, B. V. (1999). *Popular Fronts: Chicago and African-American Cultural Politics, 1935–1946.* Urbana-Champaign, University of Illinois Press.

Murphy, J. (1991). *The Proletarian Moment: The Controversy Over Leftism in Literature.* Champaign-Urban, University of Illinois Press.

Naison, M. (1983). *Communists in Harlem during the Depression.* Urbana-Champaign, University of Illinois Press.

Ngai, M. M. (2004). *Impossible Subjects: Illegal Aliens and the Making of Modern America.* Princeton, Princeton University Press.

Omi, M. and Winant, H. (1994). *Racial Formation in the United States*. New York, Routledge.

Perera, S. (2014). *No Country: Working Class Writing in an Age of Globalization*. New York, Columbia University Press.

Rabinowitz, P. (1991). *Labor & Desire: Woman's Revolutionary Fiction in Depression America*. Chapel Hill, University of North Carolina Press.

Roediger, D. (1996). *Wages of Whiteness: Race and the Making of the American Working Class*. London, Verson.

Smethurst, J. (1999). *The New Red Negro: The Literary Left and American Poetry, 1930–1946*. Oxford, Oxford University Press.

Shocket, E. (2000). 'Discovering Some New Race': Rebecca Harding Davis's 'Life in the Iron Mills' and the Literary Emergence of Working-Class Whiteness. *PMLA*, 115 (1), pp. 46–59.

Slotkin, R. (1998). *Gunfighter Nation: The Myth of the Frontier in 20th Century America*. Norman, University of Oklahoma Press.

Steinbeck, J. (2006). *The Grapes of Wrath*. New York, Penguin Books.

Tokarczyk, M. M. (2011). *Critical Approaches to Working-Class Literature*. London, Routledge.

Viramontes, H. (1996). *Under the Feet of Jesus*. New York, Plume Press.

Wald, A. (2000). Review: African Americans, Culture and Communism: part 1. *Against the Current*, [online] (May-June). Available at: https://www.solidarity-us.org/node/928 [Accessed 28 Sept 2016].

Wald, A. (2014). *Trinity of Passion: The Literary Left and the Anti-Fascist Crusade*. Chapel Hill, University of North Carolina Press.

Wright, R. and Rosskam, E. (1941). *12 Million Black Voices*. New York, Basic Books.

Wright, R. (2007). Blueprint for Negro Writing. In: H. L. Gates, ed., *The New Negro: Readings on Race, Representation, and African American Culture, 1892–1938*. Princeton, Princeton University Press, p. 269.

# Writing of a Different Class? The First 120 years of Working-Class Fiction in Finland

*Elsi Hyttinen & Kati Launis*

In 1976, the magazine *Suomen Kuvalehti* published a feature item with the title "Pirkko Saisio's introspection: We are still waiting for the great working-class author." In the article, the young debut novelist reasons that "A working-class author is an author who depicts working people and their endeavours from the point of view of a worker. . . As for me, for the time being I lack both the political awareness and the first-hand knowledge of a present-day worker's life and mindset required of a person who should wish to call themselves a working-class author" (Saisio, 1976).

Pirkko Saisio's novel *Elämänmeno* [*The Course of Life*] (1975) follows its protagonist, Marja, from childhood to early adulthood, with a class awakening as the central focus. Together with a fierce-tempered mother and a good-natured stepfather, Marja lives in a bedsit in Kallio, a distinctly working-class neighborhood in the Finnish capital, Helsinki. Saisio chose to locate Marja in a milieu of which she had first-hand knowledge; the author herself had lived in Kallio the first few years of her life, before moving to a new, respectably middle-class suburban housing development in the eastern outskirts of the city. Saisio was already a theater school-trained actor at the moment of the novel's launching, but the novel's public was eager to see the protagonist as her alter ego. This is a curious phenomenon, perhaps explained by the fact that, in the 1970s, most of the reading public would have defined a working-class author the same way as Saisio herself does in the citation above. In its eagerness to greet the arrival of the great

How to cite this book chapter:
Hyttinen, E. and Launis, K. 2017. Writing of a Different Class? The First 120 years of Working-Class Fiction in Finland. In: Lennon, J. and Nilsson, M. (eds.) *Working-Class Literature(s): Historical and International Perspectives*. Pp. 65–94. Stockholm: Stockholm University Press. DOI: https://doi.org/10.16993/bam.d. License: CC-BY

working-class author, the reading public chose to ignore Saisio's education in arts and, instead, substituted her life events with those of her protagonist. Thus, Marja's fictional childhood experiences came to serve as a proof of Pirkko Saisio's rough childhood and first-hand experience of the living conditions of the working poor. To facilitate this transferal, interviews of Saisio were sometimes accompanied by a photograph of the author standing outside the Kallio block of flats that she and Marja shared (Hyttinen, 2004).

Twenty-five years later, in an autobiographical essay, the author revisited her memories of the mid-1970s' debate: "*Elämänmeno*'s reception was positive, overwhelming, even, slightly dangerously so for a young writer. I was offered the boots of a great working-class author, they were fiercely jerked from me, and then tried on my feet again. The words flew high above and by me, like in the ceremonies of the J. H. Erkko prize for first novels where the dispute over my possible status as a working-class author was so heated that I, understanding nothing of the arguments and the aggression, had to flee for shelter in the toilets out of sheer nervousness" (Saisio, 2000, p. 353). There is something very historically specific about the image of a writer hiding in the bathroom as a heated dispute over the concepts of working-class literature and authorship is carried out in her name. The 1970s in Finland was, after the all-around cultural radicalism of the 1960s, a decade of serious attempts at bringing together class-awareness, political commitment, and art—hence the desire to find an author in whose figure all three would meet.

On the other hand, there is also a notably non-historically-specific side to the anecdote: in addition to illustrating the nature of the 1970s cultural debates, it captures an essential defining feature of the Finnish working-class literary tradition as a whole. The writers of this article claim that, in Finland, there is not really a tradition or a canon of works that could unproblematically be referred to as the working-class tradition. Rather, there is a tradition of uneasiness and heated debate provoked by every attempt at pinpointing such a continuum. What is, can, or should be considered as working-class fiction has been disputed for more than a hundred years already, with no end in sight.

Whereas in some other areas of the world debates have perhaps formed around aesthetics as a defining feature of working-class fiction, in Finland the arguments always return to "reality." Generation after generation, the question is raised: Is this truthful? Working-class literature is expected to be a truthful depiction of a worker's worldview, which, as it happens, is supposed to naturally be concordant with socialist class theories. To make this articulation look natural, the debaters have time and again turned to the figure of the author. Granted, certain types of books are more likely to trigger the debate and the uneasiness than others. Whether or not discussing these trigger-books in chronological order is the same thing as writing a Finnish working-class literary history is, perhaps not entirely surprisingly, up for debate.

## Two Fields of Literature, 1895–1918

It is impossible to talk about Finnish working-class literature (or working-class writers, or to even ask if a writer is or is not a working-class writer) in a worthwhile way before the turn of the twentieth century. As Raoul Palmgren (1966 a & b) and Aimo Roininen (1993) have shown, Finnish working-class literature only emerged at the same time as the Finnish labor movement and labor press. This, in turn, coincides with the global upsurge of working-class literary culture. Especially interesting in this respect is the rise of working-class literature in Russia, as Finland, in fact, was a part of the Russian empire from 1809 to the Finnish declaration of independence in December 1917. Even though the developments in Moscow, Saint Petersburg, and Helsinki follow similar patterns (see Clark in this anthology), they do not form a single literary movement. The Finnish and Russian languages are entirely different from each other, so most Russian influences necessarily underwent translations, both linguistic and cultural. Maxim Gorky is known to have had a considerable impact on some Finnish writers (Roininen, 1993, pp. 212–224), both as a role model and a personal acquaintance. Further, reviewing Gorky gave the Finnish press an opportunity to articulate its ideals and cultural politics in the very first years of the twentieth century when very little original Finnish working-class literature yet existed

(Roininen, 1993, p. 216). However, many of the transnational connections of the Finnish field still remain underresearched.[1] The dominating frame for research on Finnish working-class culture has been a national one, which means that even the birth of our working-class literary culture has been predominantly explained as a consequence of the developments and turns in Finnish national politics. Subsequently, much less critical effort has been put into locating the Finnish field within a larger inter- and transnational framework.

As established in Raoul Palmgren's pioneering work *Joukkosydän* [*The Collective Heart*][2] in the 1960s, it is now a commonly shared understanding that the first generation of Finnish working-class writers consists of approximately 170 writers. However, Palmgren makes a point of specifying that only a fraction of them came from a working-class context and thus met his own criteria for proper working-class authorship (Palmgren, 1965, pp. 222–223).

A renewed interest in early Finnish working-class literature begins in 1993 with the publication of Aimo Roininen's *Kirja liikkeessä* [*Book in Movement*], in which focus is shifted from the individuals to the structures supporting them and, thereby, makes their agency possible. Indeed, its subtitle reads "Literature as institution in the old working-class movement." Roininen's work has been inspirational to the generation of researchers that the writers of this article represent, as it offered a new way of delineating the limits of the phenomenon studied. No longer was it necessary to presume a unifying worldview or shared horizon of experiences for all working-class writers. Instead, one could focus on how different writers were located institutionally.

The writers who formed the emerging network of Finnish working-class literature came from different strata of the society but shared an interest in creating an alternative to bourgeois culture. Here again, Finland is no exception in the global context. As Gustav Klaus has argued, within working-class literature, writers born in the working class are rare. In his view, writers not born into the working class have contributed massively to the formation of "literature of labour" everywhere (Klaus, 1985, p. ix; Hitchcock, 1989, p. 7). Early Finnish working-class writers formed a heterogeneous group with their different backgrounds, used different literary genres, and published in both official languages, Finnish and Swedish. In Finland, Swedish was the language of the educated classes all the way to the 1870s, when the Finnish language began to rise as a language of literature. There were writers such as the playwright Elvira Willman, with her university education and roots in a family of shipowners, and Hilja (Liinamaa) Pärssinen, a teacher and the leader of the Women Workers' Union in Finland. And there were writers from lower classes—such as Kössi Kaatra, the decadent bohemian Kasperi Tanttu, the prosaist Konrad Lehtimäki, the bohemian poet and lay preacher Esa Paavo-Kallio, and the Swedish-speaking Arvid Mörne. (Hyttinen, 2015, p. 60; Palmgren, 1966a, p. 178).

Thus, not all writers who wrote working-class literature in the early years of the twentieth century had their roots in the lower classes. Conversely, quite a number of writers publishing on what research later has called "the national" or "the bourgeois" field of culture *did* (Hyttinen, 2015, p. 60). The social stratum of the intelligentsia was quite narrow: there were way too few educated upper-class families in the country for them to be able to provide the modernizing nation with all the teachers, academics, writers, critics, politicians, journalists, and other public figures it needed. The new intelligentsia came from all levels of society: upstarts flourished (Rojola, 2009). The son of a working family could, given the right twists of fate, end up as a "mainstream" poet, with nothing in his writing being an evident reminder of his roots. In our understanding, the change that took place at the beginning of the twentieth century had first and foremost to do with a reorganization of the literary field. However, whether or not working-class writers should ideally emerge from a proletarian background—or whether a dedication to the cause of the working class would suffice to turn an intellectual from the educated classes into a legitimate contributor to the working-class field of culture—has remained a hot topic, in Finland as elsewhere (see Clark and Nilsson in this collection).

The earliest examples of Finnish working-class literature were published in newspapers and journals. Most often, they consisted of poetry, but other short forms, such as stories and causeries, flourished as well. The newspapers and journals were mostly owned by organizations of the workers' movement and bore names such as *The Worker* [*Työmies*] (1895–1918, the first Finnish working-class newspaper); *A Worker's Soiree* [*Työmiehen illanvietto*] (1902–1906, a literary magazine); and the *People's Will* [*Kansan tahto*] (1906, a newspaper). Publishing in them signaled a strong desire to take part in creating the alternative field of working-class literary culture. No writer with bourgeois aspirations would have chosen them as the primary outlet for their writing.

Furthermore, a number of working-class writers wrote directly for the stage (Roininen, 1993, p. 298), as theatre was a popular working-class pastime. Especially in Helsinki, the working-class amateur theatre scene was vivid, and the National Theater offered workers cheap tickets for the third balcony, as well as whole shows at subsidized prices (Seppälä, 2010, pp. 20–27). It has been claimed that theatre was more easily accessible for the working people than books because theater, as a form, did not require as much free time and solitude as reading novels. Also, publishing a novel would have almost inevitably, regardless of their aspirations, marked the author as an agent of the bourgeois cultural field since there were yet no publishing houses run by the working-class movement or people at the time (Hyttinen, 2012, pp. 52–56). This uneasiness with book-reading is even thematized in working-class playwright Elvira Willman's 1903 debut, *Lyyli* (which premiered at the National Theater), where reading dangerously detaches a working-class girl from her class position but, in the end, does not grant her access to the higher rungs of the class ladder (Hyttinen, 2012, pp. 36–41). Only in the 1910s did the first story collections and novels written by working-class authors become available to audiences (Roininen, 1993, p. 307). The rise of the working-class press had created a string of small presses that acted as publishing houses as well, and no longer were the bourgeois establishments the only ones available for aspiring fiction writers (Roininen, 1993, pp. 369–373).

As dramatically convincing as Willman's class-conscious reutilization of the trope of *dangerous reading* (made known by Gustave Flaubert's *Madame Bovary* [1856]) was, the fact remains that Finnish workers *did* read novels and other longer forms, even if domestic working-class writers did not initially write in those genres. As literary historians have shown, in Finland the most popular and widely read literature at the end of the nineteenth century was religious (Luukkanen, 2016, pp. 421, 458), and the most borrowed book from libraries was the *Bible* (Kotilainen, 2016, p. 208). However, towards the end of the nineteenth century, the situation changed when the number of folk libraries and, soon after, working people's libraries began to increase as an outgrowth of the powerful breakthrough of the working-class movement. These developments made a large selection of books widely available. By 1916 there were over 1,000 workers' libraries in Finland, with almost 100,000 volumes available for borrowing (Roininen, 1993, p. 72).

It should be emphasized that, even when perceived within the national container, working-class literature was not born out of nowhere. It was not an isolated island of its own but part of a wider literary tradition. Raoul Palmgren (1966a, p. 5) has argued that there is "a red strand" in Finnish literature since its very beginning of folklore origins. In particular, the realist author Minna Canth (1844-1897) was a favored role model for working-class writers. But writers before Canth (such as J. L. Runeberg [1804–1877], regarded as the Finnish national poet in the nineteenth century) had depicted poor, common people. Working-class writers, however, re-wrote this earlier, Runebergian, idealistic tradition, rejecting his conception of a submissive *people* and replacing it with that of defiant *citizens* (Launis, 2009, p. 98). During the nineteenth century and before the rise of the working-class movement, there were also self-educated writers (or "common" people with very limited formal education) who represented the working people and the landless country population. For these nineteenth-century peasant writers in rural Finland, writing was a new technology, the implications of which manifested themselves in several meta-poetic ways. For example, in their texts, they often included apologies for poor writing and lack of poetic sensibilities. These writers, who lived in a semi-literate society, have been rediscovered and have become a topic of multidisciplinary research during the past ten years (Kauranen, 2013; Kuismin, 2016).

Until the early twentieth century, as research shows, the public sphere in Finland had been relatively uniform (Haapala, 1999, pp. 214–16; Lahtinen, 2006, pp. 150–54; Nieminen, 2006, p. 160) and tightly connected ideologically to nationalist interests. Only at the end of nineteenth century do we witness a quick erosion of such national monoculture. The emergence of the working-class cultural field was but one outcome of the process. An extremely important year for that "other publicity" emerging around the working-class movement was the year 1895—when the first newspaper for workers, *Työmies* [*The Worker*], was founded. Only a few years earlier, at the beginning of the 1890s, it was strongly questioned whether there would be any writers or readers for working-class publication. As *Lappeenrannan uutiset* (1895) chronicles in retrospect,

> Doubts were raised as to whether there was enough workforce available for putting together working-class literature of some kind, and, what is more, whether the poor workers of Finland had the means for supporting the endeavour enough so that the initiators would not suffer a financial loss. (*Lappeenrannan Uutiset*, 17 July 1895.)

These doubts notwithstanding, *Työmies* appeared in 1895 and was soon followed by other newspapers. The earliest hit in the Finnish National Library's Digital Collection of Newspapers using the search term *työväenkirjallisuus* [*working-class literature*] is from the same year, 1895 (*Lappeenrannan Uutiset*, 17 July 1895), and the first hit for the Swedish term *arbetarlitteratur* [*working-class literature*] is from the year 1903 (*Vasabladet*, 22 September 1903). The first real debate in the Finnish press on the definition of the term *working-class literature* (the debate that, as we argue in this article, still continues) took place in 1904 in *Työmies*. Edvard Valpas, the editor-in-chief of *Työmies* and an influential theorist of Kautskyan socialism in Finland, rejected Kössi Kaatra's poems in his article "Työväen laulaja" ["Workers' Singer"], even though Kaatra was widely regarded as the "court poet of the movement." And, in the same vein, Valpas presented a theoretical introduction to the concept of working-class literature. According to Valpas, the Finnish society of the era was not yet at the stage where real, fully-developed socialist art is possible. In his poems, Kaatra did not (according to Valpas' dire judgment) manage to measure up to the ideals of working-class literature. His poems were not ideological enough and their forms were not advanced enough. For Valpas, they were suspiciously individual and genteel (Valpas, 1904). It should perhaps be stated here that, among his contemporaries, Valpas represented the most extreme Marxist and materialist view on literature (Roininen, 1993, pp. 101–110, 377–399).

## Transnational Influences

The year 1904 seems to mark a coming of consciousness of the Finnish working-class literary field. Suddenly, working-class newspapers start publishing, on different occasions, lists of "the most famous working-class writers in our country"[3]—consisting of names such as Santtu Piri, N. R. af Ursin, Lauri Soini, Hilja Liinamaa, and Kaarlo Luukkonen. Thus, the alternative field begins its own canon formation, expressing which writers are part of "us," and what kind of literature is good and recommendable for the working-class readership (Roininen, 1993, pp. 34–37).[4] Around the same time, working-class literature emerges as a critical term in Russian and Swedish labor movements as well (see Clark and Nilsson in this collection).

The Scandinavian and, to a degree, the Russian and Anglo-American literary developments were closely followed in the Finnish working-class press (Roininen, 1993, pp. 269–284). Literature from other countries, such as Germany and France, was written about as well, but more sporadically (Roininen, 1993, pp. 284–297). The majority of Swedish writers the Finnish-language press wrote about—such as Rudolf Björnsson, Martin Koch, Maria Sandel, Elin Wägner, Gustaf Fröding, and Selma Lagerlöf—were either working-class writers or wrote about subjects presumed to be of immediate interest to a working-class readership (Roininen, 1993, p. 265). The Swedish-language working-class press in Finland went even further by following the developments of the Swedish working-class literary field. As working-class literary production in Swedish was scarce on this side of the Baltic Sea, the Swedish-language papers filled their cultural pages with reviews of Swedish working-class writers. This development begins around 1905, and during the 1910s approximately forty Swedish writers were discussed. Moreover, the papers did not only follow working-class fiction but also covered, from a class-conscious perspective, cultural debates carried out even in Swedish mainstream newspapers—introducing their readers to critics such as Bengt Lidforss, Torsten Fogelqvist, and C.A. Bolander (Roininen, 1993, p. 268).

In addition to discussing their contemporaries, Finnish intellectuals also turned their eyes toward the past decades of Nordic literature. While the 1880s' realists August Strindberg, Henrik Ibsen, and Bjørnstjerne Bjørnson were eagerly written about, it was the realist and social critical plays that were favored (Roininen, 1993, pp. 226, 269). These authors were not regarded as working-class writers, but their production was something over which class-conscious debates could be articulated. All in all, the Swedish working-class literary development was keenly followed in the Swedish-speaking Finnish press. In contrast, the coverage of Swedish working-class literature was more sporadic in the Finnish-speaking press. Quite understandably, the main focus in the Finnish-language press was on Finnish writers writing in Finnish.

Leo Tolstoi, Maxim Gorky, and Leonid Andrejev were the Russian writers most favored by the Finnish working-class movement. In Finland, their works were most often brought to the market by working-class publishers, or through cheap series by bourgeois or commercial publishers, aimed at the general public with low income. Also, working-class newspapers and journals offered a significant channel for the translations to be published as serial stories (Roininen, 1993, p. 212). American literature was of particular interest to the Finnish readership, partly because of the mass migration from Finland to the United States at the turn of the century. People were eager to get a feel of what it was like across the ocean. The most renowned names were Jack London and Upton Sinclair (Roininen, 1993, pp. 269–270). However, the cultural debates in Russia and the United States were not systematically followed by the Finnish working-class press. These literatures were first and foremost represented as translations of fictional works.

The press was, of course, not the only arena where what it meant to be a working-class writer was defined. As Jürgen Habermas has famously argued, novels also formed part of national public spheres as they emerged in the nineteenth century. Fiction thus offered a cultural arena even for "making" and valuing the working class in a dialectical relationship with the upper classes and through processes intersecting with gender, sexuality, and nationality. In fiction, what it meant to be a working-class author could be thematized, analyzed, and defined. Kössi Kaatra, for example, depicts in his autobiographical novel, *Äiti ja poika: Kuvaus köyhäinkorttelista* [*Mother and Son: A Picture of the Quarter of the Poor*] (1924), the process of *becoming* a working-class poet. For him, a working-class writer is a "poet of the masses." To become a working-class writer in Kaatra's novel, one has to receive two "visitors." The first visitor incorporates the idea that people from the "poor quarters" are not alone but belong to the working class. The second visitor is the Muse, or the spirit of poetry. Their visits help a poet to realize that the private sorrows of an individual are not enough to form the contents of poetry; a working-class poet needs to express the feelings of the entire working class, from the "viewpoint of the back yard" (Launis, 2015, pp. 14–34).[5] This is something that became a distinctive mark of working-class literature for Kaatra and, more generally, for the whole movement. This definition is remarkably close to the one given by Pirkko Saisio in the 1970s, quoted in the beginning of this article, which testifies to the extent to which most twentieth-century definitions are, in the end, versions of older understandings of culture as reflecting the social situation in which it is born.

While in the United States working-class literature has always been about the production of a class identity through modes of racial looking, as Balthaser shows in this anthology, in Finnish working-class literature class is strongly gendered. The ratio of the writers' gender alone is a good indicator of this: of the writers mentioned by name or pseudonym by Palmgren (1966b, pp. 535–536), 166 were men and only 11 were women (and of these women Maiju Lassila was known to be a pseudonym used by Algot Untola, a male writer). Furthermore, the most famous of the women writers in the field— Hilja Pärssinen, Elvira Willman, and Hilda Tihlä—came from the educated classes (Launis, 2009, p. 85). One explanation given for the low number of women writers, especially those with proletarian roots, is that they already had an outlet for their creativity in handwritten newspapers, which were popular in the societies of young working-class people (Salmi-Niklander, 2010, pp. 20–41). Another explanation is that these writers were occasionally hiding behind collective nicknames (Hyttinen & Salmi-Niklander, 2008). Finally, a more direct explanation would be that, in a society that generally allotted most of the space to bourgeois men, it was difficult for women to make a name for themselves as writers. This was especially the case for lower-class women, since raising "the woman question" was often difficult and the highlighting of this inequality posed a potential threat to class cohesion and unity.

The coexistence of the two literary fields, the bourgeois and the working-class, came to a violent end in 1918, when the Finnish civil war broke out. The previous December (1917), Finland had gained its independence from Russia. The papers were signed by Lenin, and the agreement was reached through negotiations only and without violence, with the First World War and the Russian Revolution as a backdrop. However, during the final years of Russian rule, the class conflict in Finland deepened.[6] Gaining independence opened up the question as to who should lead the country and by what means. The civil war began on 27 January 1918 and lasted approximately four months, until 15 May. It was a desperate undertaking, as neither side really had a strategy. Also, materially, in terms of equipment and weaponry, the Red front was much weaker than the White to begin with. The White front was right-wing, but it also represented the establishment. The existing infrastructure and clergy was regarded as being in their camp. The Red front was the revolutionary one, hoping to take over the state apparatuses. On both fronts, there were approximately 80,000 soldiers. Soviet Russia helped the Reds with arms shipments; the Whites received support from Germany. The support was tangible, as around 10,000 German soldiers fought alongside the White troops.[7]

Some working-class writers joined the Red troops, others took part in agitation, trying to keep up the spirits and unity of the Reds. After the Whites won the war, most writers associated with the Red front fled to Soviet Russia (or Sweden, like the above mentioned Kössi Kaatra), while some faced execution. Publishing houses were shut down. Even the make-ups, props, and wigs belonging to the working-class amateur theatres were redistributed to groups with ties to the right (Seppälä, 2010, pp. 129–130). Granted, the absolute silencing of working-class culture did not last long. Already as early as 1919, publications were distributed and some theater groups were rehearsing again (Seppälä, 2010, pp. 133–138). However, working-class culture never again established itself as an institutionally independent field the same way it had done during the first decades of the twentieth century. Rather, the bourgeois and working-class literary fields merged into one in which the battle over space, authority, and hegemony is constantly being fought.

## Working-Class Writers in the Young Republic

After the Civil War in 1918, the literary field in Finland was almost completely controlled by the victorious Whites. In fiction, the Civil War was mostly depicted from the point of view of the winners (Koskela, 1999, pp. 222–239). The labor movement was divided into the reformist Social Democratic Party and the more radical Socialist Labor Party: instead of being just *writers of the working class*, working-class authors were, in this new cultural and political reality, forced to take sides in this political division of the left. However, not all writers wanted to conflate writing about the working class, and seeking a working-class audience, with party politics. This led to a new kind of configuration of authorship on the continuum of Finnish working-class literature. The term "leftist author" was coined as a means of surpassing the party-political divide and highlighting the artistic freedom of even the authors committed to the cause of the working class (Roininen, 1999, pp. 240–241; Pynttäri, 2015, p. 128). Working-class literature was thus redefined as counter-hegemonic literature: not directly connected to party organs on either corner of the left field, but clearly antagonistic with regard to bourgeois values, politics, and literature. It is worth noticing that here, again, it was the author that had to be renamed, and all other changes on the cultural field negotiated through this renamed figure.

The 1920s was a period of cultural modernism in the spirit of "the windows open wide to Europe," to quote the motto used by the most influential literary group of the era: *Tulenkantajat* [Torch bearers]. Yet it would not take long for Finland to develop into a patriotic, right-wing society. Under the threat of war in Europe and the fear of the communist Soviet Union, laws were enacted that prohibited communism and its propagation, with the aim to deter extreme leftist activities as well as to prevent any contact with the Soviet Union the Finnish left might have. In this complex situation, a small faction of left-wing intellectuals— Raoul Palmgren, Jarno Pennanen, Kaisu-Mirjami Rydberg, Maija Savutie, Elvi Sinervo, Cay Sundström, and Arvo Turtiainen— began their battle against the bourgeois cultural elite. In 1936, this coalition of authors and artists founded a literary group known as *Kiila* [Wedge] (Salmi-Niklander & Launis, 2015, p. 7; Koivisto, 2015, pp. 99–124), and proudly claimed in their first yearbook that only now was the working man for the first time in Finland entering the literary field as both subject matter and producer of literature (Turtiainen, 1937, p. 7).

Indeed, literary scholar Veli-Matti Pynttäri points out that the rise of working-class literature in post-Civil War Finland was again accompanied by an increased critical interest in the notion of the working-class author. In 1936, *Kirjallisuuslehti,* a leftist literary magazine, published an account of a social evening attended by members of *Kiila*, where the main topic of discussion was the notion of the working-class author on a general level. However, attention soon focused on the question of who, among the contemporary writers, could be considered a "real" working-class writer (Pynttäri, 2015, p. 125). The opposing views centered on one author in particular, Toivo Pekkanen, who was born into a working-class family and rose from rather poor conditions to become a nationally recognized author. In fact, Pekkanen was eventually granted the honorary title of an Academician in 1955. Nonetheless, it was a shared opinion of *Kiila* activists that Pekkanen was not a working-class writer because he did not depict a typical proletarian. For example, in his autobiographical novel, *Tehtaan varjossa [In the Shadow of the Factory]* (1932),[8] he portrayed an individual withdrawing from questions of social class into self-examination (ibid., pp. 126–127). One year earlier, in 1935, Raoul Palmgren, the leading ideologist of the group, had defined proletarian literature through three characteristics that he was—more or less—to maintain throughout his career as a literary scholar: (1.) it must reflect proletarian vitality, (2.) it expresses a proletarian worldview, and (3.) it has a proletarian sphere of influence. Based on these criteria, Palmgren tended towards the exclusion of Pekkanen from the scope of proletarian literature on the basis of his "ideological indeterminancy"; his characters detach themselves from their social class and assume more individual concerns regarding human life. Palmgren returned to depict Pekkanen's working-class authorship in his later works. According to Pynttäri, Palmgren had a difficult, career-long relationship with Pekkanen (Pynttäri, 2015, pp. 133–138).

During the Continuation War (between Finland and the Soviet Union 1941–1944; after the Winter War 1939–1940), key members of the left-wing intelligentsia were imprisoned on charges of desertion and high treason, while many others were taken into what was called "preventive detention." After Finland lost the Continuation War, the political situation changed. Once the anti-communist laws were repealed in 1944, the Finnish Communist Party could function legally, and many of the left-wing writers and intellectuals joined either it or the SKDL (Finnish People's Democratic League). The left-wing intellectuals were unique in their own generation in terms of their internationalization, based on their universal sense of solidarity with their co-ideologists (Koivisto, 2015, pp. 99–124).

In post-war Finland, one of the most influential writers was, without a doubt, Väinö Linna. He adopted the perspectives of ordinary men on the front during the Continuation War of 1941–1944 in *Tuntematon sotilas* [*The Unknown Soldier*] (1954) and the turn-of-the-century crofters who chose the side of the Reds in the 1918 Civil War in his *Täällä Pohjantähden alla* [*Under the North Star*] (1959–1962). Both novels were unprecedentedly successful. Linna himself had working-class background. He worked in a factory and depicted in his literary works a country in which everybody worked (see Ojajärvi, forthcoming). He retraces the movement from a rural society into an industrialised, modern North European nation state that firmly believed in the growth of the economy. He also was, together with Lauri Viita, for example, part of the group of the working-class writers called "Mäkelän piiri." And yet, Linna's work was published by a mainstream publishing house and has been

characterized as "probably the last representative of the Finnish national literature" (Nummi, 1999, p. 99).

Väinö Linna did not like the notion of a working-class writer,
neither personally nor in a broader sense. In 1948, the leading
newspaper in Finland, *Helsingin Sanomat*, presented Linna as
probably "the only hundred-per-cent working-class writer in
Finland." The next year, the authoritative critic Toini Havu stated
in the same newspaper, referencing the ideas of the Swedish writer
Folke Fridell, that working-class writers should describe workers'
lives and factory work. Havu argued that writers should stay
within their own sphere and focus on "normal workers," not on
the exceptional ones. Väinö Linna critically responded to Havu's
assertions, contending that, for him, the concept of a working-class
writer (or, actually, the whole system of *labeling* writers) was a
horror. The mission of a writer was "to find his own personality,
to construct and fulfill it." The writer should not see human beings
as "class-creatures"; the writer is not a politician (Varpio, 2006,
pp. 227–231). Linna continued this line of thought in the essay
"Työläiskirjailijoista ja heidän tehtävistään" ["On Working-Class
Writers and Their Missions"] (1949), in which he strongly
emphasized the importance of the unique, personal view of
every writer. Ironically, he repudiated the entire concept of a
working-class writer because "it doesn't give many names to a
dear child but one name to many children" (Linna, 1990/1949,
p. 185).[9] Even though he disentangled his work from the strict
labels, he did not deny the importance of the social mission or task
of literature (Linna 1990/1964).

## 1960s and 1970s: History Revisited

The 1960s mark a turning point in the Finnish national
self-understanding with regard to the working-class movement.
The publication of the second part of Väinö Linna's three-volume
novel suite *Täällä pohjan tähden alla* [*Under the North Star*] in
1960 triggered an unforeseen discussion about the 1918 Finnish
Civil War and the events leading to it. Up until then, the civil
war had often been referred to as the liberation war [*vapaussota*],
and the victory of the Whites had been dubbed as victory over

Soviet Russia. Now, Linna's depiction of the peasants, workers, and other minor characters forming the Red troops brought about a whole flood of memories thus far repressed from the public sphere. Many national memory organizations such as the People's Archives, Labor Archives, and the Literary Archives of the Finnish Literature Society started collecting memory data about the war from the point of view of the common people, from either side of the front but with a focus on micro rather than macro history.

It might be debatable whether or not Linna was a working-class writer and according to which criteria; his role as someone who gave form and language to a whole new way of understanding the Finnish national past, however, is not. The public debate surrounding the second part of the North Star trilogy also created pressure on historical scholarship (Kettunen 1990, pp. 183 & 191; Nummi, 1999, p. 100), and it was only during the 1960s that the first non-biased studies on the civil war and the birth of the Finnish nation state were written.

During the same decade, in 1965, Raoul Palmgren defended his doctoral thesis on the concept of working-class literature, thus beginning the academic research tradition of the history of Finnish working-class literature. In his thesis, Palmgren discusses two words that had previously been used interchangeably as synonyms. Both translate into English as "working-class literature": *työväenkirjallisuus* and *työläiskirjallisuus*.[10] Palmgren suggests that the first should be understood as a larger umbrella under which all kinds of literature aimed primarily at working-class audiences would fit, and the latter as literature produced by, aimed at, and expressive of the working class. The following year (1966), Palmgren published his two-volume study on pre-independence Finnish working-class literature (Palmgren, 1966 a & b), putting his theoretical concepts to use.

Palmgren saw a writer's proletarian roots and origins as a defining feature for *työläiskirjallisuus*. For him, true working-class literature is literature written *by* the working-class, expressive of the "working-class worldview," rough, untamed in form, and even clumsy at times (Palmgren, 1965, pp. 222–223). The weakness contemporary research has been eager to point out in this formulation is that Palmgren seems to suggest that certain aesthetic features are *caused* by a writer's living conditions. This causal logic fits his Marxist understanding of culture as a superstructure reflecting the underlying division of labour in a society. However, this framework also allows him to view his favored forms, plotlines, and subject matters as being authentic expressions of a working-class worldview and to disregard others as being untrue (Hyttinen, 2015, pp. 59–60).

Palmgren was not the only one, of course, to try to find expressions of an authentic working-class worldview in the literature of the 1960s. However, it is not until the 1970s that this endeavor became one of the leading motives in cultural debates, as we saw in the opening anecdote of this article. Researcher Milla Peltonen claims that the two sensations surrounding the writer Hannu Salama are illustrative of the difference between the decades.

In 1964, Salama, whom Peltonen (2015, p. 167) calls "the best-known but also the most controversial Finnish working-class author" of the 1960s and 1970s, wrote a novel titled *Juhannustanssit* [*The Midsummer Dance*] that brought upon him charges of blasphemy. In the novel, a drunken character indeed gives a mock sermon and, thus, quite openly questions, and laughs at, the Christian values of 1960s Finland. That a novelist was charged with blasphemy was rare, as only a few cases were raised with regard to fictional literature during the whole of the twentieth century. Salama was sentenced to three months' imprisonment but was later pardoned by President Urho Kekkonen (Peltonen, 2015, p. 167). This first sensation was thus about the conservative society defending its values through state organs such as the court and the prison. Indeed, the radicalism of the 1960s has been described as general radicalism against the establishment. That the radicalism should have more or less articulated political aims was a thing of the 1970s (Niemi, 1999, pp. 158–171).

In 1972, Salama's novel *Siinä näkijä missä tekijä* [*Where There's a Crime, There's a Witness*] triggered the second public brouhaha of Salama's career—this time about how the working-class should be depicted. The debate resonates with Palmgren's conviction that a certain objectively definable working-class worldview exists that could and should be expressed in literature. This time, the sensation was not about the state against a rebellious individual, the debate is more correctly located within the cultural field and has to do with questions of authenticity and representability in regard to the working-class subject. Also, this time, it was not the establishment reacting to Salama's novel, but the left. As Milla Peltonen explains,

> Since the mid-1960s there had been a major conflict on the left and inside the Communist Party of Finland (SKP). The party was led by the Eurocommunist Aarne Saarinen, who had begun to modernize the party line, but a minority of members rejected this and accused the SKP leadership of revisionism. The pro-Soviet internal opposition group was also known as "Taistoists," after their leader Taisto Sinisalo. Those literary critics who supported Saarinen mainly welcomed Salama's book, as did a majority of Social-Democratic and right-wing critics. . . The Taistoist critics, in contrast, along with some veterans of the resistance movement, rejected the novel and publicly expressed their disappointment. *Siinä näkijä missä tekijä*, they claimed, was untruthful and pessimistic. (Peltonen, 2015, p. 176.)

Arguments used in the debate made references to both reality and theory. On the one hand, the veterans of the resistance movement claimed that the novel was untruthful when depicting communists as quarrelsome and even deceitful at times, when according to their experience, real communists had been decent and committed to the cause. On the other hand, Peltonen contends that younger Taistoists found that the novel did not meet their ideals of politically conscious literature (Peltonen, 2015, p. 176).

Milla Peltonen reads mostly male authors writing realist novels,[11] and as the quotation above shows, she sees a certain antagonism between them and the Taistoists. This view has, however, been challenged as well. In an anthology published in 2010, *1970-luku suomalaisessa kirjallisuudessa* [*The 1970s in Finnish Literature*], the author Marja-Leena Mikkola points out how little research there is on the variety and width of the oeuvres by authors who took part in the Taistolaiset movement (Mikkola, 2010, pp. 64–65). Indeed, their support of the movement did not mean that their production was uniform, or their worldviews overall dogmatic. Pirkko Saisio, as mentioned in the opening anecdote, was a Taistoist as well. Still, her relationship to class-conscious art as a young writer was reflective rather than didactic, and retrospectively, she has chosen to highlight her bewilderment rather than, for example, satisfaction at being named a working-class author. However, even though the generation of artists that in the 1970s became known as Taistoists still have an immense impact on Finnish cultural life, research that would inquire into the specific nature of their input remains largely to be done.

A notable phenomenon with regard to the tradition outlined here is that the Taistoist writers did not necessarily claim to be working-class by birth. However, they sought to redefine and de-mystify art so that making art could be considered labor. This is signaled even in the name they chose for the union they started in 1972, *Cultural Workers' Union* [*Kulttuurityöväen Liitto*]. They also sought an organic connection with the workers in the more traditional understanding of the word. For instance, the union published a cultural manifesto in 1975 called *Art Belongs to the People* [*Taide kuuluu kansalle*]. Also, they performed in factories and at rallies supporting strikes, their theater groups toured the country, and member Marja-Leena Mikkola wrote one of the most respected document novels in Finnish literary history, called *Heavy Cotton* [*Raskas puuvilla*] (1971). In the novel, she documents the life and working conditions of women employed in the Finnish cotton industry. A significant feature of the Taistoist movement is also that quite a large number of its most prominent writers were women. In addition to those mentioned above, Aulikki Oksanen, for example, was also an important figure, known both as a writer and a popular singer of political songs.

The heated political atmosphere had impacts on the academic world as well, in Finland as well as elsewhere. Democracy in university management was demanded, Marxist reading groups were founded. In the humanities, it suddenly became evident that talking about art was not an innocent undertaking: it had political implications. This can be seen in the works of the influential Marxist critic Pertti Karkama, who began his work during the 1970s. Whereas Raoul Palmgren was interested in the history and agents of working-class literature, Karkama turned his Marxist apparatus towards the whole of our national literary history. Thus, in his case, it was mostly methodology (not the research material) that signaled class-consciousness. Palmgren had acted as professor of literature at the University of Oulu since 1968. In 1978, Karkama became his successor.

## Working-Class Literature Today

In this anthology, Magnus Nilsson remarks that the status for, and interest in, working-class literature in Sweden hit its all-time low in the 1980s and 1990s. In Finland, the pattern is similar but not quite as dramatic. Even after the tumultuous 1970s, Pirkko Saisio, Hannu Salama, Marja-Leena Mikkola, and Aulikki Oksanen, among others, carried on writing. The Cultural Worker's Union continued publishing its own magazine, *Kulttuurivihkot* [*The Cultural Notebooks*], until 1991. Pertti Karkama continued his Marxist literary studies, attracting many disciples. Kari Sallamaa, the foreman of *Kiila* [*Wedge*] (1975–77), began his academic career in the 1980s, focusing for example on the legacy of Raoul Palmgren and the history of the first generation of *Kiila*. However, from the point of view of the 1980s' self-understanding, working-class literature was not a central phenomenon. Rather, what was regarded as interesting and new was the literature that sought to disavow the values of the 1970s. Thus, literature that wanted *not* to convey clear political messages became the hallmark of the Finnish 1980s. Postmodernism and punk were the buzzwords, and even writers who could have, in fact, been read into the working-class continuum (such as Rosa Liksom) rarely were. Instead, fragmentary style and other such features that signaled postmodernism were eagerly pinpointed as the central defining features of the 1980s' emerging generation of writers. This paved way for a more determined rejection of the concept of class in public and academic discussions during the early 1990s. This rejection expressed the principles of the neoliberal shift taking place in Finland, which argued that social classes did not *exist* anymore; we were all just individuals (Kauranen & Lahikainen, 2016, p. 46).

Since the late 1990s, several writers in Finland have once again put class difference under scrutiny. This is the phenomenon which Jussi Ojajärvi (2006; 2015) refers to as the new emergence of class in Finnish literature. Arto Salminen—as well as Kari Hotakainen, Reko Lundán, Juha Seppälä, Mari Mörö, Outi Alm, and Hanna Marjut Marttila—wrote novels in the context of the neoliberal turn of the 1980s and the great economic depression at the beginning of the 1990s in Finland. According to Ojajärvi, it was Arto Salminen who wrote, in his six novels, the angriest critique of neoliberal inequality. Salminen politicizes the subjectivities of the working class with aesthetic and literary representations (such as the figure of the dirty class) which are ambivalent in their ironic tone, and modifies the critical ethos of social realism with some naturalist and modernist stylistic influences (Ojajärvi, 2015, pp. 181–182).

Recently, the revival of literature focusing on class differences and social fragmentation has been joined by research on working-class literature, and Finnish working-class literature has become a topic of lively discussions. In addition, the annual Working-Class Literature Day has been organized in Tampere since 2010 and another in Helsinki since 2014. A special issue of the *Journal of Finnish Studies* published in 2015 (vol. 18, no. 2), titled "International Influences in Finnish Working-Class Literature and Its Research," constitutes the first ever presentation of Finnish working-class literary tradition in English. It presents the results of the revived interest in this literature from the turn of the twentieth century to the present day.

However, despite the increased interest in working-class literature in Finland in recent years, there is still no agreement on how to define it. Who counts as a working-class writer? Do we still need such a notion? Do contemporary Finnish writers describe themselves as working-class writers? What does the term imply, and what sort of images does it trigger among the writers or readers?

The publisher Robustos presented the poet Hannu Häkli as a "working-class writer from Tampere" on their web page in 2008. When asked why he chose to introduce himself as such, Häkli explained that it was because of his working-class background and the fact that he has trained "to be a so-called worker and worked in different so-called working-class trades" (Launis, 2010). Häkli, in other words, links the notion strictly to an author's life and the experience of *being* a workerworker—much like Pirkko Saisio did. Häkli also said that the notion had surprised readers because his poems do not represent the "communist pathos." Nor are they political comments. According to Mäkijärvi (2008), Häkli moves in spheres that are more sensitive than the "working-class romanticism": in nature, dreams, and affects (Launis, 2010). Another example of the continuous topicality of the subject comes from the year 2016, when the journalist Asta Leppä asked, in an essay published in Finland's leading newspaper *Helsingin Sanomat*, whether the middle class has monopolized Finnish literature. She mentions that Arto Salminen's and Hanna-Marjut Marttila's novels are not among the bestsellers of the day and asks, where are the depictions of the working or lower class, poor and marginalized, in Finnish contemporary literature. Where is today's Toivo Pekkanen or Väinö Linna? (Leppä, 2016).

As we have shown in this article, working-class fiction never simply existed as a reflection of some self-evident class-bound reality. Rather, the history of working-class literature is a history of definitions and counter-definitions; an amalgamation of political and literary histories, national tendencies, and transnational influences; politically motivated wishful thinking; and conventional and convincing portrayals of working people. What has been regarded as "authentic" has throughout this history been represented as something only about to emerge. In this respect, we have travelled far just to arrive where we started: the anticipation of the true working-class poet.

## Notes

1. Mikko Pollari's recent research is a notable exception to this rule. Pollari's starting point is explicitly in transnational theories, and his focus is on transatlantic movements between Finland and the United States in the early twentieth century (see, e.g., Pollari, 2015). For other openings towards a transnational perspective, see Salmi-Niklander & Launis, 2015.

2. Palmgren's two-volume study on the "literature of our old working-class movement" (as the subtitle of the study reads) was published in 1966. Palmgren's main interest was in cataloguing the whole field. He goes through the oeuvre of every single writer in the field, summarizing the thematics and plotlines and giving as much biographical information about the writers as he possibly can. Palmgren's work is not explicitly theoretical, unless an interest in working-class literature counts as a theoretical starting point per se. Rather, his politics and theoretical commitments are mostly implicit, such as considering the gender-specific nature of working-class women's oppression irrelevant from the point of view of what working-class fiction should depict (Hyttinen, 2015). However, Palmgren's magnum opus remains influential, as he was the first to focus academic interest on working-class writers of the pre-independence era. Palmgren went through an incredible amount of first-hand sources to be able to define the borders of the field, counting and naming the writers he considered as belonging to it.

3. For one example, see *Työmies*, 23 November 1904.

4. The same debate concerned publishers, such as Vihtori Kosonen. See Pollari, 2015, pp. 35–55.

5. Magnus Nilsson has stressed the point that the existence of the tradition of working-class writing in Sweden has given writers legitimacy for the production of subaltern, radical discourses on class. For this reason, he argues that the tradition is always in conflict with hegemonic discourses (such as nationalism), which attempt to deny the significance of class or, in the case of more recent discourses, the common view that class distinctions no longer exist (Nilsson, 2011, pp. 199–208).

6. It has, however, been claimed that the formation of red troops had more to do with local conflicts between the landed gentry and the landless poor, and that the will to fight was not necessarily motivated with any awareness of class as a larger structure (Ylikangas, 1993, pp. 8–20).

7. The Wikipedia article on the Finnish Civil War offers a research-based summary of the events of the Civil War in English: https://en.wikipedia.org/wiki/Finnish_Civil_War

8. *Tehtaan varjossa* tapped into an internationally popular trend in working-class literature. In Scandinavia, especially in Sweden, writers

such as Ivar Lo-Johansson, Eyvind Johnson, Jan Friedgård, Harry Martinson, and Gustav Sandgren published a set of autobiographical *Bildungsromane* in the 1930s. Even though Pekkanen was probably well aware of these novels, the most influental model for him was still Jack London's *Martin Eden.* (see Pynttäri, 2015, p. 132). *Martin Eden* was an important source of inspiration for the Swedish working-class writers, too (see Magnus Nilsson's chapter in this book).

9. Here, Linna is playing with a Finnish proverb that says "a dear child has many names," which means (approximately) that people can appreciate the same thing even if they use different words for describing it.

10. In Finnish press, the terms *työväenkirjailija* and *työväenkirjallisuus* (not *työläiskirjailija*) seem to be the original terms used by the contemporaries at the turn of the twentieth century. These terms convey the meaning of a "working-class author" and the "working-class literature", as in an author writing *to* workers as opposed to literature written *for* workers. In this sense, the original term in Finland refers more to the readership than to the roots and social class of the author (as emphasized later by Palmgren).

11. Peltonen studies the works of Hannu Salama, Alpo Ruuth, Lassi Sinkkonen, Samuli Paronen, and Jorma Ojaharju as the most prominent working-class writers of the era. She isolates two very different ways they relate to the realist working-class tradition of prose preceding them. Some of them carry on with the realist tradition without problematizing it—with an omniscient narrator, orderly and integrated plot, and portrayals of individuals as members of a group. Alpo Ruuth, for example, would fit this continuum (Peltonen 2015, p. 168). Others question precisely those founding blocks that stabilize a traditionally realist fictional rendition, such as the narrator's omnipotence and the causal integrity of the plot (ibid., pp. 168–169), thus remodelling the realist tradition. In postrealist novels, the act of writing is often depicted and, through such depictions, the questions of representability, narratability, and politics of writing are made visible within the narrated world. The breakthrough, argues Peltonen, of postrealism in Finnish literature takes place in the novel *Siinä näkijä missä tekijä,* in which the narration itself becomes a notable part of the action depicted (Peltonen, 2015, p. 169; Peltonen, 2008, pp. 49–53). In this respect, working-class fiction of the 1970s could be seen as making way to the postmodernist experimentality of the 1980s.

# References

Haapala, P. (1999). Työväenluokan synty. In: P. Haapala, ed., *Talous, valta ja valtio: Tutkimuksia 1800-luvun Suomesta.* Tampere, Vastapaino, pp. 199–219.

Hitchcock, P. (1989). *Working-Class Fiction in Theory and Practice. A Reading of Alan Sillitoe.* Ann Arbor, UMI Research Press.

Hyttinen, E. (2004). *Kuinka Pirkko Saisio tehdään? Naiskirjailijuus performatiivisena identiteettinä.* University of Helsinki, Finnish literature (MA thesis, unpublished).

Hyttinen, E. (2012). *Kovaa työtä ja kohtalon oikkuja. Elvira Willmanin kamppailu työläiskirjallisuuden tekijyydestä vuosisadanvaihteen Suomessa.* Turku, University of Turku

Hyttinen, E. (2015). Women in Early Capitalism and Other Irrelevant Issues: Elvira Willman's Struggle for Working-Class Authorship. *Journal of Finnish Studies* 2, pp. 56–74.

Hyttinen, E. and Salmi-Niklander, K. (2008). Nainen näkinkengässä. *Naistutkimus–Kvinnoforskning* 1, pp. 56–61.

Kaatra, K. (1924). *Äiti ja poika: Kuvaus köyhäinkorttelista.* Helsinki: Osakeyhtiö Työn kirjapaino.

Kauranen, K. (2013). Odd Man out? The Self-educated Philosopher and his Analyses of 19th-century Finland. In: A. Kuismin & M. Driscoll, eds., *White Field, Black Seeds: Nordic Literacy Practices in the Long Nineteenth-Century.* Studia Fennica Litteraria 7. Helsinki, Finnish Literature Society, pp. 120–134.

Kauranen, R. and Lahikainen, L. (2016). Luokan äänen ja hiljaisuuden muodostuminen rakenteellisesti ja kokemuksellisesti. In: A. Anttila, R. Kauranen, K. Launis and J. Ojajärvi, eds., *Luokan ääni ja hiljaisuus. Yhteiskunnallinen luokkajärjestys 2000-luvun alun Suomessa.* Tampere, Vastapaino, pp. 46–87.

Kettunen, P. (1990). Politiikan menneisyys ja poliittinen historia. In: Ahtiainen et al eds., *Historia nyt.* Helsinki, WSOY, 163–207.

Klaus, G. (1985). *Literature of Labour.* New York, St. Martin's Press.

Koivisto, H. (2015). Devotedly International – But Always Wrong: Left-Wing Intellectuals and Their Orientation toward International

Progressive Culture and Literature in the 1930s and 1940s. *Journal of Finnish Studies* 2, pp. 99–124.

Koskela, L. (1999). Kansa taisteli – valkoiset kertoivat. In: L. Rojola, ed., *Suomen kirjallisuushistoria 2. Järkiuskosta vaistojen kapinaan.* Helsinki, Finnish Literature Society, pp. 222–235.

Kotilainen, S. (2016). *Literary Skills as Local Intangible Capital: The History of a Rural Lending Library c. 1860–1920.* Helsinki, Finnish Literature Society.

Kuismin, A. (2016). Ploughing with the Pen. Metapoetic Elements in Finnish Nineteenth-Century Peasant Poetry. In: A. Edlund, T. G. Ashplant, A. Kuismin, eds., *Reading and Writing from Below: Exploring the Margins of Modernity.* Umeå, Umeå University & Royal Skyttean Society, pp. 9–24.

Lahtinen, M. (2006). *Snellmanin Suomi.* Tampere, Vastapaino.

*Lappeenrannan Uutiset* July 17, 1895. Työväenkalenteri III.

Launis, K. (2009). Työväen Maamme-kirja. In: K. Melkas, H. Grönstrand, K. Launis, M. Leskelä-Kärki, J. Ojajärvi, T. Palin, and L. Rojola, eds., *Läpikulkuihmisiä: Muotoiluja kansallisuudesta ja sivistyksestä 1900-luvun alun Suomessa.* Helsinki, Finnish Literature Society, pp. 73–106.

Launis, K. (2010). Työväenkirjallisuus ennen ja nyt. *Kiiltomato* [online] 4.5.2010. Available at: http://www.kiiltomato.net/tyovaenkirjallisuus-ennen-ja-nyt/ [Accessed 7 Dec. 2016].

Launis, K. (2015). The Making of the Finnish Working Class in Early Twentieth-Century Working-Class Literature. *Journal of Finnish Studies* 2, pp. 14–34.

Leppä, A. (2016). Passiivisuutta, ongelmien välttelyä, silmien ummistamista – onko keskiluokka ominut kirjallisuuden? *Helsingin Sanomat* July 26, 2016.

Linna, V. (1990). *Murroksia. Esseitä, puheita ja kirjoituksia.* Helsinki, WSOY.

Luukkanen, T. (2016). *Mitä maalaiskansa luki? Kirjasto, kirjat ja kirjoja lukeva yhteisö Karstulassa 1861–1918.* Helsinki, Finnish Literature Society.

Mikkola, M. (2010). Mitä sanottavaa minulla on pahasta 70-luvusta. In: K. Hypén, ed., *1970-luku suomalaisessa kirjallisuudessa*. Helsinki, Avain.

Mäkijärvi, E. (2008). Seuraamisen arvoista runoutta. *Kiiltomato* [online] 15 Dec. 2008. Available at: http://www.kiiltomato.net/hannu-hakli-seuraajat/ [Accessed 7 Dec. 2016].

Nieminen, H. (2006). *Kansallisen julkisuuden rakentuminen Suomessa 1809–1917*. Tampere, Vastapaino.

Niemi, J. (1999). Kirjallisuus ja sukupolvikapina. In: P. Lassila, ed., *Suomen kirjallisuushistoria 3. Rintamakirjeistä tietoverkkoihin*. Helsinki, Finnish Literature Society, pp. 158–171.

Nilsson, M. (2011). Arbetarlitteratur, teori, politik: Utkast till ett marxistiskt program för forskning och undervisning om svensk arbetarlitteratur. In: B. Jonsson, M. Nilsson, B. Sjöberg, and J. Vulovic, eds., *Från Nexø till Alakoski: Aspekter på nordisk arbetarlitteratur*. Lund, Absalon förlag, pp. 199–208.

Nummi, J. (1999). Väinö Linnan klassikot. In: P. Lassila, ed., *Suomen kirjallisuushistoria 3. Rintamakirjeistä tietoverkkoihin*. Helsinki, Finnish Literature Society, pp. 99–102.

Ojajärvi, J. (2006). *Supermarketin valossa: Kapitalismi, subjekti ja Minuus Mari Mörön romaanissa Kiltin yön lahjat ja Juha Seppälän novellissa "Supermarket"*. Helsinki: Finnish Literature Society.

Ojajärvi, J. (2015). The Dirty Class: The Re-intensified Antagonism of Capital and Labor, and the Politics of Arto Salminen. *Journal of Finnish Studies* 2, pp. 181–209.

Ojajärvi, J. (forthcoming). Work as a Socially and Politically Invested Figure in Finnish Literature. In: L. Haverty Rugg and K. Sanders, eds., *Nordic Literary History 3*.

Palmgren, R. (1965). *Työläiskirjallisuus*. (Proletaarikirjallisuus.) Käsite- ja aatehistoriallinen käsiteselvittely. Helsinki, WSOY.

Palmgren, R. (1966 a & b). *Joukkosydän. Vanhan työväenliikkeemme kaunokirjallisuus I-II*. Helsinki, WSOY.

Peltonen, M. (2008). *Jälkirealismin ehdoilla: Hannu Salaman Siinä näkijä missä tekijä ja Finlandia-sarja*. Turku, Uiversity of

Turku. Available at: http://urn.fi/URN:ISBN:978–951-29-3658-8 [Accessed 7 Dec. 2016].

Peltonen, M. (2015). Reshaping Finnish Working-Class Prose: Hannu Salama's *Siinä näkijä missä tekijä* as a Postrealistic Novel. *Journal of Finnish Studies* 2, pp. 166–180.

Pollari, M. (2015). The Literally International Adventures of Vihtori Kosonen. *Journal of Finnish Studies* 2, pp. 35–55.

Pynttäri, V. (2015). Recognizing Your Class – Toivo Pekkanen, Raoul Palmgren, and Literature for the Working Class. *Journal of Finnish Studies* 2, pp. 125–143.

Roininen, A. (1993). *Kirja liikkeessä: Kirjallisuus instituutiona vanhassa työväenliikkeessä (1895–1918)*. Helsinki, Finnish Literature Society.

Roininen, A. (1999). Työväenliike tuo työläiset kirjallisuuden kentälle. In: Lea Rojola, ed., *Suomen kirjallisuushistoria 2. Järkiuskosta vaistojen kapinaan*. Helsinki, Finnish Literature Society, pp. 92–105.

Rojola, L. (2009). Sivistyksen ihanuus ja kurjuus-suomalaisen nousukkaan tarina. In: K. Melkas H. Grönstrand, K. Launis, M. Leskelä-Kärki, J. Ojajärvi, T. Palin, and L. Rojola, eds., *Läpikulkuihmisiä: Muotoiluja kansalaisuudesta ja sivistyksestä 1900-luvun alun Suomessa*. Helsinki, Finnish Literature Society, pp. 10–38.

Saisio, P. (2000). Pirkko Saisio. In: R. Haavikko, ed., *Miten kirjani ovat syntyneet 4*. Helsinki, WSOY, pp. 336–367.

Saisio, P. (1976). Pirkko Saision itsetilitys: odotamme yhä suurta työläiskirjaijaa. *Suomen kuvalehti 2*.

Salmi-Niklander, K. (2010). Sanelman sisaret: Sosiaalisen tekijyyden strategioita nuorten työläisnaisten suullis-kirjallisissa verkostoissa 1910–20-luvulla. In: I. Kemppainen, K. Salmi-Niklander, and S. Tuomaala, eds., *Kirjoitettu nuoruus: Aikalaistulkintoja 1900-luvun alkupuolen nuoruudesta*. Helsinki, Finnish Youth Research Society, 20–46.

Salmi-Niklander, K. & Launis, K. (2015). New Research Trends in Finnish Working-Class Literature: Introduction. *Journal of Finnish Studies* 2, pp. 3–13.

Seppälä, M. (2010). *Suomalaisen työväenteatterin varhaisvaiheet.* Helsinki, Finnish Literature Society.

Turtiainen, A. (1937). *Kiilan albumi,* pp. 6–11.

*Työmies* November, 23, 1904. Uuden ajan kynnyksellä.

Valpas, E. (1904). Työväen laulaja. *Työmies* April 6–7, 1904.

Varpio, Y. (2006). *Väinö Linnan elämä.* Helsinki, WSOY.

[No title.] *Vasabladet* September 22, 1903.

Ylikangas, H. (1993). *Tie Tampereelle.* Helsinki, WSOY.

# The Making of Swedish Working-Class Literature

*Magnus Nilsson*

The aim of this chapter is to give an overview of the tradition of Swedish working-class literature. Today, the most common terms for working-class literature and working-class writer in Swedish are "arbetarlitteratur" [literally: "worker literature"] and "arbetarförfattare" ["worker-author"]. Historically, many different terms have been used, including "arbetardiktning" and "arbetardikt" ["worker poetry"/ "worker writing"], "proletärförfattare" ["proletarian author"], "proletärdikt" and "proletärdiktning" ["proletarian poetry"/"proletarian writing"], as well as "arbetarskald" ["worker-poet"]. Following Jan Stenkvist (1985, p. 24), I will treat these terms as synonyms, distinguishing between them only in the rare cases when specific meanings are attached to them (or when it is stylistically motivated).

The most prolific researcher within the field of Swedish working-class literature is Lars Furuland. His definition of this literature, which is the most commonly accepted one, states that it exists at the "intersection" between literatures *by*, *about* and *for workers*, and has a specific "ideological anchorage" (Furuland and Svedjedal, 2006, pp. 23–24).[1] Although he doesn't explicitly specify this ideological anchorage, he stresses – in his very first attempt at defining working-class literature – that it be written by "authors who in one way or the other had ties to the labor movement" (Furuland, 1962, p. 14). Furthermore, Furuland's research constitutes the foundation for the dominant view of working-class literature as a *tradition* beginning within the labor movement at the end of the nineteenth century and thereafter evolving into a

How to cite this book chapter:
Nilsson, M. 2017. The Making of Swedish Working-Class Literature. In: Lennon, J. and Nilsson, M. (eds.) *Working-Class Literature(s): Historical and International Perspectives*. Pp. 95–127. Stockholm: Stockholm University Press. DOI: https://doi.org/10.16993/bam.e. License: CC-BY

central strand in modern Swedish literature that stretches all the way into contemporary times (Furuland and Svedjedal, 2006; Furuland, 1991 and 1977).[2]

As Ib Bondebjerg and Anker Gemzøe (1982, p. 6) have pointed out, both the phenomenon and the concept of working-class literature "evolve and change" throughout history in ways that constantly bring "new aspects and possibilities to the fore." But, as has been emphasized by Raymond Williams (1977, p. 115; 2005, p. 39), traditions are always constructed retrospectively and constitute "intentionally selective" versions of the past in which "certain meanings and practices are chosen for emphasis" while "certain other meanings and practices are neglected and excluded." Thus, it is not to be expected that all of the aspects and possibilities alluded to by Bondebjerg and Gemzøe are made visible in the narrative about the tradition of Swedish working-class literature dominant in contemporary research and criticism. Therefore, the overview of the history of Swedish working-class literature in this chapter will include an analysis of how this literature has been conceptualized in different ways, at different times, and in different contexts. This will open up for a reconstruction of Swedish working-class literature as an ever-changing phenomenon existing within a vast field of potentialities and possibilities, rather than as an essentialist or reified category. My goal is that this mode of historicizing will not only give a richer picture of Swedish working-class literature, but also help bring to the fore historical and theoretical questions relevant for the study of the phenomenon of working-class literature in general.

## From the Labor Movement to National Literature

The starting point for the tradition of Swedish working-class literature is generally placed within what Furuland has called the labor movement's counter public sphere during the late nineteenth century (Furuland, 1977, pp. 4, 14; 1981, pp. 286–290; 1991, p. 148; Furuland and Svedjedal, 2006, pp. 24–25).[3] This literature – consisting mainly of poems and songs – was primarily viewed as a means for political agitation (Furuland, 1962, p. 290; Mral, 1985, p. 15).

Perhaps the first example of an author active within the labor movement who is described by a critic as "a proletarian writer" can be found in a 1903 article by Hjalmar Branting (the first leader of the Swedish social-democratic party) about the poet K. J. Gabrielsson (better known under his pen name "Karolus"). Branting (1930, p. 174) describes Gabrielsson as "the first worker in our country who, without leaving his class ... reached a mastery of form and a scope in his production that grants him a place in the literature of our age."

However, at least since the 1890s, authors within the Swedish labor movement had referred to themselves as proletarian or working-class poets (Furuland and Svedjedal, 2006, p. 21) and sometimes used pen names signaling either membership in the working class, for example "Miner's wife," or a commitment to socialist politics, such as "Socialist" (Mral, 1985, pp. 42–43). In some cases, these identities were also expressed in their works, as in the poem "Proletärpoetens sång" ["The Proletarian Poet's Song"] (1894) by the pseudonym Helge Röd [Red Helge] (Uhlin, 1950, p. 366), or in Robert Ågren's short story "Ur en litterär proletärs utvecklingshistoria" ["From the Story about the Development of a Literary Proletarian"] (1898).

Interestingly, authors who did not themselves come from the working class sometimes identified strongly with it in their works. One example of this can be found in the poem "Proletär" ["Proletarian"] (1905) by K. G. Ossiannilsson – a radical intellectual, who between 1903 and 1904 lead the social-democratic youth organization and whose poetry was very popular within the labor movement. Here, the speaking subject includes himself in the proletariat through the use of the possessive pronoun "our":

Proletarian – that is the title, comrades,
it is the ringing of the clog against the paving-stone.
It is imprinted on our costume, on our manners –
if it is shameful, the shame is not ours.[4] (Haste, 1977, p. 164)

In their recollections from the literary life within the early labor movement, the authors and politicians Fredrik Ström and Axel Uhlén put more emphasis on the working-class authors' politics than on their class backgrounds. Ström (1941, p. 15) argues that the term working-class writer was reserved for authors who "belonged to the movement, participated in its struggle" and "published their works in its press and through its publishing houses," and that no distinctions were made between "academic" and "uneducated" writers. Uhlén (1978, p. 6) defines working-class writers as those who "have been active in labor-movement activities and whose writing has been inspired by it, regardless of them being autodidact or not." This downplaying of the authors' backgrounds in favor of their involvement in the labor movement has been recognized in the academic research on early working-class literature. For example, in her monograph on working-class poetry published in the labor movement press before 1900 Brigitte Mral (1985) includes works by authors without working-class backgrounds, such as the socialist journalists Axel Danielsson and Atterdag Wermelin.

The first important transformation of Swedish working-class literature occurred early in the twentieth century, when a group of working-class writers started attracting attention from readers and critics outside the labor movement (mainly with realistic prose fiction) and achieved a first breakthrough for working-class literature in the national site of literature (Uhlin, 1950, p. 210; Furuland, 1977, pp. 15–16; 1991, p. 148; Furuland and Svedjedal, 2006, pp. 78–79). The most important representatives of this group were Dan Andersson, Leon Larsson, Maria Sandel, Karl Östman, Martin Koch, and Gustav Hedenvind-Eriksson. Some ten years later, another group of writers – whose most well-known representatives were Ragnar Jändel, Harry Blomberg, and Ivan Oljelund – also managed to establish themselves in the site of national literature.

Critics affiliated with the labor movement developed a discourse about these writers as working-class writers.[5] In two articles published in 1906, for example, the labor movement's then leading critic, Bengt Lidforss (1920, p. 202), described Larsson first as a "working-class" and then as a "proletarian" poet. However, he didn't use the same concepts when writing about Ossiannilsson, which indicates that he reserved them for writers who, like Larsson, were self-taught and had personal experiences of manual labor (Leopold, 2001, 130–138; 270; 330–396).[6] But Lidforss also stressed that Larsson was not only active as a writer within the labor movement: his aims were not only political but also artistic (Mattsson, 2016, p. 19). This shows that he did not only view him from a sociological or political perspective but also from an aesthetic point of view. After Lidforss' death in 1913, Erik Hedén took over his role as the most important literary critic within the labor movement. Like Lidforss, he used terms such as "working-class writer" and "working-class literature" to describe writers of working-class background – among others Koch, Andersson and Hedenvind-Eriksson – and their works, more or less regardless of their politics and subject matters (Hedén, 1917; 1927, pp. 155, 207–211). Hedén also stressed the importance of viewing working-class literature, not as a means for political propaganda, but as works of *literature*, which may also fulfill political functions (Fahlgren, 1981, p. 90).

## The Proletarian Writer Recognized and Criticized

In 1921, the literary historian Richard Steffen published an anthology of modern Swedish literature intended for use in schools. In the foreword, he argued that the most powerful and, in many ways, the most interesting achievement in the literary production of the last two decades was what he termed *proletarian writing*:

> It has been created by writers, who, although not "proletarians" in the strict sense, have emerged from the working classes, for longer or shorter periods lived the lives of workers … and thus having had the opportunity to view social conditions from the dark depths that those of higher social standing have not dared or been able to sound out. Being autodidact and naturally talented, as a rule they have, with surprising ease, overcome the difficulties of the art of expression and, with their personal experiences, added to literature new groups of motifs, new ways of expression, and new attitudes toward the mysteries of life. (Steffen 1921, p. 7)

The importance of Steffen's book for later debates about working-class literature in Sweden cannot be overestimated. Therefore, some of the key points in his argument need to be highlighted: Steffen views working-class literature as an interesting *literary* phenomenon that *added* new dimensions to national literature. His definition of the working-class writer is centered on his *working-class background* (or, at least, his personal experiences of working-class life) and on his *lack of formal education*.

Steffen's book triggered a heated debate. Some authors – most notably Oljelund, Blomberg, and Jändel – protested vehemently against being labeled proletarian writers, arguing that it placed them outside literature proper and that an author's background or political affiliation should be considered irrelevant in literary discourse (Sundin, 1969, pp. 2912, 2929–2930; Stenkvist, 1985, pp. 228–230). Others – including Koch, Hedenvind-Eriksson and Östman – accepted and appreciated the categorization (Sundin, 1969, pp. 2924–2926, 2930–2931; Stenkvist, 1985, p. 232; Fahlgren, 1981, p. 70). Hedenvind-Eriksson (1961, p. 72), for example, argued that the characterization of him as a proletarian author was correct, since he was "born a proletarian," had "lived and still lives as a proletarian," was "self-taught" and wrote about "labor." In an article allegedly written in 1921 but published in the brochure *Proletärdiktning* [*Proletarian Writing*] in 1929, Koch claimed that Steffen was "absolutely correct" in describing him as a proletarian author.

Several critics affiliated with the labor movement, including Hedén, Kjell Strömberg, and Valfrid Palmgren, defended the use of the terms *proletarian writer* and *literature* but tried to further develop them. Hedén, for example, insisted on working-class background being a central criterion (Sundin, 1969, p. 2922). Thus, he argued that the poet Ture Nerman (an academic of bourgeois background) should be excluded from the category of working-class literature (Mattsson, 2016, p. 21). However, he also argued that being born in the working class or being a "versed portrayer of workers' lives" did not automatically qualify anyone for the title of proletarian writer (Fahlgren, 1981, p. 70). Strömberg tried to downplay the authors' class backgrounds and instead focused more on the content of their works (Sundin, 1969, p. 2919). Palmgren stressed that working-class literature was a uniquely Swedish phenomenon and argued for its integration into national literature, thereby downplaying any antagonisms with bourgeois literature (Mattsson, 2016, p. 22).

According to Per-Olof Mattsson (2016, p. 28), it was Steffen who constructed the Swedish tradition of working-class literature and came up with the definition of this literature that is still accepted today. I do not agree with this.[7] Nevertheless, I do recognize that Steffen's discussion of working-class literature has had important consequences. One of these was that it triggered a debate that led to the *concept* of working-class literature becoming established in national literary discourse. An equally important consequence was that Steffen's view of working-class literature as a *strand* in Swedish literature – and not as a mere abstract category – provided a platform for its constructions as a *tradition*. Both these consequences can be illustrated with an article published by the working-class author Ola Vinberg in 1927, which constitutes the first systematic attempt to write the history of Swedish working-class literature. Vinberg accepts Steffen's definition of working-class literature, but argues that he has failed to see that it constitutes a long tradition (1927, p. 3). The starting point for "proletarian writing proper" is, according to Vinberg (1927, pp. 10–11), the political poetry – by writers such as Gabrielson and Ågren – within the labor movement. Regarding the twentieth century, Vinberg (1927, pp. 19–20) bases his understanding of the tradition of working-class literature on Steffen's, but complements it with a large number of names of (often relatively unknown) writers of both poetry and prose. More importantly, he also gives attention to some young writers who had not been noticed by Steffen, including Eyvind Johnson and Ruldolf Värnlund, who would later be viewed as central figures in the tradition of Swedish working-class literature (Vinberg, 1927, p. 22).

Värnlund and Johnson belonged to a group of authors who around 1920 started building their identities as writers by emphasizing their non-academic and working-class backgrounds. Among other things, they founded the group "De Gröna" ["The Greens"] (Björklund, 1960, p. 173) that published the literary journal *Vår Nutid* [*Our Present Times*], in which they argued that the literature of the future would be written by those who "come straight from the school of life, from the factory or the plow," the "young working-class poets." That they also argued for the necessity of "getting rid of" the academic writers then dominating Swedish literature indicates that they viewed the relationship between proletarian and bourgeois literatures as marked by conflict (Lindberger, 1986, pp. 93–94).

From 1926, the critic Sven Stople repeatedly attacked working-class literature (Nordmark, 1978, p. 17), which he defined simply as a literature written by workers that had become "dominant in our youngest literature" (Stolpe, 1928). However, because of an alleged lack of "spiritual resources" among the working-class writers, this literature was marked by an outdated style and was at odds with contemporary conditions. Great art, Stolpe further argued, had strong links to culture and education, and therefore he rejected "all democratic tendencies toward leveling within literature."

Several working-class writers – among others Erik Asklund, Josef Kjellgren, and Ivar Lo-Johansson – replied to Stolpe's attacks (Nordmark, 1978, p. 18; Vulovic, 2009, pp. 128–129). However, the most important responses were formulated by Värnlund, who did not wholeheartedly embrace the concept of "proletarian writer," but nevertheless used it to describe a group of authors to which he counted himself (Nordmark, 1978, p. 29). In his article "Vi 'proletärer' i litteraturen" ["We 'Proletarians' in Literature"] from 1927, Värnlund (1964, pp. 54–55) acknowledges that the concept of proletarian writer can be used in a derogatory way, while at the same time reminding the reader that "the majority of the world's greatest spirits have emanated from a proletariat, and created their great works without first having visited Uppsala University." He also repeats an argument put forward in *Vår nutid*, when claiming that since the working class is a "modern class," working-class writers – unlike authors belonging to other social groups – "have something to say" about the contemporary time and age (Värnlund, 1964, p. 55).

Unlike most other Swedish commentators at the time (as well as both earlier and later), Värnlund displays interest in non-Swedish working-class literature. In the article "Den internationella proletären i dikten" ["The International Proletarian in Literature"] (1930), he praised the mysterious author B. Traven's *Die Baumwollpflücker* (published in English both as *The Wobbly* and *The Cotton Pickers*, 1925) and *Das Totenschiff* [*The Death Ship*] (1926). And in another article, he acclaimed Agnes Smedley's *Daughter of Earth* (1929) and Michael Gold's *Jews Without Money* (1930) (Värnlund, 1964, pp. 83, 101). Another example of the few attempts in Swedish discussions about working-class literature to view it as a part of an international phenomenon can be found within The Workers' Educational Association, which in the 1920s offered a lecture on "Fem arbetardiktare" ["5 Working-Class Writers"] without making distinctions between their nationalities: the Swedes Koch, Andersson and Oljelund, and the Danes Jeppe Aakjær and Martin Andersen-Nexø (Åkerstedt, 1967, p. 113).

## The Golden Age

The 1930s is generally viewed as the golden age for Swedish working-class literature – a decade when this literature has its definitive breakthrough and working-class writers dominated the nation's literary life (Therborn, 1985, p. 585; Wright, 1996, p. 334; Furuland and Svedjedal, 2006, pp. 216, 316). This breakthrough can be symbolized by two events: The first is the publication in 1929 of the poetry collection *5 Unga* [*5 Youths*], in which five working-class authors – Erik Asklund, Josef Kjellgren, Artur Lundkvist, Harry Martinson and Gustav Sandgren – introduced modernist poetry in Swedish literature. The second event is the publication in 1933 of three novels – Lo-Johansson's *Godnatt, jord* [*Breaking Free*], Moa Martinson's *Kvinnor och äppelträd* [*Women and Apple Trees*], and Jan Fridegård's *En natt i juli* [*A Night in July*] – that mark the introduction of both a new kind of working-class realism and a genre to which most of the leading working-class writers of the 1930s contributed: the more or less autobiographical proletarian coming-of-age novel, which thereafter has been the perhaps most important genre in Swedish working-class literature.

The new generation of working-class writers emerging around 1930 was criticized by some left-wing intellectuals – most notably the communist journalist and author Ture Nerman. His critique has often been interpreted as a rejection of modernist forms, but at its heart, it was directed at an alleged lack of proletarian class consciousness (Nilsson, 2003, pp. 245–253). However, the most ambitious attempt by a left-wing intellectual during the 1930s to conceptualize the newest working-class literature was made by the Marxist critic Erik Blomberg. He argued that during the 1930s an "artistically significant working-class literature" emerged in Sweden, and that working-class writers had achieved dominant positions in the nation's literary life (Blomberg, 1977, p. 69). As representatives of this literature, Blomberg mentions Lo-Johansson,

Johnson, Harry and Moa Martinson, and Fridegård, all of whom he describes as proletarians writing about proletarians (Blomberg, 1977, p. 69). Both the authors' backgrounds and the subject matters of their works thus seem to have been important for Blomberg's understanding of the phenomenon of working-class literature. However, he also calls the Norwegian poet Rudolf Nilsen – who, despite growing up in a proletarian milieu, was not a worker but an academic intellectual – a "true proletarian poet" and criticizes "those who mean that only manual laborers can legitimately speak for the working class in literature" (Blomberg, 1977, pp. 234–235). In addition to this, his characterization of 1930s working-class literature as being "artistically significant" shows that he also emphasizes its aesthetical qualities.

Sometimes the working-class writers of the 1930s acted collectively. One example of this is that they debated publicly with Nerman (Matsson, 1975, pp. 63–72). They also published two collections of essays: *Ansikten* [*Faces*] (1932) and *Avsikter* [*Intentions*] (1945). In the foreword to the latter, it says that the contributors are "what one usually calls working-class writers" (Asklund et al., 1945, p. 5). In *Ansikten*, however, this term is only used in one of the contributions (Månsson et al., 1932, pp. 239). Instead, the contributors are said to belong to the group of the so-called "autodidacts" (Ibid., p. 5). It is also stressed that the collection does not aim at constructing any "collective" or "group" with a "program," at the same time as it is emphasized that the contributors are united by having experiences from similar social conditions (Ibid., p. 5). Personal experience of social hardship and, especially, the lack of formal education are also thematized in many of the contributions, and often presented as virtues. Värnlund, for example, argues that traditional culture and education are irrelevant in the modern age, and Johnson expresses similar ideas when claiming that "the proletariat" is "creating contemporary life with its hands" and one day will give culture "new life" (Ibid., pp. 180–181, 197). Another interesting comment about working-class literature is made by the only female contributor to *Ansikten*, Maj Hirdman:

> I know a wife of a statare [a poor estate worker] who could have written a novel, the like of which has never existed in Swedish literature, and perhaps will not exist in a long time. For no one else

can take her subject matter and write the book. Only she would have been able to. And that is a great loss for Swedish literature. (Månsson et al., 1932, p. 87)

Here, personal experience of working-class life is presented as a necessary prerequisite for its authentic representation in literature, at the same time as working-class literature is presented as a valuable contribution to national literature. The former idea is also expressed by Lo-Johansson in his contribution to *Avsikter*, where he argues that working-class writers have given "depth" to the representation of the proletariat in literature through their "extraction": "All realist literature presupposes, on a fundamental level, first-hand experience, but the older Swedish writers could not possibly have that about the proletariat" (Asklund et al., 1945, p. 112). The second of Hirdman's ideas is also articulated by Albert Viksten, who argues in *Avsikter* that through working-class literature "the Swedish people" have finally emerged in literature in its entirety, and that it should therefore be viewed as "a valuable contribution to a national literature in which hitherto mainly the propertied have appeared" (Ibid., p. 190). Finally, it is important to note that one of the contributors to *Avsikter*, Moa Martinson, criticizes the concept of proletarian literature. After pointing out that she is self-taught, has a proletarian background, and is politically radical, she declares that she nevertheless does not embrace the concept of proletarian writer since it "creates confusion" and "creates class difference where none exists": "There are no proletarian authors, *there are only authors*" (Ibid., p. 149, emp. in the original). Thus, all the fundamental features of Steffen's definition – according to which working-class literature is a literature produced by autodidact authors with personal experiences of working-class life that constitutes an important contribution to national literature – are present in the discussions in *Ansikten* and *Avsikter*. And so is the complaint voiced by some of those described by Steffen as proletarian writers – that such a labeling can alienate working-class writers from 'literature proper.'

Just as important as *Ansikten* and *Avsikter* were for the construction of Swedish working-class literature, were – at least in retrospect – the attempts by one working-class writer, Lo-Johansson, in several essays and articles, to define and write the history of this literature.[8] Even if the label "working-class literature" may have been used to "isolate" and "devaluate," he argues, there is no need to be ashamed of it (Lo-Johansson, 1946, pp. 207–208). He also claims that the Swedish tradition of working-class literature is unique in the world (Lo-Johansson, 1946, p. 268) but that the working-class writers, despite generally having experiences from the labor movement and from "the anonymous struggle and collective solidarity of the working masses," have not been able to break with the subjective and individualist "bourgeois" novel. Furthermore, some of them have even "become bourgeois" (Lo-Johansson, 1946, pp. 231, 269). Thus, whereas some authors feared that the title 'working-class writer' would alienate them from the established notion of literature, Lo-Johansson argued that working-class literature had not yet achieved any radical enough break with the hegemonic, bourgeois understanding of literature.

During the 1930s, several attempts were made to write the history of Swedish working-class literature and to integrate this history into that of Swedish literature. The literary historian Kjell Strömberg (1932, pp. 180–184) follows the accounts given by Steffen and Vinberg but gives Ossiannilsson a more prominent role. Additionally, Strömberg presents Strindberg as "the first proletarian author," thus implicitly downplaying the importance of the authors' working-class backgrounds. It may also be noted that Strömberg does not include the modernist poetry of 5 Unga in the tradition of working-class literature, whereas four years later, Ivar Harrie, in his attempt to write the history of Swedish working-class literature, argues that both the realistic novels by Lo-Johansson and others and the modernist poetry of 5 Unga represent the culmination of important tendencies in older working-class literature (Harrie, 1936, pp. 69–70). In a book-length study of Swedish working-class literature from 1934, Holger Ahlenius (1934, pp. 5, 262–263) describes it as being (almost) "dominant" in Swedish literature and argues that several working-class writers – for example Johnson and Harry Martinson – belong to "the most outstanding talents and the finest coming men in contemporary Swedish literature." Ahlenius contends that "the youngest generation of proletarian writers" are about to invent "their own art form, a new and special form of expression." Like Steffen, he defines working-class literature as literature written by autodidact authors emerging from the proletariat and stresses that it has enriched Swedish national literature through the introduction of hitherto unknown experiences and viewpoints. And yet, he also associates it with the increasing influence exercised by the working class in politics and in social life (Ahlenius, 1934, pp. 2, 262).

## After the Golden Age

After World War II, many of the working-class writers of the 1930s held dominant positions in Swedish literature, as evidenced, for example, by the fact that Harry Martinson, Eyvind Johnson, and Artur Lundkvist were elected members of the Swedish Academy (in 1949, 1957, and 1968 respectively) and that, in 1974, Martinson and Johnson received the Nobel Prize in literature. This was also the period when the working-class literature of the 1930s reached a mass audience through cheap editions distributed both by organizations associated with the labor movement and by commercial publishers (Furuland and Svedjedal, 2006, pp. 235–236, 507–515; Nilsson 2006, pp. 75–77). However, new working-class writers also appeared. The 1940s, for example, saw the breakthrough of the steel worker and modernist poet Stig Sjödin, the textile worker and novelist Folke Fridell, and of Lars Ahlin, whose novel *Tåbb med manifestet* [*Tåbb with the Manifesto*] (1934) gave new aesthetic and ethical impulses to Swedish working-class literature. In the 1950s, perhaps the most important addition to the tradition of working-class literature was the publication of Kurt Salomonson's novel *Grottorna* [*The Caves*] (1956), which criticized the working conditions in the Swedish mining industry.

Fridell (1970, p. 24) explicitly called for the "renewal of working-class literature" through increased engagement with "contemporary society's problems." He argued that the working-class writers of the 1930s had focused on the period before the labor movement's political breakthrough, and had mainly protested against economic poverty, but that the time had now come to criticize working conditions in the modern industry and the class injustices suffered by workers in the social-democratic welfare state (Fridell, 1970, pp. 24–26, 37). He also argued that many of the working-class writers of the previous decade had lost touch with their proletarian origins, thus stressing the importance of personal experience of labor and working-class life (Fridell, 1970, p. 25).

In a rather sympathetic response to Fridell's critique, Lo-Johansson made a series of comments regarding 1930s working-class literature. Among other things, he argued that, although "a few" authors had protested against being labeled working-class writers, the "most conscious ones" viewed it as an honorary title (Lo-Johansson, 1972, p. 89). However, Lo-Johansson's most ambitious attempt to write the history of Swedish working-class literature during this period was undertaken in his 1957 autobiographical novel *Författaren* [*The Author*]. Early in the novel, Lo-Johansson (1957, p. 6) provides a list of some fifteen names that according to him were the most important Swedish working-class writers of the 1920s and 1930s. Thereafter, more names are added throughout the narrative, including most of the contributors to *5 Unga*. Nonetheless, regarding the definition of a working-class writer, Lo-Johansson's novel is somewhat unclear. On the one hand, Hedenvind-Eriksson and Koch – the former of which came from a family of farmers, whereas the latter grew up in the petit bourgeoisie and, according to Lo-Johansson, had never really "belonged to the proletarian milieu" – are given central positions in the tradition of working-class literature (Ibid., pp. 43, 150). On the other hand, it is argued that another author, because he had worked as a clerk and attended junior secondary school, should not be viewed as a working-class writer (Ibid. 1957, p. 98).

In the 1950s and 1960s, academic literary historians began conducting research on Swedish working-class literature, and several more or less popular overviews of its history were published. Eric Uhlin's doctoral dissertation about Dan Andersson's early works from 1950 contains an extensive description of Swedish working-class literature from the first decades of the twentieth century, which, in principle, accords with the one presented by Steffen 30 years earlier. According to Uhlin (1950, pp. 210, 237), the working-class writers came from and wrote about new social strata in Swedish society. He contrasts them with writers having grown up in the bourgeoisie with academic education, while also stressing that working-class literature must be understood as a *literary* phenomenon, and arguing that its first breakthrough was intimately connected to a general aesthetic reorientation within Swedish literature. A somewhat more controversial claim is that Strindberg was "the admired model and starting point" for the working-class writers (Ibid., p. 262), which to some extent downplays the emphasis put on the working-class authors' proletarian class backgrounds. Uhlin (1950, pp. 237, 248, 262) also emphasizes foreign influence on Swedish working-class literature, mentioning, for example, Gorky's idealism and Jack London's autobiographical novel *Martin Eden* (1909). Another academic literary historian, Örjan Lindberger (1952, p. 9), also remains more or less true to Steffen and Vinberg when presenting the history of Swedish working-class literature in the introduction to the anthology *Svensk arbetardikt* [*Swedish Working-Class Writing*] from 1952, with the exception that he, like several commentators before him, also stresses that a working-class writer should, "in one way or another" have belonged to the labor movement and write about the working class. Lindberger also claims both that literature by "authors with working-class backgrounds" now constitutes the "main part of Swedish literature" and, more controversially, that in the 1940s, the history of "working-class literature proper" has come to an end (Ibid., p. 14). A similar idea is put forward by Lennart Thorsell (1957, p. 135), in an article about the "democratization" of Swedish literature, in which he argues that the "period, during which working-class literature as such blossoms and, from time to time, emphatically puts it stamp on the literary debates" is now "a closed chapter in the history of our literature."

In a popular book-length presentation of the history of Swedish working-class literature from 1952, the publisher and literary critic Åke Runnquist tries to add a few new elements to the narrative about this literature, not the least regarding the 1930s and 1940s. One example of this is that he includes both 5 Unga and some poets associated with the socialist journal *Clarté* that did not have working-class backgrounds in the tradition of working-class literature (Runnquist, 1952, pp. 142–161). An academic dissertation on the representation of labor in Swedish working-class literature published a few years later is interesting primarily because of the fact that its author, Elisabet Kågerman (1961), devotes a fair amount of energy to defining the concept of labor but not a single line to defining the concept of working-class literature. This shows that a clear correspondence between the concept of working-class literature and a literary tradition had now been established. In 1962, Furuland (1962, p. 14) published his dissertation, in which he subscribes to Lindberger's definition of working-class literature. More interesting, however, is that he highlights Alfred Kämpe as the archetypical working-class writer from the early twentieth century and as a predecessor to many younger colleagues, including several of the working-class writers of the 1930s. Simultaneously, he recognizes that there are huge differences between different generations (Furuland, 1962, pp. 304–305, 321, 338). Thus, he emphasizes both the continuity and the breaks within the tradition of Swedish working-class literature.

## Working-Class Literature in the Age of Political Radicalism

Like in several other countries, a general revival of working-class literature occurred in Sweden during the second half of the 1960s and the 1970s, in close connection to the period's rise in leftist radicalism (Nilsson, 2014a, pp. 71–74; Furuland and Svedjedal, 2006).[9] On the one hand, interest in older working-class literature increased; on the other hand, a large number of new working-class writers emerged. To the new generation of working-class writers – which published realist as well as documentary and experimental modernist works – belonged, among others, Maja Ekelöf, Göran Palm, Sara Lidman, Hans Lagerberg, Ove Allanson, Kjell Johansson, Torgny Karnstedt, Jan Fogelbäck, and Aino Trosell.

The general radicalism of the era affected the conceptualization of working-class literature through an increased focus on its relationship to politics and ideology. This is especially visible in the Marxist academic criticism from the period, which argued that all literature in a capitalist society expresses capitalist conditions and that the breakthrough for working-class literature in national Swedish literature should thus be viewed as an assimilation into bourgeois literature and ideology (Melberg, 1973, pp. 84–85, 101;

Melberg, 1975, p. 11; Holm, 1975, p. 247; Ahlmo-Nilsson, 1979, pp. 12–14; Olsson, 1979, p. 70). Interestingly enough, a similar view is expressed – but valued differently – in the award ceremony speech given by Ragnar Gierow when Johnson and Martinson were awarded the Nobel Prize in 1974. Echoing Steffen's argument from 1921, Gierow (n.d.) stated that "the many proletarian writers or working-class poets" who "broke into" Swedish literature did so, not in order to "ravish" it, but "to enrich it with their fortunes." "Their arrival," he continues, "meant an influx of experience and creative energy." And then he concludes: "A new class has conquered Parnassus. But if, by a conqueror, we mean the one who gained most from the outcome, then Parnassus has conquered a new class."

In 1977, Furuland published an overview of the history of Swedish working-class literature up to contemporary times. His account of this history begins with a lengthy discussion about Strindberg, whom he views as a role model for the Swedish working-class writers (Furuland, 1977, pp. 4–11). Regarding the question whether class background or ideology is the most important criterion for defining this literature, Furuland (1977, p. 19) tends toward the latter, arguing that such contemporary academic authors of non-proletarian background as Lidman and Palm "evidently" belong to the tradition of working-class literature. The same view is also expressed by another academic critic, Birgitta Ahlmo-Nilsson (1979, pp. 14–15), who includes Lidman and Palm in a group of academic authors belonging to the tradition of working-class literature because they write about "proletarian milieus." Regarding the 1930s, Furuland (1977, p. 17) argues for making a distinction between modernist and working-class literature. But another academic critic, Eva Adolfsson, promotes an opposite view and emphasizes that the modernist poetry constituted a central component in Swedish 1930's working-class literature (Adolfsson 1976, p. 251). During this period, one can also note an increased emphasis on two claims: that, from an international perspective, the strong tradition of Swedish working-class literature is "unique" (Ahlmo-Nilsson, 1979, p. 7), and that it constitutes a dominant strand in modern Swedish literature (Holmgren, 1982, p. 64; Adolfsson, 1976, p. 251).

## The 1980s and 1990s

In the 1980s and 1990s, the status for (and interest in) working-class literature reached an all-time-low in Sweden, a fact that is thematized in much of the period's writing about this literature. In a book about modern working-class literature, for example, the poet Arne Säll (1986, p. 8) complains about "condescending" critics reducing working-class writers to "literature's second-raters." And, in a special issue of Sweden's then most esteemed literary journal, *Bonniers Litterära Magasin*, some commentators speculated – like others had done during the decades after World War II – that the tradition was coming to an end (Jonsson, 1987, p. 388) or, at the very least, emphasized that it was in a state of crisis (Olsson, 1987, p. 396).

However, efforts were also made to present another view. Säll (1986) pointed at several new authors that should be added to the tradition, including Ragnar Järhult, Mary Andersson, Lars Åke Augustsson, Gunnar Kieri, and Per Forsman. The collection *Vägval* [*Choice of Direction*]—published in 1987 by the four working-class writers Gunder Andersson, Hans Lagerberg, Kjell Johansson, and Reidar Jönsson—contained an essay by Andersson presenting the history of Swedish working-class literature, which also listed a large number of authors, including some making their debuts in the 1980s, such Fredrik Ekelund, Eva-Lena Neiman, Åke Smedberg, and Ingmar Nylund (Andersson et al., 1987, pp. 11–44). In his contribution to a special issue of the journal *Arbetarhistoria* [*Labor History*] about working-class literature published in 1991, Bernt-Olov Andersson (1991, pp. 20–21) also presented a list of contemporary young working-class writers, which to some extent overlaps with Säll's and Lagerberg's but also includes Mats Berggren, Göran Greider, and Tony Samuelsson.

An even more ambitious attempt to extend the tradition into contemporary times was the publication in 1987 of the collection *Utsikter* [*Prospects*], which contained essays about working-class literature by 24 contemporary working-class writers. In the fore-word, its editor Jan Fogelbäck (1987, p. 9) emphasizes that the book should be viewed as a continuation of a tradition starting with *Ansikten* and *Avsikter*, but that contemporary working-class literature is different than that of the 1930s. For example, all working-class writers no longer are autodidact. Several contributors stress that changes in the composition of the working class and the class structure of Swedish society made necessary the inclusion of new social groups into working-class literature – mainly service-producing workers, but also salaried employees (Fogelbäck, 1987, pp. 35, 46, 85–86, 97). Some also argued for the need to renew the literary forms used in working-class literature or to give more attention to "existential" themes (Fogelbäck, 1987, pp. 35–37, 106, 120.). Similar arguments are put forward in *Vägval* (Andersson et al., 1987, pp. 49, 124).

In academic research, working-class literature continued to attract attention during the 1980s and 1990s, and new facets were added to the narrative about its history. One example of this is that Ebba Witt-Brattström (1988) – in a dissertation that attracted much attention and was even published as a paperback (!) – claimed that Moa Martinson should be viewed as a modernist writer, thereby recasting the relationship between realism and modernism in 1930s working-class literature.[10] Other attempts at fine-tuning the narrative about Swedish working-class literature involved highlighting female working-class writers (Adolfsson et al., 1981) or working-class writers associated with the anarchosyndicalist labor movement (Furuland et. al, 1999). In addition to this, Per-Olof Mattsson (1995) tried to shed new light on the breakthrough for working-class literature in the 1930s by connecting it to Sweden's rapid industrialization and the alleged absence of a hegemonic bourgeois culture.

The French literary historian Philippe Bouquet represents something of a dissident voice in the academic research on Swedish working-class literature during this period. In a book originally published in French, he gave an account of the history of this literature that offered some new perspectives. One example of this is that he argued that the social, political, and cultural development – especially changes in education that have eliminated the autodidact writers – had made impossible the continuation of the tradition of working-class literature after the 1930s (Bouquet, 1990, p. 145). However, in his contribution to the above-mentioned special issue of the Swedish journal for labor history, he argued instead that changes in the class structure of Swedish society had resulted in the emergence of *new kinds* of working-class literature rather than the end of the tradition (Ibid., pp. 10–12). These changes were also noted by several other contributors to the same journal issue, who argued that they made necessary a reconceptualization of the phenomenon of working-class literature. Hans Lagerberg (1991, pp. 13, 18–19) and Bernt-Olov Andersson (1991, pp. 20–21), for example, discussed whether the concept of working-class literature was useful in a situation in which the traditional working class seemed to be disappearing, and argued that working-class writers must strive to become relevant for "the new proletariat."

Regarding the conceptualization of older working-class literature, some new ideas were also put forward during this period. In her dissertation about working-class poetry published in the labor-movement press before 1900, Brigitte Mral (1985, pp. 13–14) highlighted that the definition of the concept of working-class literature had been the object of many debates and that various scholars had defined it differently. She proposed that it be understood, in explicit opposition to "bourgeois literature," as a literature thematizing the working class' (or, rather, the labor movement's) experiences, ideas, and goals. Similar definitions – which related (older) working-class literature not primarily to literature, but to working class culture in general and to the historical formation of the Swedish working class through the labor movement – were also put forward by scholars such as Håkan Bengtsson (1992, p. 12) and Stig-Lennart Godin (1994, p. 5).

In the 1980s, Lo-Johansson continued his attempts to define working-class literature and write its history. In his memoir *Tröskeln* [*The Threshold*] (1982), he gave an overview of four "generations" of working-class writers: the first consisting of writers born around 1870, such as Östman and Sandel, and the last encompassing the working-class writers of the 1930s (Lo-Johansson, 1982, pp. 88–100). According to Lo-Johansson, the latter generation constituted a numerous but heterogeneous group, including both realists and "at least some" of the modernist poets, and autodidact writers, as well as some with formal education (Ibid., pp. 99–100). He also claimed that their breakthrough was "the most important event of the century in Swedish literature," and that, from an international perspective, it was "unique" (Ibid., p. 119). Nevertheless he also pointed out a number of foreign authors that were popular among the Swedish working-class writers of the 1930s – including Michael Gold, William Saroyan, Erskine Caldwell, Isaac Babel, Mikhail Sholokhov, Richard Aldington, D.H. Lawrence, and Alfred Döblin – while arguing that it was quite simply "wrong" to view Strindberg as some sort of role-model (Ibid., pp. 211, 217). In his contribution to *Utsikter*, Lo-Johansson made, made two interesting remarks: the first was that even if Swedish working-class literature is a unique and important phenomenon, it had not received total recognition in the site of literature, and the second was that contemporary working-class writers may very well have a secondary-education degree (Fogelbäck, 1987, pp. 187, 190). In the last book he published before his death, the essay collection *Till en författare [To an Author]* (1988), Lo-Johansson further specified his view of working-class literature. Perhaps most importantly, he argued that the phenomenon of working-class literature should be understood in relation to the class structure of a capitalist society – as a literature that "fights bourgeois society" – at the same time as he highlighted that, first and foremost, a working-class novel must be a "work of art" (Lo-Johansson, 1988, pp. 6, 25, 107). He also argued that working-class literature represents not only thematic but also formal innovations in Swedish literature, mainly in the form of attempts at creating an "aesthetic of the collective" (Ibid., p. 109).

## Working-Class Literature in Contemporary Sweden

In recent years, several commentators have noticed the emergence of a new generation of working-class writers publishing works that have been positively received by both critics and readers (Williams, 2016, pp. 212–213; Nilsson, 2014b).[11] The starting point for this latest breakthrough was the publication of two (more or less) autobiographical proletarian coming-of-age novels: Susanna Alakoski's *Svinalängorna [The Pig Houses]* (2006) and Åsa Linderborg's *Mig äger ingen [I Am Owned by Nobody]* (2007). Thereafter have followed several important new contributions to the tradition of

Swedish working-class literature by, among others, Johan Jönson, Jenny Wrangborg, Kristian Lundberg, David Ericsson, and Maria Hamberg (Nilsson, 2016a; Agrell, 2016; Williams, 2016). Some central – and, in part, interconnected – features of this new working-class literature are its focus on the new "class reality" of post-industrial Sweden, its explorations of class as a multi-facetted phenomenon with strong ties to gender and ethnicity, and its focus on formal innovation (Nilsson, 2010; 2014b; 2016a).

Just before this breakthrough, two book-length studies of the history of Swedish working-class literature were published: Lars Furuland's *Svensk arbetarlitteratur* [*Swedish Working-Class Literature*] (2006), which was co-written with Johan Svedjedal, and my own *Arbetarlitteratur* [*Working-Class Literature*] (2006). Whereas the former contains what could be regarded as the most comprehensive account of the tradition of Swedish working-class literature ever published, the latter proposes a new, non-essentialist conceptualization of this literature – as literature whose reception is substantially influenced by a perceived connection to the working-class (Nilsson, 2006, pp. 25–27).[12] Following these studies, the interest in both older and newer Swedish working-class literature has increased among literary scholars. The research publications from recent years include four edited collections (Johnson et al., 2011 and 2014; Agrell et al., 2016; Hamm et al., 2017) of new research, several doctoral dissertations (Vulovic, 2009; Johansson, 2013; Mischliwietz, 2014; Hillborn, 2014), and a large number of articles. In general, this research has been anchored in already established definitions. Jimmy Vulovic (2009, p. 21) states in his dissertation about Eyvind Johnson and Rudolf Värnlund that he will not discuss questions about "what working-class literature is," which indicates that there is consensus about how they should be answered. Beata Agrell's (2016, pp. 25–26) definition of working-class literature more or less replicates Furuland's. For example, she retells his narrative of the tradition of Swedish working-class literature rather faithfully (Ibid., pp. 23–34). However, (mild) revisions are continually proposed. Johan Landgren (2014, p. 27) argues that increased attention to early working-class poetry written by women could lead to a view of the literature produced within the labor movement's counter public sphere as being more complex and dynamic than has hitherto been assumed. Johannes Björk (2014) has claimed that it might be worthwhile to speak of a pre-history to the working-class literature emerging within the labor movement's counter public sphere in the late nineteenth century. He also argues that the politics of Swedish working-class literature is best understood with the point of departure in Jacques Rancière's philosophy, as an attempt to deconstruct the ideological opposition between workers and the realm of aesthetics. Furthermore, some researchers have begun bringing to the fore how working-class writers' representations of class intersect with discourses about gender, nation, and ethnicity and how working-class literature relates to phenomena such as "immigrant" and "feminist" literature (Mattsson, 2013; Mischliwietz, 2014; Jonsson, 2014; Landgren, 2014; Nilsson, 2010).

Contemporary Swedish working-class writers have also made efforts to give working-class literature more visibility. In 2006, Tony Samuelsson (pp. 120–122, 196, 223) published a collection of essays in which he argued that, since the 1990s, the signs for a revival for working-class literature had been accumulating. Samuelsson further claimed that contemporary working-class literature – which, according to him, does not always present itself as belonging to the tradition – challenges old and rigid stereotypes about both this kind of literature and the working class. At the same time, he contends, it both upholds the high standards set by the working-class writers of the 1930s and renews the tradition emanating from them. In recent years, working-class writers have also, to an extent hitherto unparalleled, acted collectively to promote working-class literature. The main vehicle for this has been "Föreningen Arbetarskrivare" [The Association for Writing Workers]. In their anthologies from recent years, the links between contemporary and older working-class literature are often emphasized (Svanberg, 2010, p. 9; Johansson, 2012, p. 8; Johansson and Karnstedt, 2014, p. 6). However, an analysis of their content shows that both subject matters and the authors' biographies are indeed conditioned by the contemporary transformations of Swedish class society (Nilsson, 2016a, pp. 270–273). In 2015, "Föreningen Arbetarskrivare" began publishing the literary journal *Klass* [*Class*], which is entirely devoted to working-class literature and which has been a great success. Furthermore, in 2017, one of its members, Mattias Torstensson, launched the podcast "Arbetarlitteratur" ["Working-Class Literature"], which has likewise been very successful.

## The Dynamic Phenomenon of Swedish Working-Class Literature

Swedish working-class literature is a historical and heterogeneous phenomenon, consisting of works that have been associated with the working class in different ways. While some commentators have insisted on the authors' working-class backgrounds being a fundamental characteristic of this literature, others have put more emphasis on its affiliation with the labor movement, or the promotion of class consciousness and socialist politics. To some extent these different views can be related to an important distinction between two different conceptualizations of working-class literature: as primarily a political or a literary phenomenon. This distinction, in turn, has a distinct bearing on many other questions. One of these regards how the breakthrough for working-class literature in Swedish literature should be understood—as a valuable contribution to the national literary heritage, or as a challenge (successful or not) to bourgeois literature or ideology? Every definition of Swedish working-class literature, and every account of its history, run the risk of obscuring these dynamics. Therefore, the history of this literature needs to incorporate the heterogeneous process of its construction.

Parallel to the shifting conceptualizations of Swedish working-class literature, there has been a relative consensus regarding some features of its history. For instance, there is agreement that it emerged within the labor movement but later became a central strand in modern Swedish literature. The latter fact makes it unique from an international perspective. This consensus risks making invisible some aspects of the tradition of Swedish working-class literature, and limits the chances of understanding the potentialities and possibilities inherent in the concept of working-class literature. The idea about a move from the labor movement to the sphere of national literature, for example, may obscure that the labor movement has actually been an important infrastructure for Swedish working-class literature throughout its history (Nilsson, 2016c, p. 127). The insistence on the strength of the Swedish tradition risks making invisible that – as has been demonstrated above – there have been periods when it has received less attention in the site of literature. It also risks leading to a too simplistic view of the relationship between working-class and bourgeois literature. For, if Sweden remains a capitalist country (as, indeed, it does), must not the 'victory' of working-class literature mean that it was 'just' a literary phenomenon and that its potential political effects are, hence, hardly worthy of attention? And, will not the emphasis on the unique nature of Swedish working-class literature obscure the connections between working-class writers in Sweden and other countries?

Not only attention to the heterogenous history of the construction of Swedish working-class literature, but also comparisons with working-class literatures in other countries – and with research on these literatures – can contribute to highlighting the dynamic nature of the phenomenon of working-class literature. They may open up for a 'broader' understanding of this literature and make visible how it is often understood within a rather narrow national(istic) context. But they may also lead to a better understanding of what really is specific to Swedish working-class literature.

In many other countries, working-class literature is understood as a broader phenomenon than has been the case in Sweden. In research on Finnish working-class literature, for example, it is emphasized that this literature encompasses not only written and published texts, but also phenomena such as oral literature and hand-written works (Salmi-Niklander and Launis, 2015, p. 5). A similar view can also be found in contemporary U.S. research on working-class literature (Nilsson and Lennon, 2015, p. 57). Swedish research has hitherto excluded not only oral and hand-written texts, but also lowbrow literature and amateur writing, as well as new literary genres (e.g. that of the graphic novel) from discussions of working-class literature (Nilsson and Lennon, 2016, p. 56; Nilsson, 2016c, p. 125).

In Finnish research on working-class literature, international perspectives have been given relatively much attention in recent years (Salmi-Niklander and Launis, 2015). Nevertheless, the nation remains the fundamental context for the study of this literature. The author Kössi Kaatra, for instance, is described as a central character in the history of *Finnish* working-class literature, despite the fact that he lived in *Sweden* and published all his works there, from 1918 until his death in 1928 (Launis, 2015, p. 18). And, in research on Swedish working-class literature, he is not mentioned at all. Nor were – until quite recently – the Swedish working-class writers that emigrated to the USA and published their works there.[13] This inability to see past the context of national literature is also characteristic for contemporary research on U.S. working-class literature (Nilsson and Lennon, 2016, p. 55), as well as for research on many other working-class literatures. It also characterizes the discussions about the relationship between working-class and national literature in Sweden. For, not even those who view working-class literature as a challenge to the tradition of national literature have tried to conceptualize it as a transnational phenomenon relating more to *class* than to nations.

A history of Swedish working-class literature that incorporates the history of its construction makes visible that it is an ever-changing phenomenon existing within a vast field of potentials and possibilities. However, mapping the full extent of these potentials and possibilities entails more than this kind of (meta-) historicizing. It also requires that critics explore the conceptualizations that have not (or only seldom) been made. They can be made visible, for example, through international comparisons. Only when historical and international perspectives are combined will the  questions relevant for the study of both Swedish working-class literature and working-class literature(s) in general be brought to the fore.

## Notes

1. All translations of non-English quotations are my own.

2. As will be demonstrated below, Furuland draws on earlier attempts at writing the history of this literature, and his version has been disseminated and further developed by others. For a recent overview

in English of the tradition of Swedish working-class literature, see Nilsson 2014a, pp. 18–23.

3. A similar view is also expressed in research on Finnish working-class literature (Salmi-Niklander and Launis 2015, p. 5).

4. The translation of this poem is literal and does not try to capture the aesthetic values of the original.

5. It is possible that a bourgeois discourse about working-class literature also emerged at this time. However, the task of identifying and analyzing it has yet to be undertaken.

6. As I have pointed out elsewhere, this may be a product of influence from literary discourses within the German labor movement, where the term "Arbeiterdichter" [working-class poet] referred to socialist poets of working-class background (Nilsson 2016b, pp. 80–81).

7. See Nilsson 2017.

8. For an analysis of Lo-Johansson's writings about working-class literature, see Nilsson, 2017.

9. Regarding similar developments in Finland and Germany, see Salmi-Niklander and Launis 2015, p. 9; and Nilsson 2014a, pp. 91–98.

10. Similar arguments have also been put forward regarding Lo-Johansson by Hans Lagerberg (1991, p. 18; 2003, p. 46) and myself (Nilsson, 2003).

11. A similar development can be noted in Finland, where the topic of class has "reemerged" in recent years and where working-class literature is described by scholars as being "alive and well" (Ojajärvi, 2015, pp. 181–182; Salmi-Niklander and Launis, 2015, pp. 9–11).

12. This definition has later been further developed to also include the works' relationships to the tradition of working-class literature (Nilsson, 2012), as well as to the labor movement and various alternative literary spheres (Nilsson, 2017).

13. The attention given to one of them – Gösta Larsson – in recent years, may, however, indicate that this is about to change. Larsson (1898–1955) was practically unknown in Sweden until Fredrik Ekelund presented him in his novel *M/S Tiden* [M/S Time] (2008). In 2011 Larsson's best-known novel, *Ships in the River* (1946), was published in Swedish for the first time.

# References

Adolfsson, E. (1976). Det starka barnet. *Ord & Bild*, 85 (4/5), pp. 251–262.

Adolfsson, E. et. al. (1981). *Vardagsslit och drömmars språk*. Enskede: Hammarström & Åberg.

Agrell, B. (2016). Klassperspektiv i svensk arbetarprosa under 1900-talet. In: E. Igland Diesen et. al. eds., *Stempelslag*. Oslo, Novus Forlag, pp. 23–64.

Agrell, B. et. al. eds. (2016). *"Inte kan jag berätta allas historia?"*. Gothenburg, LIR.skrifter.

Ågren, R. (1898). Ur en litterär proletärs utvecklingshistoria. *Social-Demokraten*, 18–27 July.

Ahlenius, H. (1934). *Arbetaren i svensk diktning*. Stockholm, Norstedt.

Ahlmo-Nilsson, B. (1979). Inledning. In: B. Ahlmo-Nilsson ed., *Inte bara kampsång*. Lund, Liber Läromedel, pp. 8–23.

Åkerstedt, J. (1967). *Den litterate arbetaren*. Uppsala, Uppsala University.

Andersson, B. (1991). Arbetarlitteraturens framtid. *Arbetarhistoria*, 8 (2/3), pp. 20–22.

Andersson, G. et. al. (1987). *Vägval*. Stocholm Carlsson.

Asklund, E. et. al. (1945). *Avsikter*. Stockholm, Bonnier.

Bengtsson, H. (1992). *Konfrontation och försoning*. Gothenburg, Gothenburg University.

Björklund, C.J. (1960). *Orädda riddare av pennan*. Stockholm, Rabén & Sjögren.

Blomberg, E. (1977). *Folket och litteraturen och andra artiklar om litteratur*. Stockholm, PAN/Norstedt.

Bondebjerg, I. and Gemzøe, A. (1982). Arbejderlitteratur – proletarisk litteatur – socialistisk litteratur. *Kultur & Klasse*, 6 (42), pp. 5–11.

Bouquet, P. (1990). *Spaden och pennan*. Stockholm: Carlsson.

Bouquet, P. (1991). Arbetarlitteraturens vara eller icke-vara i nutiden. *Arbetarhistoria*, 8 (2/3), pp. 10–19.

Branting, H. (1930). *Tal och skrifter XI*. Stockholm, Tidens förlag.

Fahlgren, M. (1981). *Literaturkritiker i arbetarrörelsen*. Uppsala, Uppsala University.

Fogelbäck, J. ed. (1987). *Utsikter*. Stockholm, Tiden.

Fridell, F. (1970). *Återblick och framtidssyn*. Gothenburg, Författarförlaget.

Furuland, L. (1962). *Statarna i litteraturen*. Stockholm, Tiden.

Furuland, L. (1971). *Folkhögskolan – en bildningsväg för svenska författare*. Stockholm, Utbildningsförlaget.

Furuland, L. (1977). Från Strindberg till arbetarförfattarna, *Förr och nu*, 2, pp. 4–20.

Furuland, L. (1981). Svenska folkrörelser som litterära institutioner. In: J. Holmgaard ed., *Det grundtvigske bondemiljø*. Aalborg, Aalborg Universitetsforlag, pp. 283–293.

Furuland, L. (1991). *Ljus över landet och andra litteratursociologiska uppsatser*. Hedemora, Gidlunds.

Furuland, L. et. al. (1999). *Arbetarförfattarna och syndikalismen*. Stockholm, Federativ.

Furuland, L. and Svedjedal, J. (2006). *Svensk arbetarlitteratur*. Stockholm, Atlas.

Gierow, R. n.d. Award Ceremony Speech. Available at: http://www.nobelprize.org/nobel_prizes/literature/laureates/1974/press.html Accessed 5 May 2016.

Godin, S. (1994). *Klassmedvetandet i tidig svensk arbetarlitteratur*. Lund, Lund University Press.

Hamm, C. et. al., eds. (2017). *Hva er arbeiderlitteratur?: Begrepsbruk, kartlegging, forskningstradisjon*. Bergen: Alvheim og Eide.

Harrie, I. (1936). *Tjugotalet in memoriam*. Stockholm, Geber.

Haste, H. ed. (1977). *Dikter i kamptid*. Stockholm, Pogo Press.

Hedén, E. (1917). Ragnar Jändel: Till kärleken och hatet. *Social-Demokraten*, 20 July.

Hedén, E. (1927). *Litteraturkritik 2*. Stockholm, Tiden.

Hedenvind-Eriksson, G. (1961). *På minnets älv*. Uppsala, Bokgillet.

Holm, B. (1975). Efterkrigsmodernismens litterära institution. In: A. Melberg ed., *Den litterära institutionen*. Stockholm: Rabén & Sjögren, pp. 240–272.

Holmgren, O. (1982). Proletärförfattarna och den litterära institutionen. *Kultur & Klasse*, 11 (42), pp. 61–69.

Johansson, Å. and Karnstedt, T. Förord. In: V. Estby ed., *Landet som sprängdes*. Stockholm, Föreningen Arbetarskrivare, pp. 6–7.

Johansson, C-E. (2013). *Brutal social demaskering*. Tampere, Tampere University Press.

Jonsson, B. (2014). Vem talar till – och skriver för – arbetarklassens kvinnor? In: B. Jonsson et. al. eds. *Från Nexø till Alakoski*. Lund, Absalon, pp. 83–92.

Jonsson, B. et. al. (2010). Förord. In: B. Jonsson et. al. eds. *Från Nexø till Alakoski*. Lund, Absalon, pp. 9–11.

Jonsson B. et. al. eds. (2010). *Från Nexø till Alakoski*. Lund, Absalon.

Jonsson, B. et. al. eds. (2014). *Från Bruket till Yarden*. Lund, Absalon.

Jonsson, S. (1987). Varför behöver arbetare Fridman en författare? *Bonniers Litterära Magasin*, 56 (6), pp. 386–395.

Kågerman, E. (1961). *Arbetarförfattarnas syn på arbetet*. Stockholm, Svenska bokförlaget.

Leopold, L. (2001). *Skönhetsdyrkare och socialdemokrat*. Hedemora, Gidlunds.

Lagerberg, H. (1991). Hans Lagerberg, Guldålder och kris? Funderingar över arbetarlitteraturens 30-tal och 90-tal. *Arbetarhistoria*, 8 (2/3), pp. 13–19.

Landgren, J. (2014). Kollektivitet och kvinnokamp i den tidiga arbetarlyriken. In: B. Jonsson et. al. *Från Bruket till Yarden*. Lund, Absalon, pp. 25–34.

Launis, K. (2015). The Making of the Finnish Working Class in Early Twentieth-Century Working-Class Literature. *Journal of Finnish Studies*, 18 (2), pp. 14–34.

Lindberger, Ö. (1952). *Svensk arbetardikt*. Stockholm, Tiden.

Lindberger, Ö. (1986). *Norrbottningen som blev europé*. Stockholm, Bonnier.

Lo-Johansson, I. (1946). *Stridsskrifter*. Stockholm, Bonnier.

Lo-Johansson, I. (1957). *Författaren*. Stockholm, Bonnier.

Lo-Johansson, I. (1972). *Statarskolan i litteraturen*. Gothenburg, Författarförlaget.

Lo-Johansson, I. (1982). *Tröskeln*. Stockholm, Bonnier.

Lo-Johansson, I. (1988). *Till en författare*. Stockholm, Bonnier.

Matsson, R. (1975). *Svenskt 30-tal*. Stockholm, Gidlund.

Mattsson, P-O. (1995). Den svenska arbetarlitteraturen som historiskt fenomen. *Arbetarhistoria*, 8 (2/3), pp. 45–48.

Mattsson, P-O. (2013). Ett nationellt-proletärt novellepos. *Tidskrift för litteraturvetenskap*, 43 (2), pp. 61–72.

Mattsson, P-O. (2016). Konstruktionen av en svensk arbetarlitterär tradition. In: Apring, Å et. al. eds. "*Inte kan jag berätta allas historia?*" Göteborg, LIR, pp. 19–34.

Månsson, F. et. al. (1932). *Ansikten*. Stockholm, Bonnier.

Melberg, A. (1973). *På väg från realismen*. Stockholm, Gidlunds.

Melberg, A. (1975). Inledning. In: A Melberg ed. *Den litterära institutionen*. Stockholm, Rabén & Sjögren, pp. 9–29.

Mischliwietz, S. (2012). "*Att uppfinna ord*". Münster, Münster University.

Mischliwietz, S. (2014). "Finns det inga arbetare?" In: B. Jonsson et. al. *Från Bruket till Yarden*. Lund, Absalon, pp. 191–204.

Mral, B. (1985). *Frühe schwedische Arbeiterdichtung*. Uppsala, Uppsala University.

Nilsson, M. (2003). *Den moderne Ivar Lo-Johansson*. Hedemora, Gidlunds.

Nilsson, M. (2009). Radikalen och offentligheterna. In: B. Sjöberg and B. Svensson eds. *Kulturhjälten*. Stockholm, Atlantis, pp. 71–90.

Nilsson, M. (2010). *Den föreställda mångkulturen*. Hedemora, Gidlunds.

Nilsson, M. (2012). Inordning och uppror. *Tidskrift för litteraturvetenskap*, (42) 1, pp. 49–62.

Nilsson, M. (2014a). *Literature and Class*. Berlin, Humboldt-Universität.

Nilsson, M. (2014b). En ny generation – en förnyad tradition. *Samlaren*, 135, pp. 100–128.

Nilsson, M. (2016a). Den moderna(ste) svenskspråkiga arbetarlitteraturen. In: E. Igland Diesen et. al. eds. *Stempelslag*. Oslo, Novus Forlag, pp. 259–284.

Nilsson, M. (2016b). Arbeiterliteratur, Klasse und Region. In: B. Caspers et. al. eds. *Theorien, Modelle und Probleme regionaler Literaturgeschichtsschreibung*. Essen, Klartext, pp. 93–104.

Nilsson, M. (2016c). En ny arbetarlitteratur? In: Apring, Å. et. al. eds. *"Inte kan jag berätta allas historia?"* Göteborg, LIR, pp. 131–151.

Nilsson, M. (2017). Mellan klassen och parnassen. *Tidskrift för Litteraturvetenskap*, 47 (1), pp. 60–71.

Nilsson, M. and Lennon, J. 2016. Defining Working-Class Literature(s), in *New Proposals*, 8 (2), pp. 39–61.

Nordmark, D. (1978). *Samhället på scenen*. Umeå: Umeå University.

Ojajärvi, J. (2015). The Dirty Class. *Journal of Finnish Studies*, 18 (2), pp. 181–209.

Olsson, T. (1979). Proletärförfattaren – analys av en dubbelroll. In: B. Ahlmo-Nilsson ed. *Inte bara kampsång*. Lund, Liber Läromedel, pp. 57–70.

Olsson, U. (1987). Arbetar litteraturen? *Bonniers Litterära Magasin*, 56 (6), pp. 396–408.

Runnquist, Å. (1952). *Arbetarskildrare från Hedenvind till Fridell*. Stockholm, Bonnier.

Säll, A. (1986). *"Tro inte att vi är gjorda av trä"*. Stockholm, Brevskolan.

Salmi-Niklander, K. and Launis, K. (2015). New Research Trends in Finish Working-Class Literature: Introduction. *Journal of Finnish Studies*, 18 (2), pp. 3–13.

Samuelsson, T. (2006). *Arbetarklassens bästa partytrick*. Stockholm, Wahlström & Widstrand.

Stenkvist, J. (1985). *Proletärskalden*. Stockholm, Gidlunds.

Steffen, R. (1921). *Översikt av svenska litteraturen, D. 5*. Stockholm, Norstedt.

Ström, F. (1941). *Arbetardikt i kamptid*. Stockholm, Bonnier.

Strömberg, K. (1932). *Modern svensk litteratur*. Stockholm, Natur och Kultur.

Sundin, T. (1969). *Debatten kring termen proletärdiktare 1921–22*. Uppsala, Uppsala University.

Svanberg, A. (2010). Förord. In: V. Estby ed. *Skarpt läge*. Stockholm, Föreningen Arbetarskrivare, pp. 8–9.

Therborn, G. (1985). The Coming of Swedish Social Democracy. In: E. Collotti ed. *L'Internazionale Operaia e Socialista tra le due due guerre*. Milano, Feltrinelli, pp. 527–593.

Thorsell, L. (1957). Den svenska parnassens "demokratisering" och de folkliga bildningsvägarna. *Samlaren*, 98, pp. 53–125.

Uhlén, A. (1978). *Arbetardiktningens pionjärperiod 1885–1909*. Stockholm, Ordfront.

Uhlin, E. (1950). *Dan Andersson före Svarta ballader*. Stockholm, Tiden.

Värnlund, R. (1964). *Mellan tvenne världar*. Stockholm, Geber.

Vinberg, O. (1927). Den svenska proletärdiktningens gestalter. *Edda* 27, pp. 1–32.

Vulovic, J. (2009). *Ensamhet och gemenskap i förvandling*. Stockholm, Carlsson.

Williams, A. (2016). Class Revisited in Contemporary Swedish Literature. In: J. Björklund and U. Lindqvist eds. *New Dimensions of Diversity in Nordic Culture and Society*. Cambridge, Cambridge Scholar Press, pp. 212–229.

Williams, R. (1977). *Marxism and Literature*. Oxford, Oxford University Press.

Williams, R. (2005). *Culture and Materialism*. London and New York, Verso.

Witt-Brattström, E. (1988). *Skrift och drift i trettiotalet*. Stockholm, Norstedt.

Wright, R. (1996). Literature Democratized In: L. G. Warme ed. *A History of Swedish Literature*. Lincoln and London, University of Nebraska Press, pp. 333–346.

# Mexican Working-Class Literature, or The Work of Literature in Mexico

*Eugenio Di Stefano*

Working-class literature has never had a wide audience in Mexico, always overshadowed by other types of literature, such as the novel of the Mexican Revolution, the regionalist novel, and the indigenous novel. Nevertheless, there is no better place, as this chapter will suggest, to consider the status of literature and its relationship to history and ideology than from the genre of work and the worker. Approaching working-class literature as an evolving genre in relation to different modernization projects, this chapter will map out similarities and point to differences between various labor literatures—including proletarian literature in the 1930s, the testimonio (a new type first-person documentary genre) in the 1960s, and the literatures of the early 2000s—in order to argue ultimately that the genre provides a privileged space to think about labor and exploitation in Mexico.[1]

For this same reason, this chapter also argues for a reconsideration of literature (rather than of the life of workers) within this tradition of Mexican working-class literature. Throughout the century, working-class literature has emphasized the idea of authenticity of a group (e.g. proletariat, subaltern) often at the expense of literature. This can be seen, for example, when Peter Hitchcock notes that "[i]t is better that the literature of labor be barely 'literature' than for it to be barely 'labor'" (1989, p. 7). With this in mind, the last section of this chapter will focus on two contemporary novels that challenge the idea of authenticity— especially visible in theoretical accounts of the testimonio–by insisting instead on literary form. This stress on literary form,

---

How to cite this book chapter:
Di Stefano, E. 2017. Mexican Working-Class Literature, or The Work of Literature in Mexico. In: Lennon, J. and Nilsson, M. (eds.) *Working-Class Literature(s): Historical and International Perspectives.* Pp. 128–158. Stockholm: Stockholm University Press. DOI: https://doi.org/10.16993/bam.f. License: CC-BY

however, will not mean a shift away from anti-capitalist criticism, but rather an opportunity to reengage with it. As such, this chapter contends that a newfound concern with literary form emerges as a space to critique exploitation and neoliberalism in Mexico today.

## The Mexican Revolution: The Creation of a New State

In 1910, Mexico became the center of revolutionary politics in Latin America. The Mexican Revolution, the first great revolution of the twentieth century, ended the thirty-five-year dictatorship of Porfirio Díaz. During Díaz's reign [*el Porfiriato*], the country had experienced relative stability and large economic growth, although at great social cost. As Mexico sought to modernize a largely feudal system, Díaz ordered the construction of highways, railroads, and telegraph lines, all of which facilitated communication and movement of commerce, arguably strengthening the country's industrial capabilities. To achieve this objective, however, he welcomed foreign investments in Mexico, which also succeeded in reviving the mining industries and oil fields. Díaz governed, nonetheless, with an iron fist, permitting almost no political dissent and proving that, while Mexico had taken important steps toward modernization, it was still far from being a democracy. Furthermore, this economic growth did very little to improve the lives of the majority of Mexicans. Indeed, the situation during *el Porfiriato* only worsened the living conditions for many, as indigenous communal lands were privatized and sold to *terratenientes*, wealthy landowners often linked to Díaz. Modernization, in short, benefitted a small group of Mexicans at the expense of Mexico's poor.

The Mexican Revolution emerged as response to these political and economic failures. Although marked by confusion and crisis, especially during the 1920s and 1930s, the Revolution took crucial steps to ameliorate the lives of Mexicans. For instance, the Revolution proposed radical agrarian reforms, the banishment of the Catholic Church from state politics, the expropriation of foreign properties (including oil companies such as Standard Oil and Royal Dutch Shell), and the push for indigenous and mestizo rights denied since colonial times. It also pushed for massive educational reforms, as the Secretary of Public Education, José Vasconcelos, set out to build new schools, many in rural areas where poor children, primarily indigenous or mestizo, could receive an education and "mix" with criollos, the children of European descent. This type of "racial mixing" would be central to Mexico's new national identity, or what Vasconcelos called "La raza cósmica" ["the cosmic race"].[2]

Art played a crucial role in defining this new national moment, as it sought to reflect and teach Mexicans these revolutionary ideals. For this reason, Vasconcelos promoted the works of the Mexican muralists Diego Rivera, David Álvaro Siqueiros, and José Clemente Orozco, who were now commissioned to create their artwork in public buildings, including the Escuela Nacional Preparatoria. These works spoke to many of the Revolution's concerns, such as a reclaiming of pre-Columbian indigenous cultures, the condemnation of bourgeois decadence, and the fight for workers' rights. The impact of the Revolution, however, did not look the same across all art forms. In fact, within the literary field, literature in the first fifteen years after the Revolution remained mired in outdated nineteenth-century forms. Latin American *modernismo*, highly influenced by French symbolism and the Parnassian school of poets, continued to be the predominant style. Realism also had a solid literary foothold in Mexico, which began with the first Latin American novel, Fernández de Lizardi's Mexican picaresque novel *El periquillo sarniento* [*The Mangy Parrot*] (1825).[3] Informed by romanticism and naturalism, however, the early twentieth-century Mexican novel still reflected the "bourgeois morals and virtues" that had defined the years of Díaz's dictatorship (Plaskacz, 1980, p. 269).[4] What was needed was a national literature, which, much like Mexican muralism, would mark this new revolutionary moment.

For many literary critics and writers, the absence of a literature of the Revolution was both disconcerting and surprising, sparking national debates like *La polémica de 1925*. This polemic revolved around two literary groups: a cosmopolitan group of universalists, called "the Contemporaneos," and the avant-garde, politically-charged "Stridentists". The Stridentists often accused the Contemporaneos of being disconnected from national concerns and producing "effeminate" literature that looked more European than Mexican (Negrín, 1995, p. 152).[5] Mexico needed, instead, a "virile" and socially committed literature that represented the Revolution (Negrín, 1995, p. 152). For example, in 1924 Julio Jiménez Reuda laments that "It seems very strange to me that after fourteen years of revolution there has not appeared a work of poetry, prose or tragedy, whether it captures the agitations of the people in this period of bloody civil war or passionate rivalries between different interests... [Instead] [i]n half the time, Russia has created considerable works of combative or simple aesthetic expression" (Pereira, 2000, p.383). Reference to the USSR should not be surprising, since it not only had experienced its own revolution in 1917 but also had followed, as Katerina Clark's contribution to this collection shows, this political revolution with a productive aesthetic revolution ultimately consolidated in the official state style of socialist realism, a genre that reflected the ideals of the Bolshevik revolution. As we will examine further in this chapter, the USSR would be a point of reference during the 1920s and 1930s in Mexico, especially for proletarian writers who sought to create a truly revolutionary literature.[6]

For now, however, it is important to note that from this 1925 polemic, *la novela de la Revolución* [*The Novel of the Revolution*] finally emerged with the so-called discovery of Mariano Azuela's *Los de abajo* [*The Underdogs*] (1915), a "virile" realist novel that was critical of the Mexican Revolution.[7] Over the next thirty years, hundreds of revolutionary novels would be published. These novels tended to represent political and social turbulence, violence, and the overall tragedy of war.[8] These novels also discussed, and at times criticized, the lack of political objectives of the Revolution. As one character in *Los de abajo* comments, "You ask me why I am still a rebel? Well, the revolution is like a hurricane: if you're in it, you're not a man . . . you're a leaf, a dead leaf, blown by the wind" (Azuela, 2011, p. 115). There was much to criticize about the Revolution, especially during the 1920s since it had failed to make good on any of its promises—land reform, indigenous rights, and a more inclusive democracy. The novel of the Revolution sought to capture this growing disillusionment. Proletarian literature, as we will see, sought to move beyond it.

## Proletarian Literature, 1920s and 1930s

Unlike those who were penning revolutionary novels, authors from (or sympathetic with) the proletarian sector of Mexican society were less disillusioned with the Revolution. Indeed, while novels of the Revolution sought to capture and criticize the Revolution, these working-class artists, who were heavily influenced by the Bolshevik revolution, saw these failures as building blocks toward a radical social revolution. In the 1920s, proletarian writers such as Lorenzo Turrent Rozas, José Mancisidor, and Francisco Sarquis created a literature that was less about the failures of the Mexican Revolution than about a more just and egalitarian society that might be attainable after the Mexican Revolution.[9] To be sure, as the case in countries such as Finland, United States, and Russia, these artists were not always from a working-class background. Nevertheless, they shared a similar objective, insofar as they were not interested in exculpation or even in grieving the past but working toward a classless society. In this way, they criticized the novel of the Revolution (and *Los de abajo* in particular) as too restricted in its vision and not sufficiently transformative. They also interpreted the novel's pessimism as a result of Azuela's inability to grasp the true magnitude the Revolution (Plaskacz, 1980, p. 276). Although these proletarian authors also believed that the Revolution had failed in many short-term practical issues, they were convinced that it had set in motion a monumental political shift that would bring about a radical reorganization of the social structure. As such, unlike the novels of the Revolution, proletarian novels were "optimistic" because they proposed "solutions and a new reality that does not exist" (Ortega, 2008, p. 89).

Proletarian literature was as much a response to the defeatist politics of the novel of the Revolution as it was to the Mexican avant-garde, who shared similar political ideals with proletarian writers.[10] The most significant avant-garde group, Stridentists (1921–1927), who were led by Germán List Arzubide and Manuel Maple Arce, were ideologically aligned with the Bolshevik Revolution.[11] But like similar debates between the Futurists and the Traditionalists that took place in the USSR, proletarian writers in Mexico saw the experimental style of the avant-garde as a way of excluding workers and indigenous people (Soto, 1929, p. 329). Avant-garde writing was too abstract, complex, and convoluted. Furthermore, professional writers wrote avant-garde literature, which served as another form of exclusion, since they could not truly capture the worker's background and experience. In short, what was needed was a more direct and authentic form of literature that not only reflected the lives of these workers, but also was written by them.

The same concern was voiced by Turrent Rozas whose collection of short stories, *Hacia una literatura proletaria* [*Toward a Proletarian Literature*] (1932), gathered seven writers (some were non-professional) to write proletarian short stories that revealed the everyday reality and political objectives of these workers. For Turrent Rozas, the collection—and proletarian literature more generally—was positioned as a third way that moved beyond this "false dichotomy" between the universalist Contemporaneos and the nationalist Stridentists (1932, p. 7). Instead, he advocated that we "encounter a new literary expression. An expression that does not correspond to the ideology of either the universalists or the nationalists" (Turrent Rozas, 1932, p. 7). In other words, Turrent Rozas viewed this literary expression as not only providing a "global vision of the functioning of capital" but also marking an "incipient communist culture" (Negrín, 1995, pp. 155, 157).

These short stories share both a political vision and many of the same formal characteristics. All the texts, for example, have an omniscient third-person narrator. Some of the narratives deal with the tumultuous relationships between factory workers and their bosses and the events that arise because of this relationship, including strikes. Other stories in the collection take place in the countryside, away from the cities and factories. This should not be surprising since the Mexican Revolution was primarily an agrarian conflict and was fought mainly by and, nominally, for peasants. The objective of the collection, in part, is to unite these two sectors of Mexican society—the urban proletariat working in factories and the agrarian peasantry toiling in rural farms. According to the critic Bertín Ortega, this proletarian project signals "the need to reorganize the country that goes hand in hand with the need to educate them, and for these radical writers, the need to politicizes them, to teach the workers and peasants the possibilities of organization; and also to leave open the possibilities of a social revolution" (2008, p. 144). In short, the collection functions to represent the worker's reality and serves as a didactic tool for workers to achieve class consciousness.

During the 1930s, numerous Mexican proletarian texts were published, including Mancisidor's novel *La asonada* [*The Riot*] (1931) and *La ciudad roja* [*The Red City*] (1932); Francisco Sarquis's *Mezclilla* [*Denim*] (1933); Eduardo J. Correa's *La comunista de los ojos café* [*The Communist with Brown Eyes*] (1933); Miguel Bustos Cerecedo's *Un sindicato escolar. Novela corta infantil* [*A School Union: A Brief Children's Novel*] (1936); Raúl Carrancá y Trujillo's *¡Camaradas!* [*Comrades!*] (1936); Enrique Othón Díaz's *Protesta* [*Protest*] (1937); Fortino Lopez R. *Amaneceres* [*Sunrises*] (1937); Mario Pavón Flores' "El entierro" ["The burial"] and "Los gusanos rojos," [*Red Worms*] (1943, written in 1935); and Jesús Guerrero's *Los olvidados* [*The Forgotten Ones*] (1944).[12] While this increase reflects an overall upswing in proletarian publications in countries such as Sweden, Finland, and the United States, it should also be considered in relation to the progressive politics of Mexican President Lázaro Cárdenas (1934–1940), who finally implemented some of the more radical political projects that previous presidents had only talked about. These projects included large land and educational reforms, as well as the nationalization of the railroad system. Cárdenas also reinstated the Communist Party after it had been made illegal in 1929.[13] His most significant project was nationalizing the oil industry in 1938 (PEMEX), effectively kicking Standard Oil and Royal Dutch Shell out of Mexico.

Thus, proletarian literature reflected the progressive politics of the period in Mexico, which included a critique of bourgeois culture, even bourgeois literature. Like in Sweden, in Mexico there was not a systematic attempt to abandon literature completely, or even thoroughly question literature's status, which is a more visible objective, as we will see later in the 1960s with the Latin American testimonio genre.[14] Turrent Rozas, for example, suggests that "the idea is not to destroy blindly bourgeois literature, but rather to take advantage and adapt it" (1932, p. 18). This commitment to literature also means that proletarian writers were willing to experiment with forms, which as Michael Denning notes, is also visible in proletarian literature in the United States during the 1930s (2004, p. 121). In his contribution to this collection, Benjamin Balthaser signals that US criticism has attempted to treat working-class literature within a very narrow framework, which often comes at the expense of a fuller understanding of its complexity. In Mexico, this complexity has often been ignored by those who criticized proletarian literature as too schematic and ideological, or closer to political manifestos than to art. This is precisely Juan Uribe-Echeverri's criticism *La novela de la revolución mexicana [The Novel of the Mexican Revolution]* (1936) when he wonders why write fiction, when "one can write a good essay, or technical article about this material (1936, p. 77). But this type of criticism simplified the genre.

One of the more experimental texts of this period is Gustavo Ortiz Hernán's *Chimeneas [Smokestacks]* (1937).[15] In 1930, the novel had won the award for best revolutionary novel in a competition organized by the newspaper *El nacional [The National]*. The story takes place during the first years of the Revolution and centers on the proletarianization of Germán Gutiérrez who goes from being a factory bureaucrat to actively supporting his fellow factory workers as they strike. The strike fails, but the events motivate Gutiérrez to join Zapata's revolutionary troops in the South of Mexico, where he fights and ultimately dies.

*Chimeneas* departs from other proletarian literature more in style than in content. Ortiz Hernán, who once belonged to the shortly-lived Agorismo avant-garde movement (1929–1930), deploys a collage style that inserts political documents, such as the Mexican President Venustiano Carranza's 1917 land decree, as well as diagrams, drawings, and experimental photography by the famous avant-garde photographer Agustín Jiménez. The novel also openly produces a commentary on film and the work of Charlie Chaplin, in particular. In this way, unlike many of the proletarian novels that attempted to mirror society, *Chimeneas* makes its literary status visible through its experimentation. For Ortiz Hernán, however, this commitment to literary form does not make the novel any less political. According to this proletarian writer, both avant-garde's "pure art" and proletarian literature's "socialized art" are politically productive:[16]

> Pure art and socialized art are an exact reflection of battling forces within the economic and social field. Both interpret life in their own distinct way . . . Pure art responds to an economic and social past that is being eradicated, while the collective art attentively keeps an eye on the new panoramas. (Carranza, 2010, p.123)

Both "pure art" and "socialized art" are aesthetic tools for aesthetic interpretation, and political mobilization. Proletarian literature in Mexico, in other words, did incorporate different styles and aesthetic elements in order to achieve its objectives. Literature was never rejected but always understood as part of the proletarian project.

As Ortiz Hernán also makes clear, these movements are responses to the "economic and social field" (Carranza, 2010, p. 123). By the 1940s, Cárdenas' progressive term had ended and hope for a more radical revolutionary state had ended as well.[17] Tellingly, a slow-down could be seen in proletarian literature, as publications began to diminish and as other genres began to articulate and define the Mexican imaginary. Unlike in Sweden and Russia, where working-class literature had a wide audience and was regarded as a site of national literature (see Clark and Nilsson in this collection), in Mexico, this genre had never been widely read even in its heyday—a point that has also been understood in relation to a Mexican modernization project. Indeed, proletarian writers in Mexico believed that the Mexican Revolution would bring about advancements for proletarians and a true revolution; nevertheless, it remained the fact that industrial development in Mexico still lagged behind Europe and the United States. What this means is that part of the reason why proletarian literature ends can be attributed to the lack of a strong working-class movement and class consciousness (Plaskacz, 1980, p. 276). Ortiz Hernán voices a similar concern with he argues that proletarian literature can only emerge from the unity between workers and peasants, from "the classist organization of workers, sustained in its principles by dialectic materialism" (1937, p. 10). The (rise) and closure of proletarian literature, for these critics, rested more on historical developments.

But the end of the proletarian project does not mean that the representation of workers disappears, much less representations of exploitation and capital. Nor does it mean a closure of literature, or an ends of literature. That is, while the closure of proletarian literature reflected a political failure, it was never imagined as an aesthetic one. As Ortega suggests "[proletarian literature's] possibilities were closed, left partially abandoned within the current genres of Mexican literature that have favored the novel of the Mexican Revolution and Indigenous Novel as a national literary expression" (2008, p.18). The shift from proletarian literature to what Ortega had noted as "other genres" affirms that proletarian literature always considered itself to be literature. This will represent a marked difference with what happens in the 1960s, when literature comes to be understood as a reactionary force that must be eradicated.

For now, however, it should be noted that in the 1940s and 1950s, social criticism literature continues in novels by non-working class authors, such as Héctor Raúl Almanza's *Huelga blanca* [*White Strike*] (1945), Elvira de la Mora's *Tierra de hombre* [*Land of Men*] (1946) and Roberto Blanco Moheno's *Cuando Cárdenas nos dio la tierra* [*When Cárdenas Gave Us the Land*] (1952). The most important texts in this period are Juan Rulfo's *El llano en llamas* [*The Plain in Flames*] (1953), José Revueltas's *Los días terrenales* [*The Terrestrial Days*] (1949), *Ensayo sobre un proletariado sin cabeza* [*Essay about a Headless Proletariat*] (1962), and *El apando* [*The Thief*] (1969). Later still, other socially committed novels appear like Gerardo Cornejo's *La sierra y el viento* [*The Mountain and the Winds*] (1977) and Agustín Ramos's *La gran cruzada* [*The Great Crusda*] (1992).

The majority of political writing beginning in the 1940s, however, signaled a turn away from the working-class realism of the 1930s. Instead, there were indigenous-themed novels that combined nationalism and naturalism in order to idealize indigenous and mestizos. These novels include Ricardo Pozas' *Juan Pérez Jolote* (1952); Carlo Antonio Castro's *Los hombres verdaderos* [*True Men*] (1959), Rosario Castellano's *Oficio de tinieblas*

[*The Book of Lamentations*] (1962), Francisco Rojas González's *Lola Casanova* (1947), Carlos Fuentes' *La región más transparente* [*Where the Air is Clear*] (1958). There is Rulfo's so-called "mystical" novel *Pedro Páramo* (1953) that served as a critical predecessor to the magical realist texts of the 1960s (Plaskacz, 1980, p. 277). There was also the cosmopolitan poetry of Octavio Paz and his political essays that sought to locate a true Mexican identity in *Laberinto de la soledad* [*The Labyrinth of Solitude*] (1950). And there is the aforementioned novels of the Revolution and novels that directly responded to the novels of the Revolution, such as Agustin Yáñez's *Al filo del agua* [*On the Edge of the Storm*] (1947). All these texts focused on the question of the nation, especially the problem of indigenous and mestizo people and the inability of the Mexican Revolution to make good on its promises. In fact, such concerns with the failures of the Revolution would persist throughout the twentieth century.

## A Political Reawakening, an Aesthetic Revolution: The Testimonio, 1960s-1980s

By the 1940s, Mexico found itself electing more conservative PRI, *Partido Revolucionario Institucional* [*The Institutional Revolutionary Party*] leaders, who slowly rolled back Cárdenas's more progressive projects. Toward the end of the 1950s, however, social revolution was again on the political horizon, motivated by events that were taking place in Cuba. The 1959 Cuban Revolution signals a monumental political shift for the Western hemisphere. Guerrilla movements, inspired by Cuban *foquismo* soon began emerging across Latin America, even in Mexico. These guerrilla activities imagined a socialist revolution sparking with a small group and spreading like wildfire, eventually overthrowing bourgeois states and replacing them with communist ones. The Cuban Revolution brought Marxism once again to the forefront of Latin American politics; it did not, however, follow the traditional Soviet model of the 1920s and 1930s. Indeed, the Cuban Revolution, and the movements motivated by it, sought to break with the type of orthodox Soviet doctrine "whereby the task of the Communist party was to work within the political process and to organize an avant-garde of the urban proletariat until objective conditions for revolution were 'ripe'" (Colás, 1994, p. 67). This turn away from unions and proletariats from a certain theoretical position reflected Latin America's geopolitical conditions much better, since these same sectors were never as strong as they were in industrialized USSR, Sweden, or Germany. In Mexico the significance of the Cuban Revolution could be seen in the newly-formed guerrilla movements like *El partido de los pobres* [The Party of the Poor] in the state of Guerrero during the 1960s and 1970s. But perhaps the most important events centered on the student movements throughout the second-half of the 1960s, culminating with the Tlatelolco massacre in 1968 (see below).

The 1959 Cuban Revolution also changed working-class literature in ways that are still visible today. Although during the 1960s concerns about workers' exploitation and class conflict continued to be prevalent, they soon were overshadowed by a form of cultural criticism often aligned with the New Left. As we will see, this turn toward identities, decolonialism, subalternity, and civil rights often would come at the expense of class critique. For now, however, it is crucial to signal that two major aesthetic responses emerged in the 1960s: The first (the so-called "Boom" literature) might be considered as more experimental in style; the other (the testimonial narrative) was more realist, even documentary, and overtly political. The experimental Boom writers—Gabriel García Márquez, Carlos Fuentes, Julio Cortázar, José Donoso, Mario Vargas Llosa—supported the Cuban revolution; nevertheless, their innovative style had, in some sense, represented a return to avant-garde movements of the 1920s. For this reason Boom literature receives the same criticism for its stylistic exclusion of the underclass.[18] Fuentes is the best representative of this Boom generation in Mexico. His most famous novel, *La muerte de Artemio Cruz* [*The Death of Artemio Cruz*] (1963), retells the failures of Mexico and the Mexican Revolution specifically, through the life of a Mexican revolutionary, Artemio Cruz.

Testimonial literature can also be understood as a return to the proletarian literature of the 1930s, defining itself as a realist style that seeks to document and capture the reality of subalterns. But, as we will see, the emphasis will no longer be on labor and the

worker, as was the case with the working-class literature of the
1930s. The origins of the testimonio form begin in Cuba with the
Cuban Revolution, and the form testifies to a monumental revolutionary change that is taking place in Cuba. The foundational
text is Miguel Barnet's *Biografía de un Cimarrón* [*Biography of a
Runaway Slave*] (1968), which receives the first testimonio award
by Casa de las Americas in 1970. But there are other testimonios
of equal significance: Roqué Dalton's *Miguel Mármol y los sucesos
de 1932 en El Salvador* [*Miguel Marmol and the Events of 1932 in
El Salvador*] (1972), and perhaps the most famous *Me llamo
Rigoberta Menchú y así me nació la conciencia* [*I, Rigoberta
Menchú, an Indian Woman in Guatemala*] (1982). Indeed, during
the 1970s and 1980s, testimonios like Menchú's become one of
the principal mediums to denounce human rights abuses involving
torture and disappearances, which were taking place in Central
America and the Southern Cone. These later texts, including
Hernán Váldez's *Tejas Verdes* [*Diary of a Chilean Concentration
Camp*] (1974), Jacobo Timerman's *Preso sin nombre, celda sin
número* [*Prisoner without a Name, Cell without a Number*]
(1982), Alicia Partnoy's *Escuelita* [*The Little School House*]
(1986), seek less to document and to teach than to position the
reader as a witness who shares the pain of traumatic events with
its victims. For now, we should add that, like proletarian literature,
testimonios are simple, straightforward narratives, and their
"authentic" voice functions as an urgent call to mitigate a political
injustice. Sometimes nonprofessional writers pen these narratives,
but more often, ethnographers interview people and edit their
narratives.

In Mexico, the most famous testimonio is Elena Poniatowska's
*La noche de Tlatelolco: Testimonios de la historia oral* [*Massacre
in Mexico*] (1971), which deals with the events that surround the
student protests in 1968 in the Plaza of Three Cultures in Mexico
City. These mostly middle-class students were protesting authoritarian tendencies within PRI, including the state's control of unions
and workers' rights. With tensions mounting, and the impending
summer Olympics only days away—the first held in a developing
country—the Mexican government massacred over 200 students
on the night of October 2nd. The government, however, quickly

disposed of these bodies, and even today there is no official count of how many were killed. As such, the oral histories found in *La noche de Tlatelolco* serve not only as a testimony to these events but also as a call to justice.

Before *La noche de Tlatelolco*, Poniatowska had published *Hasta no verte Jesús mío* [*Here's to You, Jesusa*] (1969), a testimonial novel that is closer in content to the proletarian narratives of the 1930s. The story centers on the life of a laundress Josefina Bórquez, named Jesusa Palancares in the novel, who Poniatowska had interviewed for a year. The novel speaks to Palancares's isolation and struggles which included first fighting in the Mexican Revolution and then becoming a factory worker and later a servant. For Poniatowska, it is a story of so many excluded, the marginalized in Mexico.

There is, as already noted, an anthropological aspect to the testimonio, and its origins begin with anthropologists doing field work. Poniatowska, for example, worked with Oscar Lewis when writing his *The Children of Sanchez* (1961). But even before Poniatowska, we can see this influence in Ricardo Pozas' aforementioned novel *Juan Pérez Jolote* (1948), who was himself an anthropologist. Yet, for the testimonio critic John Beverley, it is important to distinguish this "new form" from ethnographic fieldwork (2004, p. 40). In fieldwork, subalterns function as a passive "native informant" (Ibid., p. 40); the testimonio, instead, sees the subaltern as a politically-charged subject whose real, popular voice directly testifies not only to injustices, but to the radical historical changes taking place. This point can be read as a modification of an earlier proletarian ethos that sought to give workers more political agency. As Elsi Hyttinen and Kati Launis point out in this collection, this was also the case in Finland, where working-class writers "re-wrote" earlier realist depictions of the poor as "submissive *people*" as "defiant *citizens*".

Although the testimonio is clearly a literary genre, many testimonio scholars, like Beverley, have imagined the testimonio as creating a radical "break" with literature (Ibid., p. 43). As I have shown, although critical of literature, early proletarian literature in Mexico did not necessarily problematize the ontological status of literature. Testimonio scholars, instead, argue that there has to be an ontological difference between the literature and the testimonio, which is not just categorical but, also and more importantly, political. As Magnus Nilsson astutely notes in his analysis of Swedish literature, much of this tendency can be attributed to the New Left and its systematic critique of literature. Existing literature is deemed bourgeois, effectively rendering literature's status politically irrelevant, even reactionary (2014, p. 81).[19] What this means in Mexico is that there must be a complete rejection of literature—even Boom literature, despite their authors shared ideological commitments—since literature is always considered a bourgeois form, regardless of the author's intention, political content, or even the individual reader's interpretation. As such, the testimonio is defined as extraliterary, or antiliterary, and is theorized as a rupture with literature, representation, intent, and interpretation. From this position, the emergence of the testimonio is imagined not as replacing another genre, but rather as announcing a new political form as well as an end of literature.

This ontological distinction between the testimonio and literature has been posed in different ways. Beverley, for example, argues that unlike documentary fiction and autobiography, in the testimonio "the narrative 'I' has the status of what linguists call a shifter—a linguistic function that can be assumed indiscriminately by anyone" (Beverley, 2004, p. 40). In other words, the testimonio, unlike (proletarian) literature, must be considered a collective endeavor. It is also essential, according to these scholars, that these collective subaltern voices be understood more as reality than as representations of reality; that is, they be considered authentic. For example, George Yúdice notes that the testimonio is "an authentic narrative, told by a witness who is moved to narrate by the urgency of a situation (eg. war, oppression, revolution, etc.)" and that "the speaker does not speak for or represent a community but rather performs an act of identity-formation that is simultaneously personal and collective (1996, p. 42). The subaltern voice, for Yúdice, is treated like an "authentic" emanation of the subject. What is more, for Yúdice, where other literatures (even proletarian literature) are representative, the testimonio is an "authentic narrative" that "performs" (Beverley, 2004, pp. 44, 42). The testimonio, as such, produces a different political effect on the reader, who suddenly is regarded less as a reader than as a witness—a witness who now feels the pain of the horrific events. On this account, there is no aesthetic interpretation, or if there is (as we saw above) this is not what is political about the testimonio. Indeed, aesthetic meaning and interpretation is aligned with bourgeois politics. In this way, the political effectiveness of the testimonio is found in the redescription of meaning and interpretation into effects, experience and real life.

Like proletarian literature, history informs not simply the testimonial form but its political and theoretical potential. For testimonio critics, the testimonio is an embodiment of a transition to a more just, inclusive society, where the marginalized would be incorporated into a larger political project. Beverley ends his 1989 essay, "Margin at the Center," by famously noting that:

> If the novel had a special relationship with humanism and the rise of the European bourgeoisie, testimonio is by contrast a new form of narrative literature in which we can at the same time witness and be a part of the culture of international proletarian/popular-democratic subject it its ascendancy. (2004, p. 43)

This was, as he later explains, a way of hedging his bets on Marxism, as he strongly believed events, such as the Sandinista revolutionary victory in 1979, were a clear sign of better days to come. He was, of course, mistaken. The same year in which his essay was published, the Berlin Wall would come down; and two years later, the Cold War would officially be over. Democratic liberalism had apparently won, and socialism had failed. Ideologically, nothing, as Francis Fukuyama would famously declare, would compete with liberalism again. But the writing was on the wall long before 1989. As it turns out, the 1980s had brought about an ever-growing expansion of capital. Mexico was at the forefront of this global project, as the 1982 Mexican debt crisis would radically change how debt was managed internationally. Structural changes were implemented to make free trade possible, quickly dismantling many of the international safety nets that had previously existed. By 1991, the "end of history" had arrived. And by 1995, Beverley unsurprisingly would declare that the radical potential of the testimonio had become less so, and the form, like literature before it, had now become exhausted.

At this point, it is important to summarize the similarities and differences between proletarian literature and the testimonio narrative. Theories surrounding both proletarian literature and testimonial literature understand that their respective forms emerge from historical and political developments. They are products of history and politics. Both genres also lean heavily on the question of authenticity. That is, they both imagine that a more authentic, real account of the worker or subaltern is indicative of a political shift toward a better politics.[20] The testimonio, however, goes a step further as it promotes the idea of bearing witness, where it is imagined that by feeling the pain of the other, or by seeing the world through an other's worldview, a better world can be achieved. It imagines, in other words, that empathizing or identifying with the poor or "proletarian/popular-democratic subject" serves as a critique of the structure of exploitation.[21]

This last point begins to make visible the political differences between proletarian literature and the testimonio. Unlike proletarian literature, the testimonio—especially in these later testimonial narratives—rarely produces a critique of exploitation. Instead, the testimonio (and its critics) replace structural accounts of the capitalist system with accounts of torture, pain, and abuses, or with a firm commitment to an authentic identitarian positions.[22] If for Gramsci the subaltern was a code word for the proletariat, for testimonial scholars, it clearly is not.

In fact, for these scholars, the subaltern could be queer, black, white, indigenous, disabled, migrant, rich, or poor. This does not mean that the subaltern could not also be understood as exploited. But what makes him or her essential for these testimonio scholars is that he is an authentic witness who is discriminated against for who he is, which need not (and often does not) serve as a structural critique of capitalism. On the contrary, an emphasis on discrimination often obscures class critique insofar as it insists that we imagine political conflict as a difference between those who are included or excluded from the market rather than a critique a system of exploitation that creates a gap between rich and poor.

The difference is that where a critique of exploitation is meant to lessen or eliminate this gap, a critique of discrimination is meant to change the identity of the people on top, while keeping the economic gap in place.[23] By imagining that identity is the primary conflict, the testimonio is committed less to eliminating poverty than to imagining the poor as an excluded group that needs to be included into the market. In this way, where proletarian literature's content sought to critique, or even undercut, the capitalist system, the testimonio is much more interested modifying this system to make it more "humane," while retaining its essential exploitative characteristics. In short, the testimonio becomes a mechanism to reinscribe exploitation as discrimination.

The most important aesthetic difference between Mexican proletarian literature and the testimonio is that while both are suspicious of literature, the testimonio is entirely invested in disavowing representation, literature, and aesthetic autonomy. As we suggested above, unlike proletarian literature, which did still maintain a commitment to literature and representation, the testimonio critic sees the testimonio less as representation than as reality. In so doing, it eliminates the division between art and life. It's for this reason that it also makes sense to understand the testimonio in relation less to proletarian literature than to postmodernism, which seeks to blur the lines between reality and fiction. For this reason, although it does share with United States and European postmodern texts the tendency to dismantle the idea of literature as an autonomous sphere. It also insists on imagining the world through the lens of identity rather than of exploitation.[24] The testimonio, ultimately, represents a version of this postmodern idea as it undercuts the question of fiction by emphasizing identities and reality. In short, for these postmodern scholars, there is no longer a space for fiction.

## The Work of Literature at the End of History, 1990s-2000s

Thus, the story of Mexican working-class literature throughout the century can be told in two important ways: The first is the evacuation of a normative working-class project that was representative of proletarian fiction of the 1930s and its replacement with iden-titarian narratives of the 1960s-1980s. That is, narratives of labor and exploitation are substituted by narratives about discrimina-tion and exclusion. The second is the evacuation of the aesthetic object until it supposedly disappears with the testimonio. This evacuation of the aesthetic continues today. The so-called exhaus-tion of literature (already announced by the testimonio scholars) is most visible today in the claim that literature is no different from other commodities, and readers are no different than consumers. The question of the artist, artwork, and the reader are rendered irrelevant.[25]

Indeed, Latin Americanists, such as Jon Beasley Murray and Nestor García Canclini, suggest that there is no difference be-tween art and nonart precisely because of their undifferentiated status as commodities. For these critics, everything (including lit-erature) is a commodity. This does not mean that literature doesn't have value, but it does mean that its value always seems to be in relation to the constant recognition of art as a commodity. As such, we can observe not only that labor thematically is no longer articulated as an anti-capitalist ideology, but also that an aesthetic space from which anti-capitalist projects were once formulated has been eliminated. Indeed, the force of Mexican proletarian lit-erature in the 1930s, in part, served as a claim toward an aesthetic world from which a series of political projects were proposed, imagined, revealed, and disseminated, in theory, to everyone. It was within this aesthetic world, at least as it was theorized by proletarian writers and critics, that the plight of workers could be represented in a way that was unlike other mediums and forms. Today literature, rather than a space to imagine a better world, serves primarily as a space of recognition of capital. Literature, according to these critics, functions only to reveal its commodity form.[26]

I would like to conclude by proposing a brief reading of two Mexican novels that attempt not only to distance themselves from these accounts of the art commodity but, also, to reengage with the question of labor by insisting on their status as liter-ature. This project is at the center of Valeria Luiselli's *Historia de mis dientes* [*Story of My Teeth*] (2013). The story is about

Gustavo Sánchez-Sánchez, alias *Carretera* [*Highway*], a security guard at a juice factory, who turns into the self-described "best auctioneer in the world" (2013, p. 5). The narrative spans his entire life and includes outrageous episodes of auctioning famous people's teeth—such as Plato, Jean-Jacques Rousseau, and G.K. Chesterton—through what he calls parabolic method of inventing stories to sell these objects. Highway retells stories of family members, friends, and associates, such as Julio Cortázar, Marcelo Sánchez Proust, Winifredo G. Sebald, Juan Gabriel Vázquez, Juan Villalobos, Lina Meruane and even Valeria Luiselli, the author herself. With his success as an auctioneer, and the money from his famed auctions, the toothless Highway is able to buy Marilyn Monroe's teeth, which are surgically implanted into his mouth and later removed and stolen by his son. The first part of the novel is told through the eyes of our dishonest hero and reminds readers of the picaresque novels that mark the origins of Mexican literary history. The second part of the story is told by his biographer, another narrator, Jacobo de Voraigne, who provides a more omniscient perspective of Highway's life and his death, echoing a more traditional, realist narrative style.

*Historia de mis dientes* is both experimental and entirely absurd. Nevertheless, there is an aspect of the novel that does remind us of the proletarian project of the 1930s. The real-life origins of Luiselli's novel begin with Jumex, the biggest juice producer in Mexico. Along with its juice factory, Jumex has a world-class museum, and Luiselli was asked to write something for one of the museum's exhibits. As Luiselli has suggested in interviews, these two worlds—the Jumex factory and the museum—have always been treated as separate entities and, for this project, she proposes to join them together by directly involving the workers at the plant. In order to realize this project, Luiselli would send weekly installments to a reading group of factory workers who would, in turn, comment, add stories and anecdotes, and return audio files back to her in New York, where she lives. The author would base her next installment on these comments. And this process would continue until the novel was complete. Undoubtedly, this project, in part, recalls Maxim Gorky's *Istoriia fabrik i zavodov,* or *Istoriia zavodov*) [*The History of the Factories*], established by the decree of October 1931. As Clark notes about Gorky's project in her contribution to this collection: "These histories were to be collectively written but largely comprise individual autobiographical accounts by workers of their time at the given factory or construction site; all the members of a given factory were to be, potentially, involved in writing them."

On the one hand, Luiselli's desire to engage workers (as workers) reminds us of proletarian writings of the past. On the other, this engagement is noticeably a frustrated one (as was Gorky's project, as Clark describes). At the most basic level, the publication of the novel is a result of a form of patronage, financed by a major multinational corporation to promote one of their cultural endeavors. Furthermore, *Historia de mis dientes* departs from the standard proletarian narrative that attempts to create a clear prose and a direct political message of class struggle. Luiselli's narrative is nonlinear and convoluted and, undoubtedly, is in constant conversation with literature and literary figures. Indeed, at times, one cannot help but think the novel as an inside joke from which these factory workers are meant to be excluded. When Luiselli is asked, however, if she had thought about writing in a clearer style for the workers, she responds that it would be "silly" to attempt to do so. Instead, her primary concern regarding style is to "write something that pulls them in and entertains them after a day's work at the factory. And that's a big challenge, to not lose their attention, to keep them interested and motivated so they would still come to sessions every week" ("Sink"). These explanations clearly diverge from proletarian literature, which is understood as a didactic tool to assist workers in developing political awareness, not in being entertained. In *Historia de mis dientes,* Luiselli's primary interest is that workers are entertained so they keep attending the sessions. There is no concern that they gain some form of class consciousness. What is more, this project in no way is meant for other workers outside of this project—which is just to say that the objective of entertaining these workers is so she can finish writing her novel.

It would be error, however, to deem *Historia de mis dientes* an apolitical (or a reactionary) novel because of this inauthentic account of workers, especially when considering that the authenticity of the worker, or the subaltern, does not necessarily produce a better politics. As we already noted, there is a deep compatibility between identitarianism and neoliberalism. Instead, this disavowal of authenticity marks Luiselli's first intervention on a predominant postmodern vision, especially visible in the testimonio. For Luiselli, the interest in workers is less a question of authenticity (or even recognition) than in creating artwork that distances itself from the idea of sharing an authentic experience with workers. Luiselli wants to create a work of art that is art (a project that points to its autonomy) but still holds a relationship to workers from within the text. From this position, the emphasis on literary language, and even literary referents, work against not only an identification with workers of proletarian literature but also the immediacy between the subaltern and reader that marks the testimonio.

For Luiselli, this commitment to the literary does not mean a return to art for art's sake. Instead, it is on behalf of literature where we find the most visible engagement with politics in the novel. Highway is "a lover and collector of good stories, which is the only honest way of modifying the value of an object" (Luiselli, 2013, p. 23). There is obviously an unethical dimension here. He creates fantastical stories to get people to buy anything and everything. But this is less a question of morality or ethics than a question of the present-day relationship between aesthetics and commodities. Or said differently, it is an attempt to find meaning beyond the commodity form. As the narrator Jacobo de Voraigne explains, the culmination of Highway's job as an auctioneer is his "famous allegoric method," a kind of "postcapitalist, radical recycling," in which no objects are sold. Rather, "value and meaning" are found in the stories themselves (Luiselli, 2013, p. 125). He hopes this will "save the world from its existential condition as the garbage can of history" (Luiselli, 2013, p. 125). In other words, he seeks to establish a postcapitalist project, in which, if literature is not outside of the commodity, it is, at least, understood as different from nonaesthetic objects. As I argue below, this is politically relevant, in relation to a contemporary neoliberal world that insists on dedifferentiated commodities and meaning.

Luiselli writes that *Historia de mis dientes* was inspired by both nineteenth-century literary installments, as well as the Cuban practice of cigar reading, in which people would read novels to cigar factory workers to help them pass the time as they worked. Nevertheless, what is striking about the text is that it is filled with drawings and photographs that seek to ground the project in a social referent. In turn, this also reminds us of the experimental elements of the proletarian novels of the 1930s (especially the work of Hernán Ortiz's *Chimeneas*), which incorporated photos and drawings, accentuating its aesthetic status as art. The project is a reminder that Mexican working-class literature, first and foremost, is art; and more importantly, this does not make their projects any less political. On the contrary, as Ortiz Hernán noted when discussing the difference between "pure poetry" of avant-garde literature of the Stridentist or the "socialized art" of proletarian literature, they are both "an exact reflection of battling forces within the economic and social field" (Carranza, 2010, p. 123). To be sure, very few today think that the avant-garde or realism can do what it promised in the past, but this doesn't mean that literature does not still provide some type of vantage point to gauge the "economic and social field" (Carranza, 2010, p. 123).[27]

It is from this position that we may consider recent Mexican novels that return to modernist artists as characters and modernist experimental forms in their narrative structure. Nicolás Cabral's *Catálogo de formas* [*Catalogue of Forms*] (2014) is loosely based on the life of the Mexican modernist architect and painter, Juan O'Gorman, and the various leftist artists who knew him, including Diego Rivera, Frida Kahlo, Conlon Nancarrow. This interest in modernism can easily be read as nostalgia, and yet it does seem as if there is something more at stake than simply repetition and surface. The novel spans the life of this artist—from his functionalist beginnings in the 1920s to his endorsement of a more organic style in the 1950s. But for Cabral, this exploration into O'Gorman's life functions less to highlight a past style than to find an aesthetic space that is not "born of exploitation" (Cabral, 2014, p. 61), a desire of "abstracting forms" to "banish" bourgeois history (Ibid., p. 45). Much like the story of proletarian literature, this project leads to a closure, and ultimately to the architect's madness and death. But what remains are his works of art which allow us not only to "retrace the exhaustion of Mexican modernism's utopian promise" but to imagine literature's relationship to the structure that continues to demand exploitation today (Di Stefano and Sauri, 2015, p. 155).

I would like to end this chapter by insisting that Luiselli's and Cabral's novels are not returns to either proletarian literature of the 1930s or the more recent testimonial narrative. More specifically, these are not "authentic narratives" that capture the real lives of workers or subalterns (Yúdice, 1996, p. 44). Instead, *Historia de mis dientes* and *Catálogo de formas* point to how the assertion of literature today serves as a rejection of not only authenticity, but also the idea that there is nothing beyond the commodity form. In other words, these novels function as a critique of contemporary neoliberal cultural logic. At the same time, these works offer the opportunity to revisit working-class theory and criticism. As such, we are once again reminded, as the proletarian writer Ortiz Hernán stresses, that all works of art "have class meanings and a high ability to become instruments of revolutionary struggle" (Carranza, 2010, p. 123). In the face of the commodification of everything—or at least the idea that capital is everything—the question of meaning becomes a space in which we can think beyond commodities and capitalism, a space where questions of labor and exploitation that have long been left in the garbage can of history can perhaps return. Finally, by insisting on this aesthetic space, this chapter has also sought to show how Mexican literature intersects with other national literatures, affirming that the definition of working-class literature continues to evolve as the national is imagined in relation to the global.

## Notes

1. My interest in working-class literature is not necessarily located in the belief that this genre, in itself, is more political than others; rather, it is the belief that this genre provides a space from which the limits of the aesthetic must be explored in relation to politics. For this reason, I subscribe to Magnus Nilsson's definition that working-class literature "is not constructed around some stylistic or ideological essence, but is instead made up of literary texts, which, at different times, for different reason, and in different sites, have been defined as working-class literature" (2014, p.24).

2. This cosmic identity—and the Revolution more generally—inspired many Mexicans; but it also inspired many foreigners to come to Mexico. Beginning in the 1920s, Mexico became the home of many Leftist political exiles, such as the Peruvian politician Victor Raúl Haya de la Torre, the Chilean poet Gabriela Mistral, Spanish film director Luis Buñuel, Nicaraguan revolutionary Augusto César Sandino, and Spanish novelist Max Aub. Perhaps, the most notorious leftist exile was Leon Trotsky, famously assassinated in his home in Mexico City by Ramón Mercader. Much later, the Cuban revolutionaries Fidel and Raul Castro would arrive, followed by Colombian writer Gabriel García Márquez.

3. Other realist novels followed, including Emilio Rabasa's series *Novelas mexicanas [Mexican Novels]* (1887–1888), Rafael Delgado's *Los parientes ricos [Wealthy Relatives]* (1903), and José López Portillo's *La parcela [The Plot of Land]* (1904). Social protest literature was also quite visible, such as Ricardo Flores Magón's short stories, Federico Gamboa's *Santa* (1903), and *La llaga [The Wound]* (1913), and Gregorio Lopéz y Fuentes *El indio [The Indian]* (1923).

4. All translations, unless otherwise indicated, are mine.

5. Of course, the Strindentists were themselves highly influenced by the latest European avant-gardes, including Italian Futurism, Russian Constructivism, and Spanish Ultraismo.

6. It should also not be surprising to find, for example, that aesthetic criticism in the Soviet Union looked to Mexico as a point of comparison. In 1960, to celebrate the 150th anniversary of Latin American independence, two books of literary criticism were published in the USSR: The first, *La literatura latinoamericana en la imprenta rusa [Latin American Literature in Print in Russia*, was more bibliographical, covering literature across Latin America. The second, *La novela realista mexicana [The Mexican Realist Novel]*, edited by V.N. Kuteishchikova, was a collection of articles on literary criticism and focused on realism in Mexico. For discussion of Soviet interest in Mexican literature, see Plaskacz.

7. *Los de abajo* was published in 1915, but very few knew about the novel. During the 1925 polemic, the writer Francisco Montarde rediscovered the novel. Today it is regarded as the first and most important novel of the Revolution.

8. For a comprehensive analysis of the novel of the Revolution, see Dessau.

9. See Mancisidor for a discussion on the importance of the Bolshevik revolution. Lorenzo Turrent Rozas also notes that the "referent of proletarian literature must be found in the USSR" (1932, p.7).

10. As is the case in Finland, Sweden, and Russia, the first manifestations of working-class literature in Mexico are found in poetry. Indeed, already in the early 1920s there was a handful of Mexican poets who understood themselves as very much in favor these revolutionary politics. These poets include Carlos Gutiérrez Cruz's *Sangre roja* [*Red Blood*] (1924) and Miguel Bustos Cerecedo's *Revolución* [*Revolution*] (1932). For a history of Revolutionary poetry in Mexico see, Katharina Niemeyer. As Elsi Hyttinen and Kati Launis write in this collection, theater in Finland provided an opportunity for working-class writers to produce plays, and audience members to attend them since they did not require as much time as reading novels. In Mexico, this political form of theatre was visible with the productions of *El Grupo de los siete*, The Group of Seven.

11. The most important Strident work is Maple Arce's *Vrbe. Súperpoema bolchevique en 5 cantos* [*Metropolis*] (1924), which was translated into English by John Dos Passos.

12. According to Victor Díaz Arciniegas, the primary characteristics of these proletarian narratives, are: (1) the depiction of the marginalization and exploitation of the working class; (2) the expression of a need to organize workers and unions; and (3) the representation of the organization of strikes as a tool to fight against the bourgeoisie (1979, pp. 6–8). We can add to this list that none of the novels are Bildungsromane, and love stories typically play minor roles; they also renounce "a model of individualism" in favor of vision of the collective (Ortega, 2008, p.144).

13. Moreover, Cárdenas' party, *Partido Nacional Revolucionario* (PNR), often used terminology like "class exploiter," "class warfare," "Mexican socialism" "dictatorship of the proletariat" "decomposition of capitalism" (Ortega, 2008, p.24).

14. Some testimonio scholars have rejected the idea of 'genre' because it gestures toward representation and literature. Even though this essay attempts to lay out this anti-literary testimonio project, it does

not endorse it. In other words, and against these testimonio scholars, the testimonio is a genre and literature.

15. Along with *Chimineas*, novels such as *La ciudad roja* [*The Red City*], *Protesta* [*Protest*], and *Camaradas* [*Comrades!*], incorporated avant-garde elements (Ortega, 2008, p.144).

16. These avant-garde groups sought to create a form of abstract poetry—what they called "poesia pura" ["pure poetry"], which was stripped of metaphor loaded with bourgeois ideology.

17. But there were also evident signs during Cárdenas' presidency that if the proletarian writers wanted a true revolution, he was not going to give it to them. For example, while he did legalize the Communist Party, he undermined unions and worker's autonomy and rights. Ortega notes that Cárdenas was responsible for the creation of the Confederation of Mexican Workers (CTM), making the state responsible for workers, and thus, severely limiting workers' negotiating power (2008, p. 101). He also sought to separate factory and agrarian workers in order to control both. He endorsed Manuel Ávila Camacho—a more conservative, pro-clerical leader—as his presidential successor instead of Francisco Múgica, who was considered the social conscience of Cardenismo.

18. Vargas Llosa would famously stop supporting the Cuban Revolution after the Padilla affair in 1971.

19. We can see this concern when literary critic Angel Rama in 1982 criticized the Latin American social novel of the 1930s for passively accepting these ideological constructs (qtd. in Ortega, 2008, p.44).

20. This authentic narrative can also be found in accounts of working-class literature in Russia. In Clark's contribution to this collection, she notes that Gorky urges that his readers consider when reading these working-class writers "that I am talking not of talented people, not of art, but of the truth, about life, and above all about those who are capable of action, upbeat and can love what is eternally alive and all that is growing and noble – human." Despite the claim that what these workers write is not "art," this commitment to describing their background seems to be a justification for the (lack) of literary quality, and not a complete rejection of literature or representation. Indeed, as Clark's chapter also notes, Gorky spent much of his time trying to turn workers into better writers.

21. Nilsson and Lennon are exactly right when they note that "While certainly invaluable attempts to give voice to the forgotten, if working-class literature is only viewed through this lens of 'authenticity' rather than aesthetic formulations, working-class literature may become centrally concerned about subjects rather than the processes of class formation and struggle" (2016, p. 53).

22. For a discussion on the redescription of structural critique into identification and empathy, see my chapter "Remembering Pain in Uruguay." For an analysis on the question of exploitation in Latin American literature, see Di Stefano and Sauri's "Making it Visible," (2014).

23. Within the North American context, see Michaels' *The Trouble with Diversity* (2006).

24. In the 1980s and 1990s, these postmodern characteristics can be seen in the work of Mexican writers Luis Arturo Ramos, María Luisa Puga, Brianda Domecq, Ignacio Solares, Cristina Rivera Garza, Julieta Campos, and Carmen Boullosa.

25. On the question of the commodification of literature, see Brown (2012).

26. There is another version of this exhaustion of literature argument when literature is treated as an inadequate technology to document abuses. By emphasizing this utilitarian function, literature's importance wanes in the face of other technologies, such as digital cameras and the internet. With this in mind, we should consider the importance of the most politically-charged novels that are emerging today in Mexico, especially those testimonios about maquiladoras and femicide, such as Carmen Galán Benitez's *Tierra marchita* [*Withered Land*](2002), or narcoliterature such as Yuri Herrera's *Trabajos del reino* [*Kingdom Cons*] (2004), Juan Pablo Villalobos' *Fiesta en la madriguera* [*Down the Rabbit Hole*] (2011), or even novels on Zapatistas such as Paco Ignacio Taibo and Subcomandate Marcos' *Muertos incomodos* [*The Uncomfortable Dead*] (2004). All these texts, in one way or another, point to the crisis of capital in Mexico, how it infiltrates every aspect of their (and our) lives. But they also live in a world in which literature as a mechanism to both mirror or expose reality (for example, the plight of workers) survives and competes amongst other technologies.

27. For an account on the political irrelevance of realism and avant-garde literature in Latin America today, see Ludmer.

## References

"A Story You Can Sink Your Teeth Into," (2015). *Studio 360*. Radio. WNYC, PRI.

Azuela, M. (2011). *The Underdogs: A Novel of the Mexican Revolution*. Trans. E Munguia Jr. Auckland, The Floating Press.

Beverley, J. (2004). *Testimonio: On the Politics of Truth*. Minneapolis, U of Minnesota, pp. 29–44.

*Brown, N. (2012)*. "The Work of Art in the Age of its Real Subsumption under Capital." *Nonsite.org*. http://nonsite.org/editorial/the-work-of-art-in-the-age-of-its-real-subsumption-under-capital. Accessed: Mar. 2012.

Cabral, N. (2014). *Catálogo de formas*. Mexico City, Periférica.

Carranza, L. E. (2010). *Architecture as Revolution: Episodes in the History of Modern Mexico*. Austin, University of Texas Press.

Colás, S. (1994). *Postmodernity in Latin America*. Durham, Duke University Press.

Denning, M. (2004). *Culture in the Age of Three Worlds* London: Verso.

Dessau, A. (1972). *La novela de la Revolución*. Mexico City: Fondo de Cultura Económica.

Díaz Arciniegas, V. (1979). "Cuatro novelas proletarias mexicanas; algunas consideraciones." *¡Siempre!* Iss. 1372, pp. 6–8.

Di Stefano, E. (2011). "Remembering Pain in Uruguay: What Memories Mean in Carlos Liscano's *Truck of Fools*." In: Y. Wu and S. Livescu. Lanham, MD, eds., *Human Rights, Suffering, and Aesthetics in Political Prison Literature*. Lexington Books, pp. 163–184.

Di Stefano, E. (2013). Reconsidering Aesthetic Autonomy and Interpretation as a Critique of the Latin American Left in Roberto Bolaño's *Estrella distante*. *Revista de Estudios Hispanicos*, 43 (3), pp. 463–485.

Di Stefano, E. (2014). What Can a Painting Do?: Absorption and Aesthetic Form in Fernando Botero's *Abu Ghraib* as a Response to Affect Theory and the Moral Utopia of Human Rights. *MLN*, 2 (129), pp. 412–432.

Di Stefano, E. (2014). "Making It Visible: Latin Americanist Criticism, Literature, and the Question of Exploitation Today." *Nonsite.org.* http://nonsite.org/article/making-it-visible. Accessed: Apr. 2016.

Di Stefano, E. and Sauri, E. (2015). "La furia de la materia": On the Non-Contemporaneity of Modernism in Latin America. In: M. D'Arcy and M. Nilges, eds., *The Contemporaneity of Modernism: Literature, Media, Culture.* New York, Routledge, pp. 148–164.

Hitchcock, P. (1989). *Working-Class Fiction in Theory and Practice: A Reading of Alan Sillitoe (Challenging the Literary Canon).* Rochester, University of Rochester Press.

Ludmer, J. (2010). *Aquí América latina: Una especulación.* Buenos Aires, Eterna Cadencia.

Luiselli, V. (2015). *Story of My Teeth.* Trans. C. MacSweeney. Minneapolis, Coffee House Press.

Mancisidor, J. (1933). Literatura y revolución. *Ruta: publicación mensual.* 1, pp. 8–9.

Michaels, W. B. (2007). *The Trouble with Diversity: How We Learned to Love Identity and Ignore Inequality.* New York, Holt Press.

Negrín, E. (1998). Una corriente de literatura proletaria en Xalapa. *Actas del XI Congreso de laI Asociación Internacional de Hispanistas. Edición electrónica Centro Virtual Cervantes.* 7, pp. 151–160.

Niemeyer, K. (2010). "'que agita apenas la palabra.' La poesía mexicana frente a la Revolución." *La revolución mexicana en la literatura y el cine.* In: O. C. Díaz

Nilsson, M. (2014). *Literature and Class: Aesthetical-Political Strategies in Modern Swedish Working-Class Literature.* Berlin, Nordeuropa-Institut.

Nilsson, M. and Lennon, L. (2016). Defining Working-Class Literature(s): A Comparative Approach Between U.S. Working-Class Studies and Swedish Literary History. *New Proposals: Journal of Marxism and Interdisciplinary Inquiry*, 8 (2) (April), 39–6.

Oropesa, S. A. (2003). *The Contemporaneos Group: Rewriting Mexico in the Thirties and Forties*. Austin, University of Texas Press.

Ortega, B. (2008). *Utopías inquietantes: narrativa proletaria en México en los años treinta*. Veracruz, Instituto Veracruzano de Cultura.

Ortiz Hernán, G. (1937). *Chimeneas*. Mexico City: Editorial México Nuevo.

Pereira, A. (2000). *Diccionario de literatura mexicana: siglo XX*. Mexico City, Universidad Nacional Autónoma de México.

Pérez, F. Gräfe, F. Schmidt-Welle. Madrid, eds., Bibliotheca Iberoamericana. 47–70. Web. Accessed: Mar. 2015.

Plaskacz, B. (1980). La novela realista mexicana en la crítica soviética. *Journal of Spanish Studies: Twentieth Century*, 8 (3), pp. 267–278.

Poniatowska, E. (1969). *Hasta no verte Jesús mío*. Mexico City, Ediciones Era.

Poniatowska, E. (1971). *La noche de Tlatelolco: Testimonios de la historia oral*. Mexico City, Ediciones Era.

Soto, J. S. (1929). Arte y Revolución. *Crisol*, 2 (12), pp. 392–395.

Turrent Rozas, L. (1932). *Hacia una literatura proletaria*. Xalapa, Mexico, Ediciones Integrales.

Uribe-Echeverría, J. (1936). *La novela de la revolución mexicana y novela hispanoamericana actual*. Santiago, Chile, Prensas de la Universidad de Chile.

Yúdice, G. (1996). "*Testimonio* and Postmodernism." *The Real Thing: Testimonial Discourse in Latin America*. Ed. Georg M. Gugelberger. Durham, Duke UP, pp. 42–57.

# British Working-Class Writing: Paradox and Tension as Genre Motif

*Simon Lee*

It goes without saying that the literary arts' capacity to analyze and critique contemporary cultural shifts is unparalleled, and British working-class literature grants social historians unique insight into the way class assignations are negotiated and managed. By presenting a mosaic of experience, as well as conceptualizations of class consciousness, British working-class literature mines the aspects of working-class life often overlooked in day-to-day reality. However, inherent within this literature is a paradox: competing aesthetic and political objectives that are periodically at odds. I want to suggest that this paradox echoes the persistence of class struggle, yielding an aesthetic tension that shields British working-class literature from both complacency and schematization. As other writers in this volume discuss, working-class literature is often indeterminate and contingent, and situating it within genre confines requires critical dexterity. For example, discussing Georg Lukács in his contribution to this collection, Benjamin Balthaser writes that working-class literature is "in tension with the reality it seeks to document" in a manner that produces "a dialectical vision"—a gesture that echoes Eugenio Di Stefano's recommendation to approach such literature as "an evolving genre in relation to different modernization projects" (see Di Stefano in this collection). This dialectical affiliation has been well documented by critics like Ian Haywood, who notes how the emergence of the novel as a bourgeois enterprise reflects a class bias within cultural production—one that tends to exclude working-class perspectives and authenticity in lieu of high-brow modernization and literary

**How to cite this book chapter:**
Lee, S. 2017. British Working-Class Writing: Paradox and Tension as Genre Motif. In: Lennon, J. and Nilsson, M. (eds.) *Working-Class Literature(s): Historical and International Perspectives.* Pp. 159–195. Stockholm: Stockholm University Press. DOI: https://doi.org/10.16993/bam.g. License: CC-BY

trends (1997, p. 3). These exclusions are generally offset by representational modes, such as realism, that simulate authenticity—even in the presence of authentic authorial experience—to such a degree that working-class writing that fails to foreground the jagged surface of reality often feels incomplete. Nonetheless, as Peter Hitchcock has suggested, working-class representation cannot be reduced to a set of material signifiers because class exists as a series of social relations rather than fixed traits or characteristics (2000, p. 23). Consequently, this chapter traces the emergence of British working-class literature, specifically emphasizing the way the genre sustains tension between aesthetic and political aspirations. It concludes that the very notion of an authoritative working-class literature resists formal consummation and is therefore subject to continual renovation contingent upon cultural need.

Numerous scholars have charted the general terrain of British working-class literature, pinpointing key moments and locating cultural production within the dynamics of culture itself. However, given that canonical bias has marginalized working-class voices, academic texts have sought to recover the genre through panoramic coverage rather than discrete angles or nuanced positions. For example, H. Gustav Klaus' *The Literature of Labor: Two Hundred Years of Working-Class Writing* (1985) argues for a general "literature of labor" with a particular focus on Chartist fiction while maintaining a broad perspective throughout. Similarly, Jeremy Hawthorne's edited collection *The British Working-Class Novel in the Twentieth-Century* (1984) offers a range of essays that provide a robust overview of working-class writing, leaning more toward intersectional concerns of gender and race. Ian Haywood's rich *Working-Class Fiction: From Chartism to "Trainspotting"* (1998) is as comprehensive a survey as it is a compelling entreaty for the academic legitimization of working-class writing. Texts like Martha Vicinus' *The Industrial Muse: A Study of Nineteenth Century British-Working Class Literature* (1974) and Paul Thomas Murphy's *Toward a Working-Class Canon: Literary Criticism in British Working-Class Periodicals, 1816–1858* (1994) present more period-specific synopses, focusing respectively on the impact of economic shifts on literary production while gesturing toward the formation of a burgeoning working-class literary aesthetic. Peter Hitchcock's *Working-Class Fiction in Theory and Practice: A Reading of Alan Sillitoe* (1989) historicizes the cultural dynamics that paved the way for twentieth-century working-class writing, but Hitchcock's primary concern is Sillitoe's contribution to the kitchen sink realism movement of the 1950s and 1960s. Such overviews are well supported by supplementary accounts like Jonathan Rose's *The Intellectual Life of the British Working Classes* (2001) in which patterns of literary consumption through memoirs and autobiographical writing are established. Rose emphasizes the autodidactic nature of the British working classes along the way. These approaches build on foundational work by writers like Richard Hoggart, whose acclaimed *The Uses of Literacy* (1957) not only surveyed reading habits but also argued that reading habits were responsible for shifts in the way class was experienced.

Contemporary scholarship has sharpened the focus by reevaluating overlooked works to elevate their social significance with journals such as *Women's Studies Quarterly* (1995), *Victorian Poetry* (2001), *PMLA* (2000), and *Philological Quarterly* (2013) dedicating issues to working-class writing. In addition, recent monographs have offered more nuanced analyses of working-class writing, such as John Kirk's *Twentieth Century Writing and the British Working Class* (2003) which accelerates to the 1980s and 1990s clarifying how contemporary texts respond to prior moments in the formation of working-class writing. Pamela Fox's *Class Fictions: Shame and Resistance in the British Working-Class Novel, 1890–1945* (1994) builds on Hawthorn's collection by unpacking gender relations in working-class writing and underscoring developments in the workplace throughout both wars. Nicola Wilson's recent *Home in British Working-Class Fiction* (2015) develops Fox's work on gender representation—as well as the work of sociologists, such as Joanna Bourke—by investigating the role of domestic space across a range of working-class texts. Wilson emphasizes the home's impact on the formation of class consciousness, showing how working-class fiction's tendency to privilege representations of the workplace only sheds partial light onto working-class culture as a whole. Robert del Valle Alcalá's *British Working-Class Fiction: Narratives of Refusal and the Struggle*

*Against Work* (2016) argues that mid-century working-class fiction can be read as a response to a history of economic and social oppression, insisting that working-class fiction offers correctives to the imposed limits of social stratification. My own research considers the way working-class writing responds to shifts in the built environment. I focus specifically on the way that working-class environs maintained social divisions and how fictional representations imagined alternative ways of negotiating the confines of classed spaces. The goal of this particular chapter, though, is to trace a thread running through the genealogy of British working-class texts—one whose inherent tension functions to keep the genre of working-class writing dynamic and homeostatic.

## Nineteenth-Century Literature: Formation and Development

While literary references to labor and working people certainly precede industrialization, the standard point of departure for working-class writing in Britain is the nineteenth century—a time that saw significant social and cultural shifts, the cementing of tripartite class categorization, the emergence of the novel within the arts, and the development of realism as a dominant mode of literary representation. Whereas representations of class in twentieth-century literature are relatively established, the nineteenth century reads more as a crucible, in which aesthetics and political imperatives intertwine in relation to social class. As Carmen Casaliggi and Porscha Fermanis have suggested, the challenge of comprehending the topic of class in the literature of the early nineteenth century can be attributed to disputes in the way that class itself was envisioned following the transition from feudalism to early industrial capitalism, in which economic and political dynamics were destabilized (2016, p. 40). Furthermore, professional writers in the public eye risked alignment to radicals and agitators when publishing work deemed insurrectionist or challenging to the status quo. Poet Laureate Robert Southey, for example, distanced himself from his anonymously-penned dramatic poem "Wat Tyler" when his political enemies discovered and published it under his name in 1817. This discovery prompted him to dismiss the work as the naive scribblings of an excitable schoolboy. Yet, it was Southey who, in 1831, composed a performative apologia for working-class writing, in which he simultaneously patronizes and praises the quaint vulgarity of lesser citizens (1836, p. 13). Southey's hesitancy to fully embrace working-class writers as legitimate cultural voices mirrors his own anxiety over social positioning but also reflects the new challenge of developing literary art in tandem with ideology.

As Ian Watt outlined, the eighteenth century marked the emergence and rise of the modern novel with the nineteenth century cementing its form through the birth of realism. Nineteenth-century realist texts represented working-class lives at their most organic and mercurial during this time. For Watt, the development of the novel reflects not just a trajectory within the literary arts, but an opportunity to portray diverse perspectives through verisimilitude:

> If the novel were realistic merely because it saw life from the seamy side, it would only be an inverted romance; but in fact it surely attempts to portray all the varieties of human experience, and not merely those suited to one particular literary perspective: the novel's realism does not reside in the kind of life it presents but in the way it presents it. (1957, p. 11)

In other words, style and technique are critical components of narrative mimesis, and the social value of the novel is weighed by its fidelity to the world it depicts. Despite Watt's emphasis on Daniel Defoe, Samuel Richardson, and Henry Fielding, perhaps the novel that best defines this degree of verisimilitude in terms of class demarcation is George Eliot's *Middlemarch* (1871). Eliot's text serves as a pointed rejection of early ninteenth-century Romanticism, but a fixation on interiority is what distinguishes her working-class characters from the working-class characters of many of her contemporaries whose sentimental representations sometimes bordered on caricature.

By focusing on the provincial exchanges of a tripartite class system, Eliot's novel responded to class schematics established at the time as outlined in Matthew Arnold's *Culture and Anarchy* (1869)—specifically what Arnold refers to as Barbarians (the aristocracy), Philistines (the urban middle class), and the Populace (the working class). While critics have argued that Eliot is as guilty of reproducing working-class stereotypes as her contemporaries, K.M. Newton has emphasized how Eliot's characters reflect unified outlooks and shared interests aligned to new systems of class designation (2011, p. 153). This distinction, although subtle, is reflected in the fact that Eliot's representation relies less on pathos and more on unmasking social relations that produce systems of oppression. Although Jonathan Rose has claimed that Charles Dickens's support for working-class people is understood through "the role he played in making them articulate" (2002, p. 114), Eliot moved depictions closer to reality by situating her characters in their native milieu and commenting on the social exchanges that result from their interactions. Yet, Eliot's authenticity—like that of Dickens and other professional writers from the period—was somewhat hamstrung by the author's own elevated social class, outlining a perennial concern of literary representation in general: one of credibility and rhetorical ethos. While such a concern has received significant critical scrutiny (largely resulting in its dismissal as a necessary criterion for working-class writing), the persistence of such concerns cannot be so readily abandoned. Instead, I would argue that such persistent concerns over authentic depiction contributes to the kind of productive tension at the heart of working-class writing itself.

While the rise of the novel and the alignment of realism to depictions of social class tends to reflect more canonical and established forms of nineteenth-century literary production, working-class writing can also be seen to emerge from movements where social and political objectives were prioritized over representational aesthetics. For instance, whereas Benjamin Balthaser, in his essay in this collection, notes that working-class writing in nineteenth-century America was "seldom by them and even more rarely, from their perspective", nineteenth-century British literature saw substantial contributions from legitimately working-class people in both the first and second halves of the century. One of the earliest social reform movements to form bonds with British literary production was that of the Chartists, a radical working-class movement with parliamentary reform in mind. The failure of the 1832 Reform Act to produce substantial changes to the electoral system left many working-class people disenfranchised and unable to participate in the political process. In 1838, the People's Charter was drawn by William Lovett and Francis Place, alongside members of the London Working Men's Association, with the document calling for universal suffrage and the cessation of technicalities that restricted working-class participation based on social position. After the 1839 rejection of the document by parliament, social unrest followed with subsequent petitions presented and summarily rejected. The movement dissolved in 1848 following the rejection of a final petition but with no accompanying insurrection. Despite this, a revolutionary spirit persevered with reformers continuing to advocate for and implement changes over time. Today, Chartism is seen as a catalyst of the democratic process itself, underscoring the necessity of monitoring social power dynamics and making their effects known within culture.

Texts by Yuri Kovalev, Peter Scheckner, Gustav Klaus, and Anne Janowitz, as well as the aforementioned Ian Haywood and Martha Vicinus, have explored the connections between literary production and Chartism in depth.[1] Germane to this discussion is the way that the movement viewed basic literacy as indispensable to its social objectives, reflecting not only the rise of a self-educated, articulate working-class people to counter the educated and "legitimate" output of professional writers (such as Dickens and Eliot), but also reflecting attempts at self-emancipation from imposed class confines. The Chartist movement's efficacy can be traced to its use of print media with a series of working-class newspapers like *The Poor Man's Guardian*, *The Twopenny Dispatch*, and *The Northern Star* disseminating speeches and essays as well as didactic poetry. By the time of the movement's dissolution and diffusion into other causes, the genre of Chartist fiction was established, largely penned by movement leaders as opposed to novelists and writers. Thomas Martin Wheeler's *Sunshine and Shadow: A Tale of the Nineteenth Century* is widely looked upon as one of the more successful extended works of the time. Released in serialized form in 1849, the novel outlines the decline of the movement while forcefully restating the movement's central objectives. However, it is framed in a manner that Rob Breton has described as romantic: "a political melodrama that infuses intellectualizing genres into a sensational form, telling the story of working-class autodidactism while describing shipwrecks and relying on miraculous coincidences" (2009, p. 121). While the use of sensationalist plot devices blunted the text's didactic goals, Wheeler's approach stood in contrast to representations of working-class people as sentimentalized martyrs primed for religious salvation or caricatures of class distanced from the experiences of British working-class people. Despite its narrative flights of fancy, Wheeler's text—and Chartist fiction in general—addressed contemporary concerns specific to the characters within the text, as well as the target audience that the text was aimed at. The inclusion of social issues specific to the working-class can be identified as a trope that echoes through much of the twentieth-century's working-class fiction. While the seeds of realism had yet to be fully planted within working-class literature, what emerges in Chartist fiction is an elevation of pertinent topics and concerns associated with a segment of the populace ordinarily marginalized within the arts. However, the movement also reveals the seeds of an aesthetic paradox: the challenge of bridging literary objectives of storytelling with ideological goals.

Such aesthetic challenges continued throughout the remainder of the nineteenth century—a period in which representational tropes like the use of regionalism and local dialect developed in tandem with ideological positioning and social purpose. Still, during the second half of the 19th century, literary consumption reflected an ironic divide: a preference for sensationalist, trashy novels aimed at mass-readership while literature that sought to push the envelope of verisimiltude remained notably erudite in its allegiance to established formal aesthetics. Consequently, caricature and stereotyping dominated much of the working-class representation consumed by working-class audiences of the Victorian era. Concerns of authenticity continued with the emergence of novels set in northern industrial areas by writers such as Thomas Hardy, whose own class ascension fueled his investment in fidelity and the advancement of realistic character depiction. Working-class characters, such as Jude Fawley and Tess Durbeyfield, demonstrate elevation beyond their social designation through an emphasis on self-directed, contingent morality standing in contrast to the conventional morality of the Victorian era. Yet, in spite of authors like Hardy, whose own background granted his work rhetorical ethos, the policing of social class remained strong, as noted by George Orwell who, in a 1940 interview, commented that even the most authentic working-class writers still operate within the confines of bourgeois literary production when aesthetic concerns take precedence over social objectives.[2] Despite attempts to move beyond the bourgeois prejudice and stereotyping of the social novel, there were few writers active at the time with proletariat origins who were writing for specifically working-class people.

Despite a lack of established working-class voices in mainstream publishing, working-class writing by and for working-class people thrived in the margins of the latter part of the nineteenth century. Poets like Joseph Skipsey, whose work documented the rise and impact of mining culture, went largely unnoticed despite receiving praise from luminaries like Dante Gabriel Rossetti. It was also during this time that parochial working-class writing emerged in the form of the dialect literature of the 1860s and 1870s, centered upon northern industrial towns like Durham and often associated with the phenomenon of the music hall. An example of such figures includes Edwin Waugh, whose emphasis on Lancashire dialect in poems like "Come whoam to thi childer an' me" underscore the nature of working-class life in a manner that speaks directly to a Lancashire audience. As Dave Russel has noted, dialect literature was intensely regional not just in vernacular, but also in methods of production and dissemination: "In Yorkshire, the major vehicle was the prose-oriented yearly comic almanac [whereas] in Lancashire, the monthly journal was the preferred form" (2004, pp. 118–119). Russel adds that local newspapers allowed regional writers to target specific audiences, and almanacs popularized during the 1870s led to the rise of parochial voices that lingered well into the 1950s (2004, p. 119).[3] Such texts were instrumental in establishing a strong sense of place overlooked in the more popular narratives, and the embrace of local color can be read as an analog to the more widely known regionalism emerging in late nineteenth-century American literature. However, whereas American regionalists such as Mark Twain and Kate Chopin focused on establishing a sense of place alongside narrative and character, the dialect poets' emphasis was primarily on the place itself, signaling the intimate link between language and landscape. Standing in contrast to the work of established late Victorian writers or sensationalist literature aimed at mass consumption, dialect literature reflects a kind of literature produced by and for the regions it represents—one that signals the importance of place and community as components of class consciousness.

Furthermore, Elizabeth Carolyn Miller has noted how the late Victorian period saw a rise in radical publishing as a direct counter to mass publishing, starting in the 1880s with socialist papers such as *Commonweal* and *Justice* serving as vehicles for serialized novels from writers like George Bernard Shaw and Edward Carpenter.[4] Analogous to the emergence of Finnish working-class publishing as outlined by Elsi Hyttinen and Kati Launis in this collection, the imperative was largely the same: the sustenance of alternative media currents designed to counter mass-market and more established forms of literary production.[5] The kind of novels associated with this movement, Miller points out, reflects the Chartist struggle of incorporating social messaging within popular narratives and motifs. In particular, Miller notes how novels, such as Clementina Black's *An Agitator* (1894), "collapse[s] under the weight of the bourgeois marriage plot or the novel of individual development" (2010, p. 707). Other novels of the time, Miller suggests, show signs of exploited revolutionary narratives as a spectacle by which to sell papers (2010, p. 708)—a gesture that signals the potential commodification of class identity that will form a contentious thread throughout twentieth-century working-class literature. Although the late nineteenth century can be seen as a convoluted time in terms of publishing working-class writing, the period points to the persistence of paradoxes associated with working-class literature: the disharmony of realistic representation in relation to the desire for the spectacular; the burgeoning potential to commodify and sensationalize class identity; and the irresolute parallel trajectory of aesthetic and political objectives. Whereas the early nineteenth century saw the emergence of class forms, class consciousness, and the evolution of the novel itself, the late-nineteenth century can be viewed as a time in which tropes synonymous with British working-class literature gain traction.

## Twentieth-Century Literature: Evolution and Refinement

It was the twentieth century, however, that saw the consolidation of nineteenth-century motifs into what would become known as proletariat literature. Yet due to the impact of both wars and the collapse of imperialism that followed, working-class writing continued to evolve, coming to full fruition in the late 1950s following a period in which engineered nationalism took center stage. This nationalism echoed a utopian idealism, in which conceptions of class difference established in the nineteenth century were softened in an attempt to bolster national spirits. This was accomplished, in part, through the increased commercialization of music hall writing that emerged at the end of the Victorian period. Although music hall writing veers away from more traditional literary forms, the genre serves as a key component in understanding the development of British working-class writing in that it builds on the dialect literature of the Victorian era by commercializing parochial voices and projecting them onto a national stage. The egalitarian and somewhat utopian nature of the music hall resulted in a space in which working-class values were momentarily integrated with the values of the ruling class, resulting in a temporary haven from class discrimination and difference. Music halls amplified the voice of working-class writers who would otherwise have been limited to smaller, regional audiences. And early music hall writers, such as Thomas Hudson (a grocer), John Labern (a newspaper shop owner), and Sam Collins (a chimney sweep), often doubled as performers themselves, penetrating class barriers and advancing working-class attributes for national discourse largely through a musical format that helped distract audiences from the class-specific concerns of the lyrical content. According to Richard Anthony Baker, Queen Victoria herself was reported to have shown appreciation for the melody of a military band's rendition of "Come Where the Booze is Cheaper," oblivious to the working-class sentiment of the lyrics (2014, p. 76).

However, the popularity and spread of music hall writing also positioned it as a vehicle for the broadcasting of war propaganda.[6] In this regard, it is possible to see the way working-class characteristics can be capitalized on, not just for commercial gain but for pernicious nationalism through the cooptation of class identity. Music hall performances were used to glamorize military service—especially in the years leading up to World War I—as an attempt to form a patriotic consensus. The writing of music hall content became an increasingly lucrative venture as popularity continued to boom with writers offering to "add 'a war verse' to any given song for a small fee" (Mullen, 2016, p. 153). Despite the music hall's reliance on contemporary issues, dissenting lyrics were initially kept from entering into performances but became more prominent following the war, suggesting how a genre can be reclaimed in light of commodification. The decline of the music hall during the interwar years is generally linked to the rise of cinema and the emergence of radio, but it was not until the 1950s that John Osborne offered last rites to music hall culture in his 1957 play *The Entertainer*. What this unique genre underscores is the way that regional working-class aesthetics can be seized upon and mobilized by forces external to the classes that they represent. This has significant bearing on representations of working-class people to this day and reveals the risk of systematizing class representation in a manner that can exploited for gain.

Despite the cooptation of working-class identities through music hall writing, literary representation of working-class people continued to develop in novels in a way that sustained tension between literary aesthetics and political objectives. Following writers like Thomas Hardy, whose realistic character depiction stemmed from his own lived experience, new connections between the aesthetic and the political were attempted by writers such as D.H. Lawrence, whose 1928 novel *Lady Chatterly's Lover* brought about tangible social change. *Lady Chatterly's Lover* paved the way for the inclusion of frank, taboo subject matter that would form a central motif of postwar literature. Lawrence's representations of working-class people were grounded in his own experience growing up in a working-class community in Nottingham and laboring in a factory as a clerk. However, then-contemporary critics like Christopher Caudwell aligned Lawrence with the artistic elite, due to the high-minded nature of his writing. This alignment rendered his representation of working-class people as suspect. Lawrence's use of taboo topics—especially surrounding the inter-class relations of *Lady Chatterly's Lover*—suggests a predilection to Victorian sensationalism but also reveals the complex role of gritty topics in fictional and aesthetic representations of the working-class.

Several important novels emerged during this time, however, that veered more toward the political than the aesthetic. Populist texts, such as Robert Tressell's *The Ragged-Trousered Philanthropists* (1914), found a more general readership due to a grounded use of language, yet their fidelity to the social elevation of working-class people was still questioned. Despite a slew of geographical inaccuracies and the elision of key historical events, Tressell's novel represented the broad cultural moment; and in contrast to writers like Lawrence, it reflected working-class solidarity through its depiction of shared struggle over modernist interiority and individualism. The enduring popularity of Tressell's text can be aligned to the common reader's ability to identify with the narrative in a manner that sets the aesthetic aspirations of Lawrence into stark relief. Other writers of the time, such as Harold Heslop and Henry Green, produced works that vacillated between pointed social critique and modernist experimentation. Heslop's *The Gate of a Strange Field* (1928) recounts the events of the 1926 General Strike, placing the author at the vanguard of inter-war working-class writing. As Charles Ferrall and Dougal McNeill have noted, Heslop envisioned a working-class literary revolution, declaring in 1930 at the Second Conference of Proletarian and Revolutionary Writers that texts such as his own faced an uphill struggle from editors and publishing houses which sought to attenuate revolutionary messaging (2015, p. 148). Green's *Living* (1929) can be seen as a precursor to the factory novels of the late 1950s, employing strong regional dialects to represent Birmingham factory workers to the degree that the syntax itself reflected modernist experimentation. In contrast to Tressell, though, Green's novels were not well received by the general public, selling comparatively few copies even after receiving inordinate praise from W.H. Auden and Anthony Burgess. Despite attempts by writers such as Heslop and others to authenticate a proletarian literature, the tension between competing aesthetic and political objectives kept the movement from gaining necessary traction. It was Walter Greenwood's 1933 novel, *Love on the Dole*, that brought such objectives together most saliently, seeing large commercial success through its combination of authenticity and objective realism. Furthermore, Greenwood himself declared working-class allegiance as the son of radical working-class parents. Yet, as with Lawrence at the time, critics still questioned Greenwood's dedication to a working-class audience, noting how the novel's descriptions of classed environments were written to be understood by readers who would not be familiar with such spaces (Hentea, 2014, p. 47).

While Stephen Constantine has argued that Greenwood's text was partly responsible for shifting attitudes toward working-class people and working-class conditions (1982, p. 232), the rise of the modern welfare state illuminated the plight of the working class in a manner never before seen in British history. Katrina Clark, in this volume, draws attention to the "proletarianization" of Soviet Communism following the launch of the First Five Year Plan in 1928, noting how white-collar representatives were replaced by blue-collar workers. The impact on Russian literature was a dethroning of the professional author, charging working people to produce their own stories based on their own experiences in the factory. Although no such role reversals took place in British culture, a "proletarianization" effect can be discerned in the rise of the welfare state and the elevation of working-class problems to that of a national concern. The 1942 Beveridge Report took stock of the country's national health in the midst of war, calling for nation-wide sacrifices to elevate social conditions of the working classes, as well as those most directly impacted by the Blitz. Hugely popular, the report led to dramatic renovations in terms of public health, housing, and education, raising awareness to the severity of class-specific problems. The result was that, during the austerity period following the Second World War, a shared sense of desperation emerged in which previously overlooked class concerns were foregrounded in people's minds. This period, it might be said, cleared the territory for the avalanche of working-class writing that followed.

But whereas Magnus Nilsson has noted how the interwar years represented the golden age for Swedish working-class literature due to the emergence of a specifically proletarian bildungsroman (see Nilsson in this collection), British working-class fiction of the same period lacked such aesthetic unity, emphasizing again the divide between form and function. However, the postwar years saw a culmination of working-class motifs united behind a concerted effort to move realism closer to the real. During the Second World War and the austerity period that followed, a discernible slump in realist depiction can be acknowledged and attributed to the modernist emphasis on experimentation. Additionally, the depictions of wretched lives were less salable as wretched realities washed over the country. Stuart Laing has noted how the decline in realist representation of working-class people can also be attributed to the closure of resources such as *The Left Book Club* (1948) and *Penguin New Writing* (1950)—venues that promoted topical, class-conscious texts (1986, p. 60). Consequently, the arrival of John Osborne's 1956 play *Look Back in Anger* caused pandemonium in the arts, closely followed by John Braine's novel *Room at the Top* (1957), Alan Sillitoe's *Saturday Night and Sunday Morning* (1958), and Shelagh Delaney's play *A Taste of Honey* (1958). These texts were grouped under the erroneous appellation of the "Angry Young Men," but the more appropriate descriptor is kitchen sink realism— a simultaneous challenge to and revitalization of traditional realism through the elevation of working-class authenticity via documentary-style representations of class.

The "Angry Young Man" label stems from a Royal Court Theatre press release characterizing the nature of John Osborne's most notorious protagonist. Indeed, Jimmy Porter—the play's central character—reflects an archetype that, alongside Sillitoe's Arthur Seaton, has situated him as a working-class cultural icon. Jim Dixon, the hapless protagonist of Kingsley Amis's *Lucky Jim* (1954) is often viewed as the original "Angry," but it was not until Osborne's play was released that critics looked back on *Lucky Jim* to view it within the context established by the kitchen sink movement. Amis's text certainly demonstrates aspects of the characteristic alienation expressed in the work of later "Angry" writers, but the similarity stops there. In fact, it can be argued that Keith Waterhouse's *Billy Liar* (1959) acts as a corrective by taking aspects of Jim Dixon and decanting him into a more suitable working-class context. The "Angry" texts mark a notable shift in working-class representation in that many of the characters demonstrate a distinct individual autonomy that suggests a disarticulation of the notion of class solidarity. Katrina Clark outlines a similar motif in her discussion of Soviet social realist novels of the 1930s—a genre that, while distinct from the kitchen sink movement in several ways, draws a number of allegiances—arguing that, if a working-class hero exists, it is one characterized by self-governance: "a new working-class intelligenstia to supplant the rotten old one" (see Clark in this collection). Texts such as *Saturday Night and Sunday Morning* and *A Taste of Honey* provide clear-cut examples of working-class individuals renegotiating their class identity, in the same way that Colin Wilson's nonfiction work, *The Outsider* (1956) anticipates an emergent subculture and provides a theoretical framework for the "Angry" movement. For Sillitoe's Seaton, the dilemma is whether to rebel against social morays or to acquiesce and accept his designated status as a laborer like his father. Shelagh Delaney's Jo, however, is a character who (perhaps naively) refuses her social assignation and renegotiates her identity on her own terms. Whereas Eliot, Hardy, and others emphasized the importance of the individual within class confines, the "Angry" authors shift the focus toward individuals who potentially reject their assigned status. This shift signals a fracture in monolithic class identity and ushers in a new mode of class-consciousness that, while based in anxiety and despair, carries forth an optimistic charge.

Furthermore, the texts of this period take representation to new levels. On the one hand, the degree of gritty depictions associated with kitchen sink realism can be read as an aesthetic endeavor akin to Victorian spectacularization—a way to shock audiences of the time with candid representations of working-class lives rarely seen in the arts. On the other, a social function can be ascertained in that the writers of the time, comprehending the aesthetic limits of realism, pushed literature toward a more complete and accurate representation of British culture—one in which working-class people from northern industrial areas were shown to have a culture of their own. Eugenio Di Stefano's discussion of the testimonio in 1960s South American literature draws striking parallels to the "Angry" authors in that both movements champion the role of subaltern voices within literary culture. According to Di Stefano, Testimonio is characterized by "simple, straightforward narratives" with rhetorical ethos operating "as an urgent call to mitigate a political injustice" (see Di Stefano in this collection). While the writers associated with kitchen sink realism certainly subscribe to motifs of local color and tend to rely upon archetypes, their focus is less of a direct response to injustice as it is a broad frustration to the welfare state's failure to eradicate the class concerns that the Beveridge Report sought to address. Much of the work produced during this time is deeply testimonial with writers such as Sillitoe and Delaney recreating the worlds in which they themselves were raised, lending the texts heightened legitimacy and speaking more directly to a working-class audience familiar with such environments. While nonfiction texts like George Orwell's *The Road to Wigan Pier* (1937) and Richard Hoggart's seminal *The Uses of Literacy* (1957) rely on the same kind of ethos central to the testimonio and the "Angry" text, both reveal a degree of sepia-tinged nostalgia more commonly associated with conventional representation. The texts of the kitchen sink realism movement largely sidestep nostalgia by presenting lived experience and the struggles unique to working-class people in a notably matter-of-fact way. Given this, the period in which Britain moved from postwar austerity to postwar affluence marks perhaps the most defined and forceful example of a unified proletarian literature to date.

Having said that, the kitchen sink era and the approaches its writers favored are not without their inconsistencies. As a relatively brief moment in cultural history, combined with the youthful antagonism of the movement, the period reads as electrified but with frayed wiring. It would be a stretch to suggest that kitchen sink realism offered a cohesive philosophy as (aside from *Declaration*— a 1957 collection of essays penned by prominent figures of the movement) no singular manifesto or galvanized approach can be identified. Furthermore, despite the genuine class-based challenges faced by several of the movement's key figures, some were quick to distance themselves from their origins while keeping working-class culture central to their narratives. To suggest such a move as a betrayal to cultural origins would be unwise, but it does underscore once more the commercial viability of working-class representations and the ease by which such representations can be mobilized for aesthetic rather than political gain. Ironically, it was socially elevated writers such as Colin MacInnes who offered some of the most consistently vital and authentic depictions of working-class life during and after this time in *The London Novels* (1957–1960). MacInnes bridged on-the-ground journalism with narrative storytelling and surveyed the impact of urban gentrification on working-class people prior to the term entering into the lexicon. Similarly, E.R. Braithwaite's autobiographical *To Sir, with Love* (1959) offers a rare perspective on class and race by contrasting postwar London with colonial cultures. Braithwaite's novel stands out because of its depiction of a highly educated Guyanese immigrant helping underserved white working-class young men. This depiction underscores the complex intersections of race and class in Britain at the time. Despite such disparities between aesthetic and political objectives, the kitchen sink movement can be seen as a vector of past working-class literary tropes: the emphasis on gritty, visceral representation; the unflinching use of taboo subject material; the paradox of the individual within the collective; and personal testimony channeled as artistic and class-based insurrection.

To provide a comprehensive overview of the years that followed the kitchen sink movement is beyond the purview of this chapter, but the movement can be understood as a watershed—one whose impact can be felt throughout the five decades that followed across multiple media forms. The endurance of gritty television soap operas like Tony Warren's *Coronation Street* (1960-) and the emergence of the British New Wave film movement based upon adaptations of kitchen sink texts helped to cement the profound impact of the movement beyond its chronological parentheses. Comprehensive links can be drawn between the popular *Wednesday Play* series (1964–1970) and the emergence of Channel 4 television (1982) and its accompanying films—many of which were structured upon the work of the kitchen sink authors and relied upon the genre tropes codified during the period. Televised adaptations of novels like Nell Dunn's 1963 *Up the Junction* for the BBC (1965) had direct impact on British life, such as foregrounding conversations around illicit abortions that led to the legalization of the procedure in 1967. The culmination of tropes galvanized during the 1950s and 1960s served literature well in terms of its efficacy to represent working-class culture as it was experienced. And whereas Magnus Nilsson in this collection registers a decline in Swedish working-class literature of the 1980s and 1990s, the Thatcher years in Britain saw an increase in working-class representation to oppose the political expediency of deindustrialization and neoliberalism by narrativizing its impact on communities in detail. Texts like Pat Barker's *Union Street* (1982) responded to the ensuing poverty of northern industrial regions stripped of their livelihood, whereas *The Century's Daughter* (1986) launched a thinly veiled attack on Tory policies. Work by James Kelman and Irvine Welsh followed a similar trajectory of raising working-class grit to the foreground as a response to the kind of political rhetoric of the time, in which the inhabitants of working-class communities decimated by deindustrialization were belittled for relying on social security nets established in the postwar years. The anger and social frustration expressed through the working-class literature of the 1950s and 1960s provided a working model for the 1980s and 1990s. It could not be more appropriate for today's world.

Furthermore, the rise in working-class representation of the 1980s is fraught with racial tension as, following Conservative MP Enoch Powell's rabid "Rivers of Blood" speech in April of 1968, working-class identities were mobilized as part of a nationalist effort to maintain a traditional English heritage through the reduction and reversal of immigration. Powell's contention was that prior waves of immigration posed an impending threat to British culture, responsible, he claimed, for an increase in violent crime in urban centers. In the words of Paul Gilroy, Powell's stance on immigration policy and his vocal opposition to the 1965 Race Relations Act—legislation that outlawed discrimination on the grounds of ethnicity and race—made claims that it "assists in the process of making Britain great again" in that it "restores an ethnic symmetry to a world distorted by imperial adventure and migration" (1992, p. 46). Powell's populist rhetoric aimed to link British working-class culture to nationalist concerns, suggesting that issues, such as unemployment, were the fault of non-white immigrants—the implications of which led to a series of hate crimes carried out amidst chants of the MP's surname. These claims found a surprising surge of support from white dock workers, miners, and laborers, who, according to Camilla Schofield, lacked the critical capacity to recognize their own manipulation by false rhetoric and narratives of disenfranchisement (2013, p. 241). As Gilroy adds, it was not until the 1980s that many of these working-class supporters came to realize their role as political pawns and that, in terms of policy, they were viewed no differently from the racialized Other that Powell's speech scapegoated (1992, p. 34). Following the speech, Powell was promptly relieved from his position by then-party leader Edward Heath and his rhetoric widely condemned by his peers. Although Margaret Thatcher, the MP for the North London region of Finchley at the time, admitted that parts of Powell's speech were provocative, Powell's influence is perceptible through her subsequent politics of disenfranchisement, deindustrialization, and an emphasis on nationalism and retrograde cultural nostalgia masquerading as heritage. In response, the 1980s saw a rise in multicultural and ethnic writing that complicated notions of British working-class cultural identities while commenting on Thatcher's neoliberal ideals of wealth acquisition, entrepreneurship, and forceful push toward individual responsibility under the guise of union busting and the dismantling of the welfare state. Screenplays such as Hanif Kureishi's *My Beautiful Laundrette* (1985) emphasized such incongruous ideals by placing cultural hybridity and community in conversation with seemingly irreconcilable notions of Randian libertarianism. Adapted as an award-winning and highly successful film by Stephen Frears, Kureishi's text reveals the inherent conflict of a proposed cultural identity that looks backwards while attempting to move ahead— one that underscores Thatcher's vision for British culture.

Nevertheless, British working-class literature at the turn of the twenty-first century suggests adjustments to the formula established in the 1950s, specifically through the amplification of past literary devices to a level that borders on hyperbole by moving representation from documentary-style realism to a state of exaggerated shock. One result from such a move is that the dividing line between drama and comedy becomes increasingly blurred in alignment with what has been termed as the New Sincerity and Post-Ironic movements. Additionally, the use of taboo subject material becomes so egregious that identification and schadenfreude are simultaneously engaged, depending on the reader's social position. In other words, twenty-first-century working-class writing retreats from realism, moving instead into the realm of caricature seen in nineteenth-century novels. This shift is motivated, it seems, by the commercial imperatives of overdetermined appeal. The fact that Paul Abbott's Channel 4 series *Shameless* (2004–2013) won acclaim for both comedy and drama underscores the notion that the viewers' social positions dictate how the show is received: For working-class people, the world it depicts is grimly familiar; for others, the show is something else entirely. Twenty-first-century texts continue to favor gritty representations but now on a higher scale, resulting in working-class writing that pushes the envelope in terms of narrative shock value. Theater critic Aleks Sierz has discussed the rise of what he terms "In-Yer-Face Theatre,"or the kind of writing that "grabs the audience by the scruff of the neck and shakes it until it gets the message" (2001, p. 4). Writers like Sarah Kane and Mark Ravenhill produced work that merged aspects of the edgier kitchen sink drama of the 1960s such as Edward Bond's *Saved* (1965) with Artaud's *Theatre of Cruelty* through an amplification of sadistic sex, gratuitous violence, coarse dialog, and an undermining of narrative conventions—a post-ironic take on working-class literature of the past. While shock aesthetics are clearly at the heart of such representation—most pronounced in the commercial success of shows like *Shameless* or *Skins*, both of which saw phenomenal ratings and adaptations for international markets—the political aspirations of such extreme representation is considerably more opaque.

Similarly, Richard Milward's novel *Apples* (2007) tells the story of young people on a North Yorkshire housing estate in which class stereotypes run amok. Largely narrated in first-person by two teenagers, the depiction of classed space and class crisis is intensified to levels that border on parody. The fact that Milward's text emerged around the same period as *Shameless* and followed much of the same narrative logic, underscores the commercial appeal of gritty class-based representation that treads a fine line between depiction and cultural tourism. In the novel, Adam's domestic abuse at the hands of his father is presented in a manner that is both horrifying and darkly humorous, often within the same sentence. Eve's drug abuse and promiscuity dispenses vicarious thrills to the reader but in a manner that is just as troubling as Adam's harm. Poignantly, these depictions are emblematic of very real social problems that still plague parts of the country affected by the deindustrialization of the 1980s. The degree by which comedy masks tragedy and vice versa is therefore rendered unclear. But the text characterizes a contemporary approach to representations of class that are aggressive and relentless in their grittiness, supplementing the lived-monotony of kitchen sink realism with a latent, disturbing brutality. On the one hand, it may appear that the barrage of aesthetic grit thrown into the realist machine in twenty-first-century British working-class writing appears as a purely commercial and soulless endeavor—one that either undermines realist representation or amplifies it to the level of simulacra, fully disengaged from the reality it portrays and devoid of any political objective. On the other hand, it reveals a critical component consistent across British working-class writing: the dynamic nature of representation that responds to both aesthetic and cultural shifts within the contextual moment. Given this, British working-class cultural production, by embracing tension between aesthetic and political objectives, maintains homeostatic flux that is critical to its longevity. To return to Peter Hitchcock's claim that working-class representation cannot be reducible to a series of material signifiers due to the fact that class is experienced as shifting social relations (2000, p. 23), the continual renovation of and resistance to a galvanized formal aesthetics reflects such a claim.

## Persistent Paradox and the Dynamic Tensions of Working-Class Writing

Paradox and indeterminism, then, can be considered as characteristics threaded throughout the lineage of British working-class writing, emblematic of the kind of questions of authenticity that have plagued critical responses to working-class literature and, more significantly, underscoring the genre's capacity to adapt to cultural and aesthetic shifts in real time. Gauging the interplay between the form and the function of British working-class literature begins with an understanding of how such texts were received by the British public and the demands placed on cultural production. Chartist writing, for example, was aimed at a general audience in the hopes of enacting social change. Nonetheless, its success was hampered by the writers' inability to make largely didactic texts work within the framework of popular literary conventions. As Edmund Richardson has noted, Chartist writing was viewed as anachronistic in that reformist movements relied upon retrograde motifs in which "looking back to antiquity became a way to argue passionately for contemporary change" (2015, p. 118). Classical themes were presumed to add literary gravitas, but references to the ancient world were too outmoded to be taken seriously by readers of contemporary fiction. In this regard, the Chartists' failure to reconcile dual objectives implies a technical shortcoming— permissible given that the majority of the Chartist authors were not fiction writers at all. But in the context of working-class literature that followed, such early attempts at the reconciliation of form and function can perhaps be read as the catalyst of a productive tension inherent within working-class writing today.

Advances in publishing allowed for the expansion of print media to Victorian audiences, and many of the texts of the time were written with a wide readership in mind that bridged age, class, and gender. Although the novel as a format was still under construction during the Romantic period, innovations in distribution awarded Victorians wide access to texts. Novels, such as those penned by Dickens and Eliot, were popularized through serialization—a process that not only sustained readers' attentions over time but also reduced production cost. The result was increased access for middle- and working-class audiences. Consequently, the most commercial novels of the period often functioned as spectacles aimed at mass consumption, and in order to produce the spectacular effect, authentic depictions of class were sidelined in lieu of narrative structure and technical effects.

As a result, representations of working-class people in popular Victorian novels were rarely more than two-dimensional foils— props against which to establish more centralized characters. Positioning working-class characters in such a manner allowed the focus to remain on the spectacular form of the plot but lessened representational authenticity, limiting the text's function to produce tangible social effects.

The upshot of working-class audiences' appetite for sensational representation was addressed by Richard Hoggart who argued that consumption of commercial fiction resulted a "massifying" effect, or one that worked against the interests of working-class people by rendering them docile. Although attempts to counteract passive consumption of popular novels can be discerned throughout the working-class literature of the Victorian period, aesthetic form dominated over social function. And it was not until the kitchen sink movement that function was somewhat reconciled in texts where characters, scenarios, and problems directly reflected working-class lived experience. While it should be noted that several kitchen sink writers deployed social positioning to further their own aesthetic agenda, Kenneth Tynan's praise of John Osborne's infamous protagonist is telling:

> The salient thing about Jimmy Porter was that we—the under-thirty generation in Britain—recognised him on sight. We had met him; we had pub-crawled with him; we had shared bed-sitting-rooms with him. For the first time the theatre was speaking to us in our own language, on our own terms" (Lichtenstein and Schregenberger, 2006, p. 284).

In their ability to connect with working-class people in a meaningful manner, postwar working-class texts restored equilibrium between aesthetic and political objectives through their capacity to exist alongside conventionally established literary forms while short-circuiting the massifying effect of popular media. This was accomplished by foregrounding working-class lives in a manner that reflected the new visibility of the underclass in the age of the modern welfare state. Whereas the readership of the past—which included working-class people—welcomed working-class caricature as part and parcel of dominant literary trends, mid-twentieth-century literature signified an alignment of mimetic representation to then-current cultural concerns.

Yet the degree by which postwar working-class writers were motivated to diversify cultural representation in relation to their desire to undermine literary and theatrical conventions is rendered somewhat opaque, underscoring the productive tension of aesthetic and political objectives. Postwar writers were not simply writing for a marginalized audience as an altruistic venture; their aesthetic was equally grounded in artistic disobedience and a lucrative rebellion that put them on the literary map. Given the striking influence of mid-century cultural production on today's representations of the working-class, it is crucial to acknowledge the ease by which working-class grit can be packaged as a salable identity. This is especially significant given the way class-based narratives of the post-Thatcher years tend to amplify such representations as part of their enduring popularity. In this sense, the tension engaged between aesthetic and political objectives reads less as an effort to assuage discord and more as a strategic attempt at maximizing audience reception through broad appeal. Having said that, the texts of the 1950s and 1960s also laid the groundwork for important youth subcultural movements, so the upshot of enlarging target audiences through overdetermination is as much a gesture of ethics and social function as it is a gesture of commercial or aesthetic aggrandizement. A working-class text conveys significance in different ways depending on the social position of the reader. Consequently, the tension between aesthetic and political objectives can be read as less of an attempt at unification; instead, it functions more as a complication—a suspension that undermines, usurps, and revamps established literary norms and expectations throughout the evolution of working-class literature. Ultimately, what this suggests is that an intentional vacillation between form and function can be read as a persistent trope which responds to trends in both in society and the arts but also responds to trends in readership as well.

In addition to the effect of supply and demand, themes and motifs common to the genre also reflect historical contingency, underscoring British working-class literature's reluctance to be reduced to a set of formal components. As noted prior, working-class writing mirrors aesthetic techniques perceptible in other literary forms. However, the genre tends to politicize such techniques in order to increase their social function—a move recognizable in the use of taboo subject matter. When aesthetic motifs of formally established styles are adopted, they are often augmented for increased impact, either by revealing the limits of the original motif or reemphasizing its social dimensions. Such manipulation of motifs can be read as an opportunity to enrich prior literary techniques, while sustaining the tension between aesthetic and political objectives. Whereas Katrina Clark notes how Soviet writer Maxim Gorky sought to develop working-class writerly voices in opposition to established literary norms (see Clark in this collection), British working-class writing tends to work within established norms, updating rather than usurping them. For example, whereas realism of the past might skimp on working-class characterization for the sake of the plot, twentieth-century working-class texts grant extra dimension to working-class characters at the plot's expense, often by importing present-day social issues into their characters' psychological makeup. In this regard, working-class literature decouples from traditional realism through pointed, radical class advocacy. Its representations are more like insertions than repudiations, suggesting that the objective is not to redefine literary modes but to mobilize them more effectively.[7]

However, it is the postwar period that also reveals the paradox between the use of taboo topics to draw attention to social concerns and the potential to commodify such concerns for aesthetic elevation. Arguably, the writers associated with kitchen sink realism benefited from subject material that both challenged conventional morality and questioned the capacity of conventional morality to account for the lives of the entire populace. As virtually every film that emerged from the kitchen sink movement received a contemporary X rating—and many of the novels that they were based upon fell under similar scrutiny—the fine line between authentic representation of working-class issues and the exploitation of taboo as a marketable motif was rendered less clear. The 1959 trial of D.H. Lawrence's *Lady Chatterley's Lover* played a critical role in the loosening of publishing restraints, granting writers greater leniency in relation to content. Furthermore, Richard Hoggart, testifying in the Lawrence trial, noted how the perceived shock of the novel was abrogated once the reader accepted the fact that the shock emanated not from the coarse language of the working-class characters, but from the mere existence of working-class characters within bourgeois environments. The shock effect was less the result of the text itself, and more the result of residual Victorian values that persisted well into the twentieth century. Given this, it is possible to see how the use of not just taboo topics but of vivid depictions of working-class life could act as marketable lure for upcoming writers looking to make a cultural impact. Discerning whether such motifs were deployed to raise social awareness of the dire conditions of working-class realities, to provide a more accurate overview of the British populace in the arts, or to simply shock audiences in a manner that echoed Victorian sensationalism, is rendered equivocal through the kind of paradoxical tensions permeating working-class literary aesthetics.

Yet the most recognizable trope associated with the form— realism—reveals a critique of literary techniques that pushes realism further than ever before. Benjamin Balthaser, in this collection, offers a strong argument against the conflation of realism with working-class literature by raising the question of form and function. Citing Georg Lukacs, Balthaser posits that class emancipation through writing should stem from literary secession— a clean break in which a uniquely subjective working-class voice can emerge distinct from established traditions (see Balthaser in this collection). While such concerns are apt—that a proletariat writerly voice might be compromised were it to emerge from within a bourgeois framework—the argument parallels the distinction between subculture and counterculture. Whereas counterculture operates in direct opposition to established norms, subculture emerges from within, carrying the potential to manipulate the dominant culture in the process. Much of the British working-class literature of the mid-twentieth century both anticipated and shaped radical subcultural developments that began in the 1960s with the rise of youth subculture. Having said that, advances made in British working-class literature also serve to reveal the limits of realism in its capacity to push literary representation beyond the realm of aesthetic effect and into the realm of direct social usage.

While realism's capacity to capture the real has long been contested, it might be said that gradations of verisimilitude exist, allowing for a rethinking of cultural fiction as indices of potential sociological data. Such gradations are based upon relative proximity to the real that raises questions as to whether ethnographic narratives like Hoggart's *The Uses of Literacy* are any closer to the real than works of fiction produced by authors with first-hand lived experience. [8] In his brief study of verisimilitude in crime fiction, Tsvetan Todorov argues that written language can never attain the real as it will always be subjected to a subordinate referent, be it the "truth" of genre confines, public consensus of opinion, or verisimilitude's own rhetorical aim to sustain a mask of truth. In other words, language can depict authentically (realist fiction, for example), and can recount factual data (the lived struggles of working-class people, for example), but it is always subservient to the internal, autonomous laws of the medium. However, as Todorov reminds us, his own treatise of verisimilitude is not immune to this kind of interpellation. It holds allegiance first and foremost to the established confines of academic discourse, yet his "sentences participate in a different, a higher verisimilitude, and in that they resemble the truth" (1977, p. 88). [9] In this regard, Balthaser's call for literary secession could result in a literature that is still subjected to rules of language and usage, never fully escaping the ideological influence of dominant culture or established literary conventions. Similarly, Peter Hitchcock considers the tension between political and cultural representation to be "a theoretical knot for literary criticism," warning steadfastly against the conflation of representation and culture (2000, p. 22). While working-class literature does not untangle this theoretical knot per se, its awareness of realism's limits—and its desire to push against those limits as a bourgeois construction to be challenged—does suggest that concerns of realism's efficacy are still up for discussion and that the genre has the capacity to advance realist motifs further.

In agreement with Hoggart's concern over romanticized depictions of class (as well as the commercial viability of exploiting class identity), Tony Davies has noted how realist depictions in pre- and inter-war fiction have "often taken the form of a sentimental populism which seeks to conscript a radically simplified and un-historical conception of the working class" (1984, p. 126). Davies adds that, like realism, representations of working-class people are still demonstrations of "an aesthetic *ideology* with a specific history and discourse" (p. 126). Obviously, this claim mirrors the ideological snare of verisimilitude sketched by Todorov, but Davies suggests that postwar representations of the working-class discard the sentimentality of the past to develop more visceral, graphic approaches while embracing the kind of "them and us" vexations of distrust outlined in Hoggart as recurring themes (1984, p. 126). For Davies, the prominence of characteristically gritty subject matter reflects "a more authentic tradition of prole-tarian realism: a profound suspicion of bourgeois ideologies and processes, particularly those that aspire to 'represent' the working class and its interests" (1984, p. 127). Davies clarifies that he is not seeking to conflate fact, fiction, and stereotypes, but rather to illuminate points of intersection that grant cultural fiction extra-literary worth, noting provocatively that

> There is nothing at all to be gained from observing the academic protocol that questions of literary genre and tradition are one thing, those of political history and understanding another, and that they should have as little to do with one another as possible. The problem is rather to grasp both the *difference* and the insep-arable through shifting kinds of *relatedness* between the terms; not in order to construct another 'theory of realism', but in an attempt to understand how and why a set of meanings mobilized by key words has become, historically, the locus of important and still unfinished transactions in the fields of culture and politics: in political culture, in cultural politics (1984, p. 127).

For Davies, characterizations of the working-class in postwar British fiction reflect less of a romanticized archetype in that fiction and lived experience become increasingly intertwined through the merging of social realism (a formal style) with *socialist* realism. This ideology coincides with the socialist imperatives underway in the development of the welfare state (1984, p. 131). Furthermore, the collaborative nature of the movement conveys an unusually high dedication to fidelity with documentary filmmakers, such as

Tony Richardson, Karel Reisz, and Lindsay Anderson directing adaptations of the realist theatre of John Osborne and Shelagh Delaney while working with novelists like Alan Sillitoe and screenwriters such as Harold Pinter to produce films designed to be "more relevant than those made in the popular national cinema" (Dancyger, 2014, p. 138). Although delineations do exist, there is an unmistakable impression of alliance during this period aimed at the intensification of realism and elevating verisimilitude to a level never before seen in British culture—one that is sustained through homeostatic tension. Therefore, if realism can be said to function on the sliding scale that Todorov conjectures, it would be at this particular moment that *gritty representation* in cultural fiction would parallel the *representationally gritty* ethnographic nonfiction approaches, such as that of Hoggart.

So, consistent from the Chartists to the present time is the question of intent: Is British working-class literature an aesthetic endeavor with self-aggrandizement in mind, or do working-class texts aim to engender social change through pointed social critique? What this survey hopes to have acknowledged is that, at any given moment, working-class literature reveals oppositional tracks that intertwine but rarely cohere. Therefore, as Sherry Linkon has noted of American working-class literature, such texts often require an effort to parse form and function, with Linkon adding how scholars of working-class texts should focus on "describing the qualities of working-class literary texts, rather than policing boundaries that define who has the authority to write them" (2010, n.p.).

However, as with concerns over the efficacy of literary realism, debates over the spiky topic of authority and legitimacy are difficult to jettison entirely. Citing architectural historian Luis E. Carranza, Eugenio Di Stefano reminds us in this volume that both formal experimentation and social function are inherently political, and Benjamin Balthaser outlines, in his essay, the negative impact of white authors representing ethnic minorities through the subsequent "racial dis-identification" observable in work by writers of color in the 1930s. Whereas it is widely accepted in critical studies of literature that non-working-class writers can represent working-class people and their attendant concerns with fidelity, such a claim does not hold so readily in terms of other social classifications, such as race or gender. Instead, concerns surrounding legitimacy reflect distinctions still made today between social classifications that clearly signify (such as race and gender) and classifications that do not (such as social stratification). Having said that, Linkon's point—that questions of authenticity should avoid rigid judgment—is well taken in terms of British working-class literature, especially during the Victorian era in which bourgeois writers' tendencies to stereotype working-class people are complicated by their genuine desire to enact progressive social change. In the twentieth century, this is complicated even further by "authentically" working-class writers who, in using their experience to further their own thematics, are granted social ascendency.[10] My point here is not to resuscitate settled debates surrounding legitimacy in the study of working-class literature, but to suggest that such concerns can be read as *productive dynamics unique to the genre.*

## Conclusion: The Direction of British Working-Class Literature

In British society today, class is as politically charged a topic as ever. Although class boundaries are less stable than at the point of their formation, the capacity of literature to both critique and imagine future expressions of class consciousness is hard to ignore. Renewed interest in class-conscious independent presses and the arrival of collectives, such as the Northern Fiction Alliance, echo the heterodox publications of the Chartist movement, as well as the rise of the radical press at the turn of the twentieth century. This development suggests that continued efforts to present voices at the margins of established literary circuits are critical to class representation. While working-class imagery has become increasingly commodified as of late alongside the fetishization of Otherness, nontraditional voices and outlets endeavor to maintain homeostatic balance and prevent the total commodification of cultural histories and regional character. For example, in the wake of Brexit, novelist and essayist Nikesh Shukla suggested a collection from multiethnic working-class writers that was quickly crowd-funded for release through Dead Ink Press with Dead Ink director, Nathan Connolly, aiming for an anthology that "disproves myths and allows writers to challenge preconceptions about what it is like to be thought of as working class in twenty-first-century Britain" (Onwuemezi, 2016, n.p.). The mere existence of such projects and the production of minority ethnic working-class writing reaffirms the continual need to assess and monitor representations of class that follow aesthetic trajectories aimed at cashing in, suggesting how working-class representation should always exist within a state of dynamic tension.

What this chapter hopes to have accomplished is to reveal the way that British working-class literature presents a challenge to the literary techniques upon which it relies, mobilizing indeterminacy in a manner that renders such literature as historically contingent and dialogic. By adding grit to the realist mode, working-class literature proves to be less of a problem of definition and more of a problem of categorization in that working-class texts refuse what are ultimately bourgeois artistic categories. The continual tension enacted between style, authenticity, and political objective is not a bug but a feature of working-class literature, addressing the difficulty of aligning ideological messaging with the kind of interpretative and symbolic frameworks associated with the literary arts. This tension, I suggest, mandates that working-class fiction continues to adapt to contemporary social concerns through the use of adapted literary techniques, refusing a fixed formal aesthetic and, therefore, curtailing the potential for commodification. The result is a state of aesthetic flux in which style, authenticity, and political objectives are rendered fluid without one focus necessarily privileging the other. In other words, a bourgeois writer can represent the conditions of working-class experience with fidelity just as an authentically working-class writer can exploit his or her own class experience for a bourgeois cause. Therefore, the work of identifying what it is that makes a text proletarian is ultimately the work of the reader. Despite the emergence of tropes and technical choices clearly perceptible within a genealogy of British working-class writing, attempts to place a formal ceiling on such works is to restrict the kind of tensions that the genre requires to succeed.

## Notes

1. For anthologies, Ian Haywood's three collections are the most comprehensive (1995's *The Literature of Struggle: An Anthology of Chartist Fiction* and two volumes of *Chartist Fiction* from 1999 and 2001 respectively). For additional critical writing on the topic, the Summer 2001 edition of *Victorian Poetry* was devoted to working-class poetics with five contributions specifically looking at Chartist writing.

2. George Orwell, in a 1940 interview with Desmond Hawkins, registered a discrepancy in class-conscious writing movements, stating that "I don't think the people who throw this expression about mean literature written by proletarians. W. H. Davies was a proletarian, but he would not be called a proletarian writer. Paul Potts would be called a proletarian writer, but he is not a proletarian. The reason why I am doubtful of the whole conception is that I don't believe the proletariat can create an independent literature while they are not the dominant class. I believe that their literature is and must be bourgeois literature with a slightly different slant" (1968, p. 38).

3. As Russel points out, echoes of dialectical literature in the form of almanacs can be identified in the rise of comics such as *Viz*, in which both class and dialect are mercilessly skewered in questionable ways.

4. Miller also registers persistent canonical bias against working-class literature, noting how influential socialist papers like the *Clarion* have seen little in the way of academic scrutiny because they were aimed at and read by predominantly working-class audiences from the north (2010, p. 705).

5. It is worth noting here that the rise of radical publishing epitomizes a motif identifiable throughout working-class writing (as well as other forms of media production): an oppositional, subcultural gesture that serves to challenge dominant media forms, resulting in a continuous tension that prevents the commodification of the form.

6. Specifically, the Second Boer War (1899). While mentions of war—including the First Boer War (1880)—showed up in earlier Music Hall content, it was the second that certified its capacity as a tool of the state.

7. The insertion of class-specific social issues finds its origins in the Chartists and is developed in Late-Victorian realism, but an amplification

can be identified within the 1950s and 1960s through the forceful embrace of taboo topics that serve to offset the class dominance of the arts. Topics such as abortion, domestic violence, alcoholism, and adultery were foregrounded during this time—a move that pushed the envelope of realism but also provided a spectacularized shock effect to audiences accustomed to morally homogenized media. It might be said that intensified realism, under the guise of kitchen sink realism, exposed the limits of traditional, bourgeois literary realism—an effect attained through the complicating of aesthetic and political goals.

8. For example, the difference between a documentary film that takes creative liberties in narration and a work of fiction that strives for absolute authenticity is, I would argue, up for debate.

9. Given that Todorov argues that the comprehension of verisimilitude as simply "consistent with reality" is a naïve perspective that should be discarded (1997, 82), it follows that a gradational spectrum of verisimilitude can—and should—be considered.

10. Writers such as Sillitoe, for example, distanced themselves from the culture central to their work, while authors like MacInnes—an upper-middle class writer—produced novels that depict class inequality with journalistic precision and was one of very few writers in working-class literary history whose work deals specifically with race.

## References

Alcalá, R. del V. (2016). *British Working-Class Fiction: Narratives of Refusal and the Struggle Against Work.* London, Bloomsbury Academic.

Baker, R.A. (2014). *British Music Hall: An Illustrated History.* Barnsley, Pen & Sword Books Ltd.

Braithwaite, E.R. (1959). *To Sir, with Love.* London, The Bodley Head.

Breton, R. (2009). Genre in the Chartist Periodical. In: A. Krishnamurthy, ed., *The Working-Class Intellectual in Eighteenth- and Nineteenth-Century Britain.* Surrey, Ashgate, pp. 109–128.

Breton, R. (2016). *The Oppositional Aesthetics of Chartist Fiction: Reading Against the Middle-Class Novel.* Burlington, Ashgate.

Casaliggi, C. and Fermanis, P. (2016). *Romanticism: A Literary and Cultural History.* Abingdon, Routledge.

Caudwell, C. (1971). *Studies and Further Studies in a Dying Culture.* New York, Monthly Review Press.

Constantine, S. (1982). 'Love on the Dole' and its Reception in the 1930s. *Literature and History,* 8 (2), pp. 232–247.

Dancyger, K. (2014). *The Technique of Film and Video Editing: History, Theory, and Practice.* CRC Press, Boca Raton.

Davies, T. (1984). Unfinished Business: Realism and Working-Class Writing. In: J. Hawthorne, ed., *The British Working-Class Novel in the Twentieth Century.* London, Edward Arnold, pp. 125–136.

Eliot, G. (1998). *Middlemarch.* Ware, Wordsworth Editions.

Ferrall, C. and McNeill, D. (2015). *Writing the 1926 General Strike.* Cambridge, Cambridge University Press.

Foster, D.W. (1992). *Contemporary Argentine Cinema.* Columbia, University of Missouri Press.

Fox, P. (1994). *Class Fictions: Shame and Resistance in the British Working-Class Novel, 1890–1945.* Durham, Duke University Press.

Gilroy, P. (1992). *There Ain't No Black in the Union Jack: The Cultural Politics of Race and Nation.* Abingdon, Routledge.

Hawthorne, J. (1984). *The British Working-Class Novel in the Twentieth Century.* London, Edward Arnold.

Haywood, I. (1997). *Working Class Fiction: From Chartism to Trainspotting.* Plymouth, Northcote House Publishers.

Hentea, M. (2014). *Henry Green at the Limits of Modernism.* Sussex, Sussex Academic Press.

Hitchcock, P. (1989). *Working Class Fiction in Theory and Practice: A Reading of Alan Sillitoe.* Rochester, University of Rochester Press.

Hitchcock, P. (2000). They Must Be Represented? Problems in Theories of Working-Class Representation. *PMLA,* 115 (1), pp. 20–32.

Hoggart, R. (2009). *The Uses of Literacy: Aspects of Working-Class Life.* London, Penguin Classics.

Janowitz, A. (1998). *Lyric and Labour in the Romantic Tradition.* Cambridge, Cambridge University Press.

Kirk, J. (2003). *Twentieth-Century Writing and the British Working Class.* Chicago, University of Chicago Press.

Klaus, H.G. (1985). *The Literature of Labour: Two Hundred Years of Working-Class Writing.* New York, Harvester Press.

Kovalev, Y. (1956). *An Anthology of Chartist Literature.* Moscow, Foreign Languages Publishing House.

Kureishi, H. (1996). *My Beautiful Laundrette and Other Writing.* London, Faber & Faber.

Laing, S. (1986). *Representations of Working Class Life, 1957–1964.* London, Palgrave Macmillan.

Lichtenstein, C. and Schregenberger, T. (2006). *As Found: The Discovery of the Ordinary: British Architecture and Art of the 1950s, New Brutalism, Independent Group, Free Cinema, Angry Young Men.* Baden, Lars Müller Publishers.

Linkon, S.L. (2010). *Why Working-Class Literature Matters.* [Blog] Working-Class Perspectives. Available at: https://workingclass studies.wordpress.com/2010/02/22/why-working-class-literature-matters [Accessed 23 March 2015].

Mahoney, C. (2010). *A Companion to Romantic Poetry.* Oxford, Wiley-Blackwell.

Miller, E.C. (2010). Literature and the Late-Victorian Radical Press. *Literature Compass*, 7 (8), pp. 702–712.

Milward, R. (2008). *Apples: A Novel.* New York, Canongate.

Mullen, J. (2016). *The Show Must Go On! Popular Song in Britain During the First World War.* Abingdon, Routledge.

Murphy, P.T. (1994). *Toward a Working-class Canon: Literary Criticism in British Working-class Periodicals, 1816–1858.* Columbus, Ohio State University Press.

Newton, K.M. (2011). *Modernizing George Eliot: The Writer as Artist, Intellectual, Proto-Modernist, Cultural Critic.* London, Bloomsbury Academic.

Onwuemezi, N. (2016). *Northern Fiction Alliance Launches for Indies*. [Blog] The Bookseller. Available at: http://www.thebook seller.com/news/indies-launch-northern-fiction-alliance-371476 [Accessed 19 Oct. 2016].

Orwell, G. (1968). The Proletarian Writer: Discussion Between George Orwell and Desmond Hawkins. In: I. Angus and S. Orwell, eds., *George Orwell: Volume 2, My Country Right or Left, 1940–1943*. Boston, David R. Godine, pp. 38–44.

Richardson, E. (2015). Political Writing and Class. In: N. Vance and J. Wallace, eds., *The Oxford History of Classical Reception in English Literature: Volume 4: 1790–1880*. Oxford, Oxford University Press, pp. 103–129.

Rose, J. (2002). *The Intellectual Life of the British Working Classes*. New Haven, Yale University Press.

Russell, D. (2004). *Looking North: Northern England and the National Imagination*. Manchester, Manchester University Press.

Scheckner, P. ed. (1989). *An Anthology of Chartist Poetry: Poetry of the British Working Class, 1830s–1850s*. New Jersey, Associated University Presses.

Schofield, C. (2013). *Enoch Powell and the Making of Postcolonial Britain*. Cambridge, Cambridge University Press.

Sierz, A. (2001). *In-Yer-Face Theatre: British Drama Today*. London, Faber & Faber.

Southey, R. and Jones, J. (1836). *Lives of Uneducated Poets, to Which are Added Attempts in Verse*. London, H. G. Bohn.

Todorov, T. (1977). *The Poetics of Prose*. Translated from French by R. Howard. Ithaca, Cornell University Press.

Vicinus, M. (1974). *The Industrial Muse: A Study of Nineteenth Century British Working-Class Literature*. London, Croom Helm.

Watt, I. (1957). *The Rise of the Novel: Studies in Defoe, Richardson and Fielding*. Berkeley, University of California Press.

Williams, R. (1958). Realism and the Contemporary Novel. *Universities and Left Review*, 4, pp. 22–25.

Wilson, N. (2015). *Home in British Working-Class Fiction*. Abingdon, Routledge.

# Afterword

*John Lennon & Magnus Nilsson*

As stated in the introduction, the aim of this collection is to give a broad and rich picture of the many-facetted phenomenon of working-class literature(s), to disrupt narrow understandings of the concept and phenomenon, and to identify and discuss some of the most important theoretical and historical questions brought to the fore by the study of this literature. Doing so, we argue, makes possible the forging of a more robust, politically useful and theoretically elaborate understanding of this phenomenon. Below follows a discussion of how the collected essays have contributed to fulfilling this aim.

## The Hetero- and Homogeneities of Working-Class Literature(s)

The essays collected here demonstrate clearly that there are real and important differences between works and traditions that have been or could be conceptualized as working-class literature. This is brought to the fore by comparisons between working-class literatures from different countries. The 1930s, for example, may have been a golden age for proletarian literature in many countries, but the literature produced during this decade by working-class writers in countries, such as Sweden, The Soviet Union, and the U.S., is highly diverse. Historical accounts also make visible this heterogeneity. In Russia/The Soviet Union, the history of proletarian literature contains poems by self-educated workers, documentary sketches

How to cite this book chapter:
Lennon, J. and Nilsson, M. 2017. Afterword. In: Lennon, J. and Nilsson, M. (eds.) *Working-Class Literature(s): Historical and International Perspectives*. Pp. 197–206. Stockholm: Stockholm University Press. DOI: https://doi.org/10.16993/bam.h. License: CC-BY

from factories, and novels by communist intellectuals. Mexican working-class literature encompasses both proletarian novels and testimonios. And in Britain, Chartist fiction, as well as Kitchen Sink realism, belong to the tradition of working-class writing.

This heterogeneity is, of course, a result of differences in context. Chartist fiction and Kitchen Sink realism belong to different epochs and are products of different social, political, and aesthetic conditions. The Whites' victory in the Finnish civil war led to the destruction of the institutionally autonomous field of working-class culture, thereby fundamentally changing the course of the history of the country's working-class literature. Despite 1930s proletarian literature in the U.S. being influenced by the literary debates in the Soviet Union at the time, the major social and political differences between the two countries helped produce radically different types of literature. It is, however, important to realize that this heterogeneity is not only a result of differences between countries and historical epochs, but that it also exists within any given historical situation. The period following (and, to some extent, preceding) the Russian revolution, for example, saw a plethora of proletarian literary organizations that promoted aesthetically different kinds of literature, and in the 1930s, Swedish working-class writers published realistic novels as well as modernist poetry and documentary works.

Parallel to these differences and heterogeneities, there are also marked and important similarities between working-class literatures from different countries and epochs. Some of these can be attributed to similarities of context. The emergence of working-class poetry within the labor movements in Russia, Sweden, and Finland during the last decades of the nineteenth century, for example, is probably a result of similar material conditions. For workers lacking formal education, economic resources, and leisure time, poetry was a more accessible genre than the novel. Poetry could also easily be distributed within the labor movement – published in newspapers, printed on leaflets, read at rallies. In the U.S, for example, the I.W.W.'s *Little Red Songbook* and the plethora of songs and poetry produced by Woody Guthrie are testament to the orality of literature for working-class audiences.

Other similarities were the results of international influence. The most prominent example of this is the influence of the Bolshevik

Revolution upon the way writers from a number of countries wrote and thought about literature. As Eugenio Di Stefano points out in his contribution to this collection, the USSR was "a point of reference during the 1920s and 1930s in Mexico, especially for proletarian writers who sought to create a truly revolutionary literature." As evidenced in several of the other essays, this was also true in other countries, including the U.S. and Finland.

What all of the texts in this collection gesture toward in different degrees is the push and pull of international influences upon national literatures. In his essay about U.S. working-class literature, Benjamin Balthaser highlights how "discussions of working-class U.S. literature run within two parallel if not necessarily connected trajectories": one that "responds to the call for a global 'proletarian literature'," and one that is autochthonous. This conceptualization of U.S. working-class literature, which recognizes both its national specificity and its international connections, frames a central concern of this collection, and the essays help qualify and place this frame in greater focus. Each essay, in essence, is also highlighting the parallel (though not necessarily connected) trajectories of national and international influences upon the literature from their particular country and showing how difficult it is to pin down a universal definition of working-class literature.

Taken as a whole, the collection helps tease out some of these similarities and differences between various working-class literatures. It is a complicated process with numerous facets, some of which are:

1. The responses to the "call for a global 'proletarian literature'" have always been conditioned by national circumstances. A comparison between Balthaser and Di Stefano's accounts of the histories of U.S. and Mexican working-class literatures, for example, shows that the answers to the call for an international proletarian literature in these two countries were in no way identical. And, whereas these responses were relatively strong in the U.S., they were – as can be seen in Nilsson's essay – not so in Sweden. One probable

reason for this is that in the U.S., the development of prole-tarian literature was closely connected to the cultural policy of the Communist Party, and thus to the discussions about proletarian literature within the international communist movement. In Sweden in the 1930s, on the other hand, working-class writers had stronger anchorage in the field of literary production than in that of party politics.

2. Even if the two trajectories identified by Balthaser are rel-atively distinct, they are also intertwined. The specific an-swers in the U.S. to the call for an international proletar-ian literature have, of course, become integrated into the domestic tradition. And the same goes for those answers formulated in Finland, Mexico, or any other country. Thus, while the distinction between the call for an internation-al proletarian literature and more homegrown traditions of working-class literature does have analytical value as a means for conceptualizing the conditions under which working-class literatures have emerged, it should not be taken to imply that it would be possible to distinguish do-mestic and foreign components within those literatures.

3. While writers in other countries have certainly been influ-enced by the understanding of proletarian literature within the Soviet Union, this understanding was, in fact, far from univocal. As demonstrated by Clark in this volume, the de-bates about proletarian literature in Russia and the Soviet Union during the first decades of the twentieth century were heated and heterogeneous. Furthermore, they were not self-contained. As Clark points out, Gorky's thinking about proletarian literature may, for example, very well have been inspired by that of the American publisher and politician Hamilton Holt. And the very fact that large parts of the communist intelligentsia in the Soviet Union had spent years in exile makes it reasonable to assume that their ideas about literature were influenced by discussions in other countries.

4. Even if discussions within the Soviet Union have been an important point of reference for working-class writers in other countries, none of the contributors to this volume have identified any substantial impact from the perhaps

most important literary doctrine emerging there—namely that of socialist realism. Nilsson points out that, according to Ivar Lo-Johansson, Mikhail Sholokhov – whose *Tikhiy Don* [*And Quiet Flows the Don/Quietly Flows the Don*] is one of the most important examples of socialist realism – was popular among Swedish working-class writers in the 1930s. However, many of these writers were in fact very critical of socialist realism. After having visited the Union of Soviet Writers' Congress in 1934, for example, the later Nobel laureate Harry Martinson (1940, pp. 11, 17–18) pitied Sholokhov (who also would receive the Nobel Prize) for being forced by the government to "write about tractors." He described Gorky – who in the 1930s propagated the doctrine of socialist realism – as "a burned-out and sick writer" who, because of his loyalty to the communist state, spoke against his own literary ideals. Furthermore, in several of his novels, another prominent Swedish working-class writer – Ivar Lo-Johansson – entered into a highly critical dialogue with socialist realist works. In *Bara en mor* [*Only a Mother*] (1938), for example, he "inverts" the story told in Gorky's *Mat'* [*The Mother*] (1906) (Nilsson, 2003, p. 150). In Gorky's novel, a poor and ignorant woman's maternal love leads her to embrace socialism. Lo-Johansson instead describes a woman who, because of her poverty, ignorance, and commitment to being a loving mother, is alienated from the labor movement. In the novel *Traktorn* [*The Tractor*] (1943), Lo-Johansson tells a story that is very similar to the one told in Sholokhov's *Podnyataja Tselina* [*Vigin Soil Upturned*] (1935), while negating the mythic/utopian ideology which, as has been demonstrated by Clark (1981), is a central feature of socialist realism.

5.  The call for an international proletarian literature is far from the only form of external influence on national working-class literatures. Hyttinen and Launis, for example, show that both Swedish working-class literature and discussions in Sweden about this literature received a fair amount of attention in the Finnish labor-movement press, and thus influenced the development of Finnish

working-class literature. And working-class literatures have, of course, also been influenced by more general literary trends. Examples of this can be found in Di Stefano's and Nilsson's essays, which demonstrate, to take only one example, that, in the 1970s, both Mexican and Swedish working-class writers experimented with documentary forms.

These insights constitute a good foundation for the exploration of one of the central themes in this collection of texts about working-class literatures: that these literatures display both similarities and differences, that they are connected but distinct, and that they constitute a class of literature that is fundamentally heterogeneous.

## Working-Class Literature(s) – Under Construction

While it is important for us to recognize and explore the similarities and differences between working-class texts from various countries, it is equally important to examine how different working-class literatures have been conceptualized. Clark and Nilsson make this their main object of study by tracking the meanings given to the term "proletarian" in debates about literature in Russia and the Soviet Union and by analyzing how Swedish working-class literature has been conceptualized in different ways at different times and in different contexts. Simon Lee highlights how, in Britain, the notion of working-class literature "resists formal consummation" and is "subject to continual renovation," whereas Hyttinen and Launis describe the history of Finnish working-class literature as "a history of definitions and counter-definitions" and thus – much like Nilsson – argue that the history of this literature cannot be told in isolation from that of how it has been conceptualized.

Hyttinen and Launis also stress that the conceptual history of working-class literature is marked by *conflict*, not the least through their memorable anecdote about a working-class writer hiding in the bathroom during a heated debate among critics about whether or not she is truly worthy of that title. However, as demonstrated by Nilsson and Clark, as well as by Hyttinen and Launis, not all working-class authors have been hiding. Rather, many have actively taken part in the struggles over how the phenomenon of working-class literature should be defined and understood. These struggles have also involved critics, academics, and political activists. And they have often been deeply political, especially when they – as often has been the case – have concerned not what working-class literature is, but what it *should be*. Gorky's ideas about a proletarian literature by workers through which communist intellectuals could come into contact with new ideas, for example, express a different political ideology than does the organization "October's" promotion of a proletarian literature, whose primary aim was to agitate for party commitment among workers, or the doctrine of socialist realism. As Clark demonstrates, the latter focuses more on literature's connections to communist doctrine than on its thematizing of working-class experience. And the conceptualization by some Swedish critics of working-class literature as a valuable contribution to the country's national literary history has different political implications than other critics' understanding of it as a means for the political liberation of the working class.

Literary scholars – including those of us who have contributed to this collection – are generally less interested in what working-class literature should be than in what it is and has been. Thus, it might appear to be at least somewhat problematic that our definitions are often highly divergent. To some extent this can be explained by the fact that they are constructed as responses to different aspects of that highly diverse phenomenon that is working-class literature(s). The study of U.S. working-class literature will generate other understandings of the concept of working-class literature than the study of working-class writing in the U.K., and scholars focusing on contemporary working-class literatures will develop different conceptual apparatuses than those of their colleagues researching proletarian writing from the 1930s. But literary scholarship is never purely responsive; it also actively contributes to the construction of its objects of study. And thus, it is political. But whereas the politics of the conceptualization of working-class literature has often concerned itself with what it *should* be, the politics of scholarly debates often focus (or should focus) more on what it *could* be.

204 Working-Class Literature(s): Historical and International Perspectives

The most general political implication of working-class literature (and the academic study of it) is that it brings to the fore questions about class, class injustice, and class politics. However, class is a historical, ever-changing process. The class injustices suffered by workers in nineteenth-century Britain are not the same as those to which working-class communities in Mexico or Finland are subjected today. Similarly, the political situations in which various kinds of working-class literature have emerged have been different, which has resulted in the development of different aesthetical-political strategies. Thus, reified working-class literature(s) and reified understandings of this literature will obscure rather than highlight class. By using a comparative – and, perhaps, even a speculative – approach, we, as literary scholars, can avoid this danger.

This volume contains several explicit challenges to accepted understandings of the phenomenon of working-class literature, the implications of which are not only academic in a narrow sense, but also political. One of these is Balthaser's reading of *The Autobiography of Malcolm X* (1965) as "one of the most important U.S. working class novels of the 20th century," which self-consciously challenges "ideas of both working-class literary tradition as well as the political meaning of its genealogy." Examples of less explicit revisions of the canon and concept of working-class literature include Lee's incorporation of George Eliot and Ken Loach in his overview of British working-class writing and Di Stefano's analysis of the genre of testimonio within the context of Mexican working-class literature. These inclusions will certainly cause some scholars to disagree with the authors' conceptual formulations; we hope this will spur a continued healthy and vibrant debate.

Another important aspect of the presentation of working-class literature(s) in this collection, which some might consider revisionist, is the lack of discussion of its/their relationship to socialist realism. The main reason for this is that (as has been pointed out above) the doctrine of socialist realism does not seem to have played any important role for the development of the working-class literature(s) in the countries discussed here (with the exception, obviously, of the Soviet Union). This is hardly surprising. As Clark demonstrates in her essay, the proclamation of socialist realism as an official literary ideology marked a move away from understanding "proletarian" literature as a literature connected to the working class and toward an emphasis on its ties to the communist party. Thus, it was not necessarily appealing to authors and critics committed to *working-class* literature. And thus, it does not necessarily belong to the *category* of working-class literature(s), even when this literature – as is the case in this collection – is defined as a fundamentally heterogeneous phenomenon.

Balthaser legitimizes his expansion of the field of U.S. working-class literature through the inclusion of *The Autobiography of Malcolm X* by arguing that it represents "not a rupture so much as a fulfillment of 20th century traditions of self-conscious working class writing." We, however, view his revisionist attitude as rather radical and read his analysis as a *reconfiguration* of both the concept and tradition of U.S. working-class literature and of Malcolm X's autobiography. By reading *The Autobiography of Malcolm X* as working-class literature, Balthaser makes visible its relationship not only to race, but also to class, while simultaneously highlighting that U.S. working-class literature has always been about the production of class identities through modes of racial looking. Through similar maneuvers, Hyttinen and Launis show how Finnish working-class literature relates not only to class, but also to questions about gender. Thus, the innovative revisionist analyses of working-class literature presented in this collection not only bring questions about class to the fore, but also make visible how class is overdetermined by phenomena such as race and gender. This is a good illustration of the fact that research on working-class literature has the potential to make valuable contributions to contemporary academic and political discussions. This is certainly needed. In our current historical moment, right wing and alt-right candidates have strengthened their positions or even swept into power, riding the nationalist momentum that has exploited the large chasms between the classes. In the U.S., Donald Trump, a billionaire who literally lives in a penthouse that is partially gold-encrusted, convinced a large number of working-class voters that he is going to be their champion. In Sweden, a right-wing party with roots in National Socialism has become a strong political force among workers. It is clear that class, and the disparity between the classes, has been ignored or misconstrued in political discussions. The election results are one outcome of this. Examining and comparing working-class literature(s) from around the globe—literature by and about the working-class—is one tactic (of many) to help combat the ways that class has been marginalized or miscomprehended in both academia and political discussions.

Tampa and Malmö, 1 August 2017,
John Lennon and Magnus Nilsson

## References

Clark, K. (1981). *The Soviet Novel: History as Ritual*. Chicago and London, University of Chicago Press.

Martinson, H. (1941). *Den förlorade Jaguaren*. Stockholm, Norstedts.

Nilsson, M. (2003). *Den moderne Ivar Lo-Johansson: Modernisering, modernitet och modernism i statarromanerna*. Hedemora, Gidlunds.

# Contributors

**Benjamin Balthaser** is Associate Professor of Multi-Ethnic U.S. literature, Post at Indiana University-South Bend. His December 2015 book from University of Michigan Press, *Anti-Imperialist Modernism: Race and Transnational Radical Culture from the Great Depression to the Cold War*, explores connections between cross-border, anti-imperialist movements and the making of modernist culture at mid-century. Critical and creative work of his appeared in journals or collections such as such as *American Quarterly*, *Boston Review*, *Jacobin*, *The Oxford History of the Novel in English*, *Criticism*, *Cultural Logic*, *The Massachusetts Review*, and elsewhere. He is also the author of a collection of poems about Jewish victims of the Cold War blacklist entitled *Dedication*, that appeared from Partisan Press in the fall of 2011, and is currently working on a critical manuscript entitled *The Dialectics of Race: Modernism and the Search for a Racial Subject*.

**Katerina Clark** is Professor of Comparative Literature and of Slavic Languages and Literatures at Yale University, and has previously taught at SUNY Buffalo, Wesleyan University, the University of Texas at Austin, Indiana University and Berkeley. Among her most important publications – all of which have been, or are in the process of being, translated into several languages – are: *The Soviet Novel: History As Ritual* (1981), *Mikhail Bakhtin* (with Michael Holquist, 1984), *Petersburg, Crucible of Cultural Revolution* (1995), and *Moscow, the Fourth Rome: Stalinism, Cosmopolitanism and the Evolution of Soviet Culture, 1931–1941* (2011). She is currently working on a book project tentatively titled *Eurasia without Borders?: Leftist Internationalists and Their Cultural Interactions, 1917–1943*, which looks at attempts to found a "socialist global ecumene," which was to be closely allied with the anticolonial cause.

**Eugenio Di Stefano** is an Associate Professor of Latin American Literature and Culture at the University of Nebraska at Omaha. He has published articles on human rights, the work of Roberto Bolaño, and the politics of aesthetic form in *MLN, Revista de Estudios Hispánicos,* and *Nonsite* (co-authored with Emilio Sauri). He is also the author of the book, *The Vanishing Frame: Latin American Culture and Theory in the Postdictatorial Era* (University of Texas Press), which examines art and politics in the aftermath of the recent dictatorships in Argentina, Chile and Uruguay. ORCID: 0000-0001-6588-233X

**Elsi Hyttinen** gained her PhD at the University of Turku, Finland, and has worked as research fellow, university teacher and lector in Finnish literature. Her research interests cover working-class and queer literary history, feminist criticism, posthumanist theory, and archives. She is the author of *Kovaa työtä ja kohtalon oikkuja. Elvira Willmanin taistelu työläiskirjallisuuden tekijyydestä* [Hard work and twists of fate. Elvira Willman's struggle for working-class authorship] (2012) and the co-editor of *Lukemattomat sivut. Kirjallisuuden arkistot käytössä* [Countless pages. Using literary archives] (2010), and has published several articles in national and international peer-reviewed publications including the *Lambda Nordica* and the *Journal of Finnish Studies.* Hyttinen is currently writing a collection of essays on depictions of Finnish-American migrancy in 19th and early 20th century Finnish fiction.

**Kati Launis,** Ph.D., is a University Researcher at the University of Eastern Finland, and a Docent of Finnish Literature at the University of Turku. She is the author of *Kerrotut naiset. Suomen ensimmäiset naisten kirjoittamat romaanit naiseuden määrittelijöinä* [*Narrated Women: The First Novels Written by Women in Finland Defining Womanhood* (2005) and numerous articles on Finnish working-class writers, 19th century female writers, and Gothic fiction. She is currently working in the Research consortium "LibDat: Towards a more advanced loaning and reading culture and its information service. A study, based on digital material, of contemporary Finnish loaning and reading culture" (Academy of Finland, 2019–21). ORCID: 0000-0002-8498-7361

**Simon Lee** researches British cultural production of the 20th and 21st-centuries, focusing on issues of class in relation to the built environment. His recent work centers on the kitchen sink realism movement and its impact on contemporary working-class representation, specifically the movement's tending to aesthetic and ethical impulses to reconfigure verisimilitude. He has published on authors such as Colin MacInnes, Shelagh Delaney, John Osborne, Alan Sillitoe, and Nell Dunn, and is presently writing an article on X-rated certification in the British New Wave. He currently teaches at the University of California, Riverside, where he completed his dissertation in June of 2017.

**John Lennon** is an Associate Professor of English at the University of South Florida. His research is principally concerned with how marginalized individuals exert a politicized voice in collectivized actions. Dr. Lennon's monograph, *Boxcar Politics: The Hobo in Literature and Culture 1869–1956* examines the hobo as a resistive working-class figure. His work has appeared in various edited volumes and journals including *Cultural Studies Review, New Proposals: Journal of Marxism and Interdisciplinary Inquiry, American Studies, Rhizomes,* and *Acoma.* He is currently at work on a new book length project examining conflict graffiti from a global perspective. For this project he has received various grants to travel to Egypt, Lebanon, Israel, Palestine, England, Sweden, Brazil and Germany. Follow him at @hoboacademic. ORCID: 0000-0002-6472-98

**Magnus Nilsson** is Professor of Comparative Literature at Malmö University, Sweden. He has published a large number of books, book chapters and articles on working-class literature and on questions regarding the relationship between literature and class, including the monographs *Den föreställda mångkulturen: Klass och etnicitet i svensk samtidsprosa* [Imagined Cultural Diversity: Class and Ethnicity in Contemporary Swedish Prose Fiction] (2010) and

*Literature and Class: Aesthetical-Political Strategies in Modern Swedish Working-Class Literature* (2014). He is coordinating a Nordic network for research on working-class literature, which since 2010 has organized five conferences and published four edited collections. His other research interests include comics and heavy metal. ORCID: 0000-0001-5848-2231

# Index

5 *Unga* 103, 106, 108–109

5 *Youths* 103, 106, 108–109

12 *Million Black Voices* 54–55

1970-*luku suomalaisessa Kirjallisuudessa* 83

*The 1970s in Finnish Literature* 83

**A**

Aakjær, Jeppe 103

Abbott, Paul 179

*Abriss einer Geschichte der deutschen Arbeiterliteratur* xi

Adi, Hakim 38

Adolfsson, Eva 111, 113

Af Ursin, N. R. 73

*An Agitator* 168

Agrell, Beata xii, 115–116

Ågren, Robert 97, 101

Ahlenius, Holger 106–107

Ahlin, Lars 107

Ahlmo-Nilsson, B. 110–111

Äiti ja poika: Kuvaus Köyhäinkorttelista 75

Åkerstedt, J. 103

Alakoski, Susanna 115

Alcalá, Robert del Valle 161

Aldington, Richard 115

*Al filo del agua* 138

Algren, Nelson 52

Allanson, Ove 110

Alm, Outi 86

Almanza, Héctor Raúl 136

*Amaneceres* 134

*America is in the Heart* 52, 54

*American Rust* 59

*American Working-Class Literature* xii, 32

Amis, Kingsley 173–174

Andersen-Nexø, Martin 103

Anderson, Lindsay 188

Anderson, Sherwood 51

Andersson, Bernt-Olov 112, 114

Andersson, Dan 98–99, 103, 108, 112–113

Andersson, Gunder 112

Andersson, Mary 112

*And Quiet Flows the Don/ Quietly Flows the Don* 200

Andrejev, Leonid 74

Anisimov, Iv. 27 (endnote)

*Ansikten* 104–105, 112

Anthony, Mark x

*Apples* 179

*Arbetarhistoria* 112

*Arbetarlitteratur* 116

Arce, Manuel Maple 132, 153 (endnote)

Arciniegas, Victor Díaz 153 (endnote)

Arnold, Matthew 163–164
Artaud, Antonin 179
*Art Belongs to the People* 84
Arzubide, Germán List 132
Asklund, Erik 102–105
Attaway, William 39
Aub, Max 152 (endnote)
Auden, W. H. 172
Augustsson, Lars Åke 112
*The Author* 108
"The Author as Producer" 15
*The Autobiography of Malcolm X* xv, 32–35, 39–40, 55–56, 59–60, 204–205
*Avsikter* 104–105, 112
*Awake and Sing* 52
Azhaev, Vasilii 25
Azuela, Mariano 131

**B**
Babel, Isaac 115
Bachilo, I. 17
Bacon, David 56, 61 (endnote)
Baker, Richard Anthony 169
Balthaser, Benjamin xv, 135, 159, 164, 185–186, 188, 199–200, 204–205
*Bara en mor* 201
Baraka, Amiri 32
Barker, Pat 177
Barnet, Miguel 140
*Barrio Boy* 56
*My Beautiful Laundrette* 178
*Belomorsko-Baltiiskii kanal imeni Stalina* 18–19
Belye odezhdy 26

Bengtsson, Håkan 114
Benitez, Carmen Galán 155 (endnote)
Benjamin, Walter 15
Berdiaev, Nikolai 25
Berggren, Mats 112
Bergson 25
Berman, Marshall 36
Beverley, John 141–144
*Beyond Desire* 51
*Bible* 71
Billy Liar 174
*Biografía de un Cimarrón* 140
*Biography of a Runaway Slave* 140
Björk, Johannes 117
Bjørnson, Bjørnstjerne 74
Björnsson, Rudolf 73, 101
Black, Clementina 168
*The Black Jacobins* 60 (endnote)
Blomberg, Harry 98, 100, 103–104
"Blueprint for Negro Writing" 35, 43–45
Bogdanov, Alexander 5
Bogdat'eva, E. 8
Bolander, C. A. 74
Bond, Edward 179
Bondebjerg, Ib 96
*Bonniers Litterära Magasin* 112
*The Book of Lamentations* 138
*Book in Movement* 68
Boullosa, Carmen 155 (endnote)
Bouquet, Philippe 113–114
Bourke, Joanna 161

Bowen-Struyk, Heather xii
Braine, John 173
Braithwaite, E. R. 176
Branting, Hjalmar 97
Brat'ia Ershovy 26
Breaking Free 103
Bredel, Willi 35
Breitman, George 55–56
Breton, Rob 165–166
Brezhnev, Leonid 26
British Working-Class Fiction 161–162
The British Working-Class Novel in the Twentieth-Century 160
Brodskii 8
Brown, N. 155 (endnote)
Brown, Sterling 39
Bulosan, Carlos 52, 54
Buñuel, Luis 152 (endnote)
"The Burial" 134
Burgess, Anthony 172
Burke, Fielding 51
Burke, Kenneth 35
"Byli gory vysokoi" 27 (endnote)

C
Cabral, Nicolás 150–151
"Cadres Decide Everything" 21
Cahan, Abraham 47
Caldwell, Erskine 115
Call Home the Heart 51
Call it Sleep 52
Camacho, Manuel Ávila 154 (endnote)

¡Camaradas! 134, 154 (endnote)
Campos, Julieta 155 (endnote)
Canclini, Nestor García 146
Canth, Minna 71
Capital 55
Cárdenas, Lázaro 134, 136, 153–154 (endnotes)
Carpenter, Edward 168
Carranza, Luis E. 135–136, 150–151, 188
Casaliggi, Carmen 161
Castellano, Rosario 137
Castro, Carlo Antonio 137
Castro, Fidel 152 (endnote)
Castro, Raul 152 (endnote)
Catálogo de formas 150–151
Catalogue of Forms 150–151
Caudwell, Christopher 171
The Caves 107
Cement 10–13, 20, 25
The Century's Daughter 177
Cerecedo, Miguel Bustos 134, 153 (endnote)
Chaplin, Charlie 135
Chesterton, G. K. 147
The Children of Sanchez 141
Chimeneas 135, 150, 154 (endnote)
Choice of Direction 112
Chopin, Kate 167–168
Christ in Concrete 52–53, 57
City of Night 56
Clark, Katerina xiv-xv, 27 (endnote), 35, 67, 73, 131, 148, 154 (endnote), 172, 174, 184, 200–204

*Clarion* 191 (endnote)

*Clarté* 109

*Class* 118

*Class Fictions* 161

Cleaver, Eldridge 32

Colás, S. 139

Coles, Niclas xii

*The Collective Heart* 68

Collins, Sam 169

"Come whoam to thi childer an' me" 167

*Commonweal* 168

*The Communist with Brown Eyes* 134

*Comrades!* 134, 154 (endnote)

Connolly, Nathan 190

Constantine, Stephen 172

Cornejo, Gerardo 137

*Coronation Street* 176

Correa, Eduardo J. 134

Cortázar, Julio 139, 147

*The Course of Life* 65–66

*Critical Approaches to American Working-Class Literature* xii, 31

Cruz, Carlos Gutiérrez 153 (endnote)

*Cuando* Cárdenas *nos dio la tierra* 137

Cullen, Countee 39

*The Cultural Front* 41, 46

*The Cultural Notebooks* 85

Cultural Revolution in Russia, 1928–1931 27 (endnote)

*Culture and Anarchy* 163

**D**

Daleko 25

Dalton, Roqué 140

Dancyger, K. 188

Daniels, R. 48

Danielsson, Axel 98

*Das Totenschiff* 102

*Daughter of Earth* 102

Davies, Tony 186–187

Davies, W. H. 191 (endnote)

Davis, Frank Marshall 38

Davis, Ossie 39

Davis, Rebecca Harding 36–37, 42

*The Death of Artemio Cruz* 139

*The Death Ship* 102

Defoe, Daniel 163

de la Mora, Elvira 137

Delaney, Shelagh 173–175, 188

de la Torre, Victor Raúl Haya 152 (endnote)

Delgado, Rafael 152 (endnote)

de Lizardi, Fernández 130

*Denim* 134

"Den internationella proletären i dikten" 102

Denning, Michael 16, 35, 39, 41, 46, 51–52, 56, 60, 61 (endnote), 135

Dessau, A. 153 (endnote)

*Diary of a Chilean Concentration Camp* 140

Díaz, Enrique Othón 134

Díaz, Porfirio 129–130

Dickens, Charles 164–165, 181

Di Donato, Pietro 52–53, 55, 57

*Die Baumwollpflücker* 102
Di Stefano, Eugenio xvi, 150–
151, 155 (endnote), 159, 175,
188, 198, 201, 204
Döblin, Alfred 115
Dobrenko, E. 16
Domecq, Brianda 155 (endnote)
Donoso, José 139
Dostoevsky 6
Douglass, Frederick 37–39
*Down the Rabbit Hole* 155
(endnote)
Du Bois, W.E.B. 36–39, 43
Dudintsev, V. 26
Dunbar-Oritz, Roxanne 53
Dunn, Nell 177
*Dutchman* 32

**E**
Ekelöf, Maja 110
Ekelund, Fredrik 112, 121
(endnote)
*Elämänmeno* 65–66
Eliot, George 163–165, 174,
181, 204
Ellison, Ralph 39
*El apando* 137
"El entierro" 134
*El indio* 152 (endnote)
*El llano en llamas* 137
*El nacional* 135
*El periquillo sarniento* 130
*Energiia* 15
*Energy* (also, *Power*) 15
Engel 75
*En natt i juli* 103

*Ensayo sobre un proletariado
sin cabeza* 137
*The Entertainer* 170
Ericsson, David 115–116
Ernst, Thomas xi
*The Ershov Brothers* 26
*Escuelita* 140
Espada, Martín 57
*Essay about a Headless
Proletariat* 137

**F**
*Faces* 104
Fahlgren, M. 99–100
*Far from Moscow* 25
Farrell, James 52, 55
Fermanis, Porscha 162
Ferrall, Charles 171
"Fetish of Being Outside" 35, 45
Fielding, Henry 163
*Fiesta en la madriguera* 155
(endnote)
Fitzhugh, George 36
Flaubert, Gustave 70
Flores, Mario Pavón 134
Fogelbäck, Jan 110, 112–113
Fogelqvist, Torsten 74
Foley, Barbara 31, 38, 52, 57, 61
(endnote)
*Författaren* 108
*The Forgotten Ones* 134
Forsman, Per 112
Fox, Pamela 161
Frank, Semyon 25
Frears, Stephen 178
Fridell, Folke 80, 107–108

Friedgård, Jan 89 (endnote), 103–104

Fröding, Gustaf 73

"From the Story about the Development of a Literary Proletarian" 97

Fuentes, Carlos 138–139, 152 (endnote)

Fukuyama, Francis 143

Furuland, Lars 95–98, 103, 107, 109–111, 113, 116, 120 (endnote)

*The Future* 8

**G**

Gabrielsson, K. J. (also, "Karolus") 97, 101

*The Gadfly* 22

Galarza, Ernesto 56

Gamboa, Federico 152 (endnote)

García, Diana 57

Garrison, W.L. 38

Garza, Cristina Rivera 155 (endnote)

Gastev, Alexei 8

*The Gate of a Strange Field* 171

*The Gathering Storm* 43, 51–52

Gauzner, G. 19

*Gazeta-kopeika* 3

Gemzøe, Anker 96

*Gidrotsentral* 15

Gierow, Ragnar 111

Gilroy, Paul 177–178

Gladkov, Fedor 10–13, 15, 25

Godin, Stig-Lennart 114

*Godnatt, jord* 103

Gold, Mike 35, 43, 45–51, 55–57, 61 (endnote), 102, 115

González, Francisco Rojas 138

Gorbachev, G. 10

Gor'kii, A.M. 17

Gorky, Maxim 3–6, 8, 16–20, 22, 67, 74, 109, 147–148, 154 (endnote), 184, 200–203

Gramsci 2, 144

*Grapes of Wrath* 53–54

*The Great Crusda* 137

Green, Henry 171

Greenwood, Walter 172

Greider, Göran 112

*Griadushchee* 8

Grossman, Vasilii 22–23

*Grottorna* 107

Guerrero, Jesús 134

Guthrie, Woody 198

Gutiérrez, Germán 135

**H**

Haapala, P. 71–72

Habermas, Jürgen 74

*Hacia una literatura proletaria* 133

Häkli, Hannu 86–87

Haley, Alex 32–33, 40

*The Half that has Never Been Told* 60 (endnote)

Hall, Stuart 31, 39

Hamberg, Maria 115–116

Hamm, C. xii, xvii, 116, 123

*Hammer and Hoe* 61 (endnote)

Hansberry, Lorraine 39
Hardy, Thomas 166–167, 170, 174
Harrie, Ivar 106
*Hasta no verte Jesús mío* 141
Haste, H. 97
Havu, Toini 80
Hawkins, Desmond 191 (endnote)
Hawthorne, Jeremy 160
Hayden, Robert 39
Haywood, Ian 159–160, 165, 191 (endnote)
*A Hazard of New Fortunes* 38, 42
Heather, Edward 178
*Heavy Cotton* 84
Hedén, Erik 99–100
Hedenvind-Eriksson, Gustav 98–100, 108
Hegel 41
Helge Röd (pseudonym) 97
*Helsingin Sanomat* 80, 87
Hentea, M. 172
*Here's to You, Jesusa* 141
Hernán, Gustavo Ortiz 135–136, 151
Herrera, Juan Felipe 57
Herrera, Yuri 155 (endnote)
Heslop, Harold 171–172
Hillborn, E. 116
Himes, Chester 39, 52
Hirdman, Maj 104–105
*Historia de mis dientes* 146–149, 151
*The Historical Novel* 40–41

"The History of the Civil War" 16
*History and Class Consciousness* xv, 41, 59
"The History of the Factories" 16–20, 23, 147–148
Hitchcock, Peter 68, 128, 160–161, 180, 186
Hoggart, Richard 161, 175, 182, 184–188
Holm, B. 110–111
Holmgren, O. 111
Holt, Hamilton 5, 200
*Home in British Working-Class Fiction* 161
Hotakainen, Kari 86
Howells, William Dean 38, 42
*How the Steel Was Tempered* 11–12, 21–22
Hudson, Thomas 169
*Huelga blanca* 137
Hughes, Langston 39
*HydroCentral* 15
Hyttinen, Elsi xii, xv–xvi, 66, 69–70, 76, 82, 88 (endnote), 141, 153 (endnote), 168, 201–202, 205

**I**

*I Am Owned by Nobody* 115
*I, Rigoberta Menchú, an Indian Woman in Guatemala* 140
Ibsen, Henrik 74
*If He Hollers* 52
*Incidents in the Life of a Slave Girl* 37
*The Independent* 5

*The Indian* 152 (endnote)
*The Industrial Muse* 160
*The Intellectual Life of the British Working Classes* 161
*Intentions* 104
"The International Proletarian in Literature" 102
*In the Shadow of the Factory* 78
*Istoriia fabrik i zavodov* (or *Istoriia zavodov*) 16–20, 23, 147–148

**J**

*Jacobin* 60
Jacobs, Harriet 37
Jacobson, M.F. 48
James, C.L.R. 36–37, 60 (endnote)
Jameson, Frederic 41–42
Jändel, Ragnar 98, 100
Janowitz, Anne 165
Järhult, Ragnar 112
*The Jazz Singer* 47
*Jews without Money* 43, 45–51, 57, 61 (endnote), 102
Jiménez, Agustín 135
Johansson, Kjell 110, 112, 116–117
*John Henry Days* 59
Johnson, Eyvind 101, 103, 106–107, 111, 116
Jönson, Johan 115–116
Jonsson, B. xii, 112, 117
Jönsson, Reidar 112
*Joukkosydän* 68
*Journal of Finnish Studies* xiii, 86

*Juan Pérez Jolote* 137, 141
*Juhannustanssit* 82
*Justice* 168

**K**

Kaatra, Kössi 69, 72–73, 75–76, 120
*Kadry reshaiut vse* 21
Kågerman, Elisabet 110
Kahlo, Frida 150
*Kak zakalialas's stal'* 11–12, 21–22
Kämpe, Alfred 110
Kane, Sarah 179
*Kansan tahto* 70
Kaplan, Amy 38
Karnstedt, Torgny 107, 117
Karkama, Pertti 84–85
Karlsson, Mats xii
Kataev, Valentin 15–16, 18, 23
Kauranen, K. 71, 85
Kauranen, R. 71, 85
Kekkonen, Urho 82
Kelley, Robin D. G. 33, 38, 60 (endnote)
Kelman, James 177
Kettunen, P. 80–81
Khrushchev 26
Kieri, Gunnar 112
*Kiila* 85
*Kingdom Cons* 155 (endnote)
Kirillov, Vladimir 8
*Kirja liikkeessä* 68
*Kirjallisuuslehti* 78
Kirk, John 161
Kjellgren, Josef 102–103

"Kniga o pafose novogo stroitel'stva. 'Vremia, vpered.'" 27 (endnote)

*Klass* 118

Klaus, H. Gustav 68, 160, 165

Koch, Martin 73, 98–100, 103, 108

Kochetov, Vsevolod 26

Koivisto, H. 78

Koskela, L. 76

Kosonen, Vihtori 88 (endnote)

Kotilainen, S. 71

Kovalev, Yuri 165

Kuismin, A. 71

*Kulttuurivihkot* 85

Kureishi, Hanif 178

Kuteishchikova, V. N. 152 (endnote)

*Kvinnor och äppelträd* 103

**L**

*La asonada* 134

*Laberinto de la soledad* 138

Labern, John 168

*Labor History* 112

*The Labyrinth of Solitude* 138

*La ciudad roja* 134, 154 (endnote)

Laclau, Ernesto 35

*La comunista de los ojos café* 134

*Lady Chatterley's Lover* 170–171, 184

Lagerberg, Hans 110, 112, 114, 121 (endnote)

Lagerlöf, Selma 73

*La gran cruzada* 137

Lahikainen, L. 85

Lahtinen, M. 71–72

Laing, Stuart 173

*La literatura latinoamericana en la imprenta rusa* 152 (endnote)

*La llaga* 152 (endnote)

*La muerte de Artemio Cruz* 139

Landgren, Johan 116–117

*Land of Men* 137

*La noche de Tlatelolco* 140–141

*La novela de la revolución Mexicana* 135

*La novela realista Mexicana* 152 (endnote)

*Lantern* 37–38

*La parcela* 152 (endnote)

*Lappeenrannan uutiset* 72

*La region mas transparente* 138

Larsson, Gösta 121 (endnote)

Larsson, Leon 98

*La sierra y el viento* 137

Lassila, Maiju (also, Algot Untola) 75

*Latin American Literature in Print in Russia* 152 (endnote)

Launis, Kati xii, xv-xvi, 71, 75, 78, 86–87, 87 (endnote), 119–120, 121 (endnote), 141, 153 (endnote), 168, 201–202, 205

Lawrence, D. H. 115, 170–172, 184–185

Lee, Simon xvi-xvii, 202, 204

*The Left Book Club* 173

Lehtimäki, Konrad 69

Leopold, L. 98

Leppä, A. 87

Lenin 5–6, 13–14

Lennon, John xi, 119–120, 155 (endnote)

Lepidus, Marcus Aemilius x

Le Sueur, Meridel 35–36, 45–46

Lewis, Oscar 141

Libedinskii, Iurii 10–11, 13

*The Liberator* 45

Lichtenstein, C. 182

Lidforss, Bengt 74, 98–99

Lidman, Sara 110–111

"Life in the Iron Mills" 36–37, 42

*The Life Stories of Americans as Told by Themselves* 5

Liinamaa, Hilja 73

Liksom, Rosa 85

Lindberger, Örjan 101, 109–110

Linderborg, Åsa 115

Linkon, Sherry x, 188–189

Linna, Väinö 79–81, 87, 89 (endnote)

*Literature and Revolution* 14

*Literatura i revoliutsiia* 14

*The Literature of Labor* 160

*The Literature of Struggle* 191 (endnote)

"Little Heroes and Big Deeds" 27 (endnote)

*Little Red Songbook* 198

*The Little School House* 140

*Living* 171

Llosa, Mario Vargas 139

Loach, Ken 204

Locke, Alain 39

Lo-Johansson, Ivar 89 (endnote), 102–103, 105–106, 108, 114–115, 121 (endnote), 201

*Lola Casanova* 138

*Look Back in Anger* 173

López Robles, Fortino 134

Lovett, William 165

Llosa, Vargas 154 (endnote)

London, Jack 74, 89 (endnote), 109

*The London Novels* 176

Lopéz, Gregorio 152 (endnote)

Lorde, Audrey 39

*Los de abajo* 131–132, 152 (endnote)

*Los días terrenales* 137

"Los gusanos rojos" 134

*Los hombres verdaderos* 137

*Los olvidados* 134

*Los parientes ricos* 152 (endnote)

Lossky, Nikolai 25

*Love on the Dole* 172

Lowe, Lisa 56

*Lucky Jim* 173–174

Ludkvist, Artur 103, 107

Ludmer, J. 155 (endnote)

Luiselli, Valeria 146–149, 151

Lukács, Georg xv, 40–44, 46, 159, 185

Lumpkin, Grace 51

Lunacharsky, Anatoly 5

Lundán, Reko 86

Lundberg, Kristian 115–116

Luukkanen, T. 71

Luukkonen, Kaarlo 73
Lysenko, Trofim 26
*Lyyli* 70

**M**
MacInnes, Colin 176
*Madame Bovary* 70
Magón, Ricardo Flores 152 (endnote)
Mäkijärvi, E. 87
Malcolm X 31–35, 40, 43–44, 55–56,
Malley, L. 8
Malyshkinm, Aleksandr 23–25
Mancisidor, José 132, 134, 153 (endnote)
*The Mangy Parrot* 130
Månsson, F. 104–105
Marable, M. 34
Marcos, Subcomandate 155 (endnote)
"Margin at the Center" 143
Markels, Julian x
Márquez, Gabriel García 139, 152 (endnote)
*Martin Eden* 89 (endnote), 109
Martinson, Harry 89 (endnote), 103–104, 106–107, 111, 201
Martinson, Moa 104–105, 113
Marttila, Hanna Marjut 86–87
Marx, Karl 55, 75
*Massacre in Mexico* 140–141
*Mat'* 201
Mattsson, Per-Olof 98, 100, 104, 113, 117
Maxwell, William 48

McKay, Claude 39
McNeill, Dougal 171
Melberg, A. 110–111
*Me llamo Rigoberta Menchú y así me nació la conciencia* 140
Mercader, Ramón 152 (endnote)
Meruane, Lina 147
*Metropolis* 153 (endnote)
*Mexican Novels* 152 (endnote)
*The Mexican Realist Novel* 152 (endnote)
Meyers, Philip 59
*Mezclilla* 134
Michaels, W. B. 55 (endnote)
*Middlemarch* 163
*The Midsummer Dance* 72
*Mig* äger *ingen* 115
*Miguel Marmol and the events of 1932 in El Salvador* 140
*Miguel Mármol y los sucesos de 1932 en El Salvador* 140
Mikkola, Marja-Leena 83–85
Miller, Elizabeth Carolyn 168, 191 (endnote)
Milward, Richard 179
Mirskii, D. 17
Mischliwietz, S. 116–117
Mistral, Gabriela 152
Moheno, Roberto Blanco 137
Monroe, Marilyn 147
Montarde, Francisco 152 (endnote)
Mörne, Arvid 69
Mörö, Mari 86
*Moskvy* 25

*The Mother* 3–4, 22, 201

*Mother and Son: A Picture of the Quarter of the Poor* 75

Mouffe, Chantal 35

*The Mountain and the Winds* 137

Mral, Brigitte 96–98, 114

*M/S Tiden* 121 (endnote)

*M/S Time* 121 (endnote)

*Muertos incomodos* 155 (endnote)

Múgica, Francisco 154 (endnote)

Mullen, Bill V. 31, 38, 170

*Murder at the Sleepy Lagoon* 60 (endnote)

Murphy, James 40

Murphy, Paul Thomas 160

Murray, Jon Beasley 146

"My rastem iz zheleza" 8

**N**

$N_{+1}$ 60

Naison, M. 32, 38, 60 (endnote)

Nancarrow, Conlon 150

*Na postu* (also, *Na literaturnom postu*) 9

*The Narrative of the Life of Frederick Douglass, an American Slave* 37–39

*Nashi pesni* 3

*The National* 135

*Native Son* 52, 54

Nedelia 10

Negrín, E. 130–131, 133

Neiman, Eva-Lena 112

*Ne khlebom edinym* 26

Nerman, Ture 100, 103–104

*Never Come Morning* 52

*The New Masses* 45

*The New Red Negro* 60 (endnote)

Newton, K.M. 164

Ngai, Mae M. 48, 56

Niemeyer, Katharina 153 (endnote)

Niemi, J. 82

Nieminen, H. 71–72

Nietzsche 25

*A Night in July* 103

Nilsson, Magnus xi-xii, xvi, 73, 85, 88–89 (endnotes), 103, 107, 110, 115–117, 119–120, 120–121 (endnotes), 142, 151 (endnote), 155 (endnote), 173, 177, 200–202

Nishchinskii 18

*No Country* xiii

Nordmark, D. 101–102

*The Northern Star* 165

*Not by Bread Alone* 26

*Novelas mexicanas* 152 (endnote)

*The Novel of the Mexican Revolution* 135

Nummi 81

Nylund, Ingmar 112

**O**

Octavian, Augustus x

Odets, Clifford 52

*Oficio de tinieblas* 137–138

O'Gorman, Juan 150

Oljelund, Ivan 98, 100, 103
Omi, Michael 40
*On Guard* (also, *On Literary Guard*) 9
Ojajärvi, Jussi 86, 121 (endnote)
Oksanen, Aulikki 84–85
Olsson, U. 110–112
*O pisateliakh-samouchkakh* 4
*On the Edge of the Storm* 138
*Only a Mother* 201
"On Self-Educated Writers" 4
Onwuemezi, N. 190
Orozco, José Clemente 130
Ortega, Bertín 132–134, 137, 153–154 (endnotes)
Ortiz, Hernán 150
Orwell, George 167, 175, 191 (endnote)
Osborne, John 170, 173, 182, 188
Ossiannilsson, K. G. 97–98, 106
Östman, Karl 98, 100, 114
Ostrovsky, Nikolai 11
*Our Present Times* 101
*The Outsider* 174
"On Working-Class Writers and Their Missions" 80

**P**

Paavo-Kallio, Esa 69
Pagán, Eduardo 33, 60 (endnote)
Page, Myra 43, 51
Palm, Göran 110–111
Palmgren, Raoul 67–69, 71, 75, 78–79, 81–82, 84–85, 88–89 (endnotes)

Palmgren, Valfrid 100
Pärssinen, Hilja 69, 75
Partnoy, Alicia 140
"Party Organization and Party Literature" 13–14
"Partorganizatsiia v bor'be za bol'shevistskuiu istoriiu zavodov" 27 (endnote)
Passos, John Dos 35, 153 (endnote)
*Pedro Páramo* 138
Peiss, Kathy 33, 60 (endnote)
Pekkanen, Toivo 78–79, 87, 89 (endnote)
Peltonen, Milla 82–83, 89 (endnote)
*Penguin New Writing* 173
Pennanen, Jarno 78
*People of the Backwoods* 23–25
*People's Will* 70
Pereira, A. 131
Perera, Sonali xiii, 59
Perry, Samuel xii
*Pervyi proletarskii sbornik* 3
Petry, Ann 52, 54–55
*Philological Quarterly* 161
*The Pig Houses* 115
Pinter, Harold 188
"Pirkko Saisio's introspection" 65
Piri, Santtu 73
Place, Francis 165
*The Plain in Flames* 137
Plaskacz, B. 130, 132, 136, 138, 152 (endnote)

Plato 147

*The Plot of the Land* 152 (endnote)

*PMLA* 161

*Podnyataja Tselina* 201

Pollari, Mikko 87–88 (endnote)

Poniatowska, Elena 140–141

*The Poor Man's Guardian* 165

Portillo, José López 152 (endnote)

Potts, Paul 191 (endnote)

Powell, Enoch 177–178

Pozas, Ricardo 137, 141

*Preso sin nombre, celda sin número* 140

*Prisoner without a Name, Cell without a Number* 140

*Prison Notebooks* 2

"Proletär" 97

*Proletärdiktning* 100

"Proletarian" 97

*Proletarian Writing* 100

"The Proletarian Poet's Song" 97

"Proletärpoetens sång" 97

*Proletarskii sbornik* 3

*Prospects* 112

*Protest* 134, 154 (endnote)

*Protesta* 134, 154 (endnote)

Proust, Marcelo Sánchez 147

Puga, María Luisa 155 (endnote)

Pynttäri, Veli-Matti 77–79, 89 (endnote)Rabasa, Emilio 152 (endnote)

**R**

Rabinovich, I. 18

*Race Rebels* 60–61 (endnote)

*The Ragged-Trousered Philanthropists* 171

Rancière, Jacques 117

Rama, Angel 154 (endnote)

Ramos, Agustín 137

Ramos, Luis Arturo 155 (endnote)

*Raskas puuvilla* 84

Ravenhill, Mark 179

Rechy, John 56

*Red Blood* 153 (endnote)

*The Red City* 134, 154 (endnote)

*Redwedge* 60

*Red Worms* 134

Reisz, Karel 188

*Revolución* 153 (endnote)

*Revolution* 153 (endnote)

Revueltas, José 137

Richardson, Edmund 181

Richardson, Samuel 163

Richardson, Tony 188

Riis, Jacob, 37

*The Riot* 134

Rivera, Diego 130, 150

"Rivers of Blood" 177–178

*The Road to Wigan Pier* 175

Robeson, Paul 39

Roediger, David 36

Roininen, Aimo 67–68, 70–71, 73–74, 77

Rojola, L. 69

*Room at the Top* 173
Roosevelt, Theodore (Teddy) 50
Rose, Jonathan 161, 164
Rossetti, Dante Gabriel 167
Roth, Philip 52
Roumain, Jacques 35
Rousseau, Jean-Jacques 147
Rozas, Lorenzo Turrent
  132–135, 153 (endnote)
Rueda, Julio Jiménez 131
Rulfo, Juan 137–138
Runeberg, J. L. 71
Runnquist, Åke 109
Russel, Dave 167, 191 (endnote)
Russo, J. x
Ruuth, Alpo 89 (endnote)
Rydberg, Kaisu-Mirjami 78

**S**
Safranski, Rüdiger xi
Saisio, Pirkko 65–66, 75, 83–85
Salama, Hannu 82–83, 85
Säll, Arne 112
Sallamma, Kari 85
Salmi-Niklander, K. 75–76,
  78, 87 (endnote), 119–120,
  120–121 (endnotes)
Salminen, Arto 86–87
Salomonson, Kurt 107
Samuelsson, Tony 112, 117
Sandel, Maria 73, 98, 114
Sandgren, Gustav 89 (endnote),
  103
Sandino, Augusto César 152
  (endnote)
*Sangre roja* 153 (endnote)

Santa 152 (endnote)
Sarquis, Francisco 132, 134
Saroyan, William 115
*Saturday Night and Sunday
  Morning* 173–174
Sauri, E. 150–151, 155
  (endnote)
*Saved* 179
Savutie, Maija 78
Scheckner, Peter 165
Schocket, Eric 36
Schofield, Camilla 178
*A School Union* 134
Schregenberger, T. 182
Sebald, Winifredo G. 147
"Segodnia" 22
Seppälä, Juha 86
Seppälä, M. 70, 76–77
Shaginian, Marietta 15
*Shameless* 179–180
Shaw, George Bernard 168
*Ships in the River* 121 (endnote)
Shklovsky, Victor 19
Sholokhov, Mikhail 115,
  200–201
Shukla, Nikesh 189
Sierz, Aleks 179
*Siinä näkijä missä tekijä* 82–83
Simms, William Gilmore 36
Sinclair, Upton 74
Sinervo, Elvi 78
Siqueiros, David Álvaro 130
Sjödin, Stig 107
Skipsey, Joseph 167
Slotkin, Richard 49

Smedberg, Åke 112
Smedley, Agnes 35, 102
Smethurst, James 38, 60 (endnote)
*Smokestacks* 135
*The Social Construction of American Realism* 38
Soini, Lauri 73
Solares, Ignacio 155 (endnote)
Soto, Gary 57
Soto, J. S. 133
*Soul on Ice* 32
Southey, Robert 162–163
*The Soviet Novel* 19–21
"Sozdadim" 18
Stalin 21–22, 25–26
Steffen, Richard 99–101, 105–106, 109, 111
Stein, L. 5
Steinbeck, John 53–54
Steinberg, M. D. 3, 8
Stenkvist, Jan 95, 100
*Stepan Kol'chugin* 22–23
Sillitoe, Alan 161, 173–175, 188, 192 (endnote)
Stolpe, Sven 101–102
*Story of My Teeth* 146–147
*The Street* 52, 54
Stieg, Gerald xi
*Strike!* 51
Strindberg, August 74, 106, 115
Ström, F. 97–98
Strömberg, Kjell 100, 106
*Studien zur Entwicklung der Arbeiterliteratur in der Bundesrepublik* xi

*The Studs Lonigan Trilogy* 52
Sunao, Tokunago 35
Sundin, T. 100
Sundström, Cay 78
*Sunrises* 134
*Sunshine and Shadow* 165
Suomen Kuvalehti 65
Svanberg, A. 117
Svedjedal, Johan 95–98, 103, 107, 110, 116
*Svensk arbetardikt* 109
*Svensk arbetarlitteratur* 116
*Svinalängorna* 115
*Swedish Working-Class Literature* 116
*Swedish Working-Class Writing* 109

**T**

*Täällä Pohjantähden alla* 79
*Tåbb med manifestet* 107
*Tåbb with the Manifesto* 107
Taft, P. 5
Taibo, Paco Ignacio 155 (endnote)
*Taide kuuluu kansalle* 84
Tanttu, Kasperi 69
*A Taste of Honey* 173–174
*Tejas Verdes* 140
*Tehtaan varjossa* 78, 88 (endnote)
*The Terrestrial Days* 137
Thatcher, Margaret 177–178, 183
*Theatre of Cruelty* 179
Therborn, G. 103
*The Thief* 137

Thorsell, Lennart 109
*The Threshold* 114
*Tierra de hombre* 137
*Tierra marchita* 155 (endnote)
Tihlä, Hilda 75
*Tikhiy Don* 200
*Till en författare* 115
*Time, Forward!* 15–16
Timerman, Jacobo 140
*To an Author* 115
Todorov, Tsvetan 186, 188, 192 (endnote)
Tokarczyk, Michelle xii, 31, 59
Tolstoi, Leo 74
*To Make my Bread* 51–52
Torstensson, Mattias 118
*To Sir, With Love* 176
"Toward Proletarian Art" 35, 46
*Toward a Proletarian Literature* 133
"Toward a Revolutionary Symbolism" 35
*Toward a Working-Class Canon* 160
*Trabajos del reino* 155 (endnote)
*The Tractor* 201
*Traktorn* 201
Traven, B. 102
Tressell, Robert 171
Trosell, Aino 110
*Tröskeln* 114
Trotsky, Leon 14, 152 (endnote)
*The Trouble with Diversity* 155 (endnote)
*True Men* 137
Trujillo, Raúl Carrancá y 134

Trump, Donald x, 205
Tsement 10
*Tuntematon sotilas* 79
*Turkey* 137
Turtiainen, Arvo 78
Twain, Mark 167–168
*Twentieth Century Writing and the British Working Class* 161
*The Twopenny Dispatch* 165
Tynan, Kenneth 182
"Työläiskirjailijoista ja heidän tehtävistään" 80–81
*Työmiehen illanvietto* 70
*Työmies* 70, 72, 88 (endnote)
"Työväen laulaja" 72

**U**
Uhlén, A. 98
Uhlin, Eric 97–98, 108–109
*The Uncomfortable Dead* 155 (endnote)
*The Underdogs* 131–132
*Under the Feet of Jesus* 57–59
*Under the North Star* 79–81
*Union Street* 177
*The Unknown Soldier* 79
*Un sindicato escolar. Novela corta infantil* 134
*Up the Junction* 177
"Ur en litterär proletärs utvecklingshistoria" 97
Uribe-Echeverría, Juan 135
*The Uses of Literacy* 161, 175, 186
"Uskorit" 17
*Utsikter* 112, 115

**V**

*Vägval* 112–113

Váldez, Hernán 140

Valdez, Luis 57

Vallejo, Cesar 35

Valpas, Edvard 72–73

*Vanishing Moments* 36

Värnlund, Rudolf 101–102, 104, 116

*Vår Nutid* 101–102

Varpio, Y. 80

Vasconcelos, José 130

Vázquez, Juan Gabriel 147

Vicinus, Martha 160, 165

*Victorian Poetry* 161

Viksten, Albert 105

Villalobos, Juan 147, 155 (endnote)

Vinberg, Ola 101, 106, 109

"Vi 'proletärer' i litteraturen" 102

Viramontes, Helena 57–59

*Virgin Soil Upturned* 201

Volkov, A. 3

Vorse, Mary Heaton 51

Voynich, Ethel 22

*Vrbe. Súperpoema bolchevique en 5 cantos* 153 (endnote)

*Vremia, Vpered!* 15–16

Vulovic, Jimmy 102, 116

**W**

*The Wages of Whiteness* 36

Wägner, Elin 73

Wald, Alan 31, 38–39, 61 (endnote)

Warren, Tony 176

Waterhouse, Keith 174

"Wat Tyler" 162

Watt, Ian 163

Waugh, Edwin 167

*Wealthy Relatives* 152 (endnote)

*Wedge* 85

*A Week* 10–11

"A Week" 10–11, 13

"We Grow Out of Iron" 8

Welsh, Irvine 177

"We 'Proletarians' in Literature" 102

Wermelin, Atterdag 98

West, Dorothy 39

Wheeler, Thomas Martin 165–166

*When Cárdenas Gave Us the Land* 137

*Where the Air is Clear* 138

*Where There's a Crime, There's a Witness* 82–83

*White Garments*, or *Raiments* 26

Whitehead, Colson 59

*The White-Sea Baltic Canal* 18–19

*White Strike* 137

Whitman, Walt 46

Williams, A. 115–116

Williams, Raymond 96

Willman, Elvira 69–71, 75

Wilson, Colin 174

Wilson, Nicola 161

Winant, Howard 40

*Withered Land* 155 (endnote)

Witt-Brattström, Ebba 113

Witte, Bernd xi

*The Wobbly* (also, *The Cotton Pickers*) 102

*Women and Apple Trees* 103

*Women's Studies Quarterly* 161

*The Worker* 70, 72

"Workers' Singer" 72

*A Worker's Soiree* 70

*Working-Class Fiction* 160

*Working-Class Fiction in Theory and Practice* 161

*Working-Class Literature* 116

*The Wound* 152 (endnote)

Wrangborg, Jenny 115–116

Wright, Richard 35, 38–39, 43–46, 52, 54–55, 103

**Y**

Yáñez, Agustin 138

*Yekl* 46

Ylikangas, H. 88 (endnote)

Yúdice, George 142–143, 151

**Z**

Zandy, Janet xii

Zapata 135

*The Zhurbins* 26

*Zhurbiny* 26

*Zoot Suit* 60 (endnote)